P9-CEP-034

Ability Testing in Developing Countries

Paul A. Schwarz
Robert E. Krug

Ability Testing in Developing Countries

A Handbook of Principles and Techniques

PRAEGER SPECIAL STUDIES IN INTERNATIONAL ECONOMICS AND DEVELOPMENT

Praeger Publishers New York Washington London

PRAEGER PUBLISHERS
111 Fourth Avenue, New York, N.Y. 10003, U.S.A.
5, Cromwell Place, London S.W.7, England

Published in the United States of America in 1972
by Praeger Publishers, Inc.

Library of Congress Catalog Card Number: 70-182993

Printed in the United States of America

PREFACE

This handbook is based on an eight-year program of research and development supported by the Agency for International Development, and carried out by the American Institutes for Research. The opinions expressed as a result of the study are not necessarily those of the Agency for International Development, however. The objectives were, first, to devise techniques of aptitude testing that could be applied in cultures in which standard ability tests are not fully effective; and, then, to assist in the application of these techniques to human resource development programs in the developing countries.

The research proceeded through four major phases, as follows:

Phase I was a feasibility study to determine whether the probability of devising effective testing methods in these countries was sufficiently high to warrant the fairly substantial developmental investment that might be required. It was begun in July, 1960, in Nigeria, which had been selected as a suitable model country, and it lasted approximately nine months. The results included a set of principles for constructing aptitude tests in the Nigerian culture, a series of twelve prototype tests that had been developed in accordance with these principles for purposes of experimental evaluation, and evaluative data that showed these tests to be reasonably effective. The development of appropriate testing devices appeared to be an entirely feasible proposition.

Phase II consisted of the further developmental research that was necessary to translate these prototype tests into operational forms and to devise measures of other important aptitudes that had not been included in the feasibility study. It lasted from October, 1961, to June, 1963, and resulted in a set of twenty-one ability tests, which we termed the I-D Aptitude Series. As part of the research, these tests were validated and normed for a wide range of practical applications throughout Nigeria; by the end of Phase II, a number of operational testing services were actually being provided to education and training establishments, and to private employers. Additional validity studies were carried out in Ghana, Liberia, Tunisia, and Mali as a first step toward extending the program to other African countries.

Phase III was the first stage of the institution-building effort that, through a variety of successor projects, is still being carried forward today. It began in November, 1963, with the objective of establishing a Nigerian center for aptitude testing that could take full responsibility for the continuing development of the program, under the supervision of a Nigerian professional staff and with entirely local financing. In July, 1964, the Nigerian Aptitude Testing Unit began operations as an affiliate of the West African Examinations Council; and in January, 1966, it became an integral part of that organization as its Office for Test Development and Research. Under this expanded charter, the unit was responsible for all of the council's test development programs—achievement as well as aptitude tests—and began to provide services outside Nigeria to the three other member countries of Ghana, Gambia, and Sierra Leone. Concurrently, but as an entirely separate effort, the Liberian Testing Center was also developed.

Phase IV was the major "generalization phase" of the research, designed to extend the program beyond Africa to other parts of the developing world. It was planned basically as a replication of the Nigerian studies in these countries, and was carried out during the period May, 1966, to June, 1968, in Brazil, Korea, and Thailand, which had agreed to participate as the new model countries. The objectives were, first, to develop a testing program in each of these countries that would have immediate local benefits and perhaps later serve also as a regional resource for similar efforts in other locations; and, second, to obtain the broad base of crosscultural data that would be needed to expand the I-D testing approaches to more or less universally applicable procedures. As part of the second objective, a handbook of testing methods appropriate to the developing countries—i.e., the present volume—was also to be prepared.

Chronologically, then, this handbook is a product of Phase IV. But characterizing its content as such would be misleading. For, when the initial generalizability studies revealed that the techniques developed in Africa were equally effective in these new model countries, the effort was shifted to practical applications and institution-building and further methodological innovation was not attempted. The developmental research necessary for the Brazil, Korea, and Thailand projects had in effect already been carried out in the African countries, and all of the sections of the handbook that describe methodological adaptations of standard testing approaches are based on these earlier studies.

The reason for this ready generalizability of the I-D testing approaches, no doubt, lay in the substantially more difficult adaptation problems that had been encountered in the African setting. In Africa, the tests had to be given in the second language of the examinees, and much more of the research had to be carried out in remote rural locations. That techniques effective for second-language examinees in rural Africa would be adequate for most applications elsewhere is, in retrospect, not really surprising.

At the same time, however, these factors also suggest that certain of the adaptations incorporated in the I-D techniques may not be necessary for adequate testing in a less challenging setting. Some of the more economical features of the standard testing approaches can perhaps be reintroduced for greater efficiency in such locations. Preliminary studies of this possibility were included in the Phase IV research, but the specific conditions under which a certain modification is or is not required have not yet been determined.

Similarly, the highly practical orientation of the research does not permit us to say that the I-D techniques are the only effective approach to test adaptation, or even the one that is best. When we found that a certain procedure provided results of sufficient accuracy for operational use, we generally stopped that aspect of the research and did not look for something better. And we have therefore felt constrained to temper the typical "Thou shalt . . . " style of a prescriptive handbook with the more modest "It was found that . . . " approach of a descriptive report.

In the planning of the handbook itself, two major decisions had to be made. The first concerned the audience to which the content should be addressed. The national development planner, the technical assistance official, the educator or the employer, the senior testing specialist, the recent graduate of advanced measurement courses—all of whom play an important role in the expansion of testing in a developing country—would clearly be interested in different aspects of the research, and would find maximum utility in different kinds and depths of discussions. The second and somewhat related decision concerned the degree to which the handbook should be self-sufficient in presenting the essentials of testing, including techniques (e.g., statistical analyses) that are unaffected by cultural variations, and the degree to which it should concentrate on the unique aspects of testing in a developing country, requiring the reader less familiar with measurement practices to consult other sources.

On the first issue, we decided that instead of addressing the entire handbook to the interests of a single audience or to a "happy mean" of the interests of a number of different audiences, we would try to organize the material into reasonably modular chapters, and address each to the audience for which it is mainly intended. Thus, the style and focus of the discussion varies throughout the volume, and the following brief overview may be helpful:

Chapters 1 and 3 are concerned with the conditions under which test adaptation should or should not be considered, from a measurement point of view. The former is addressed to the generalist who has to approve or finance testing research, the latter to the specialist responsible for its implementation. We suggest that the generalist read Chapter 1 and skip Chapter 3, and that the specialist read both chapters.

Chapters 2 and 8 are concerned with the desirability of investing in testing reform, from a cost-effectiveness point of view. Both are written mainly for the administrator or financier, but should be of interest also to specialists responsible for the design of a testing program (Chapter 2) or the development of a testing center (Chapter 8).

Chapters 4 and 5 summarize the methodology of test adaptation developed as the main outcome of the research; Chapter 6 illustrates the application of these principles and techniques to nineteen aptitude tests. The major developmental studies carried out in Africa and the generalizability studies carried out in Brazil, Korea, and Thailand are also described as part of the discussion. The intended audience is the practicing test constructor.

Chapters 7 and 9 are addressed to the administrators and specialists responsible for the final step of translating the completed test instruments into operational testing programs. Chapter 7 is concerned with the technical aspects of validating and combining tests, and is by far the most esoteric chapter with respect to measurement theory and practice. Chapter 9 is concerned with the organization and management of large-scale testing operations in a developing country.

Overall, the handbook is intended to serve both as a comprehensive overview of the technical and organizational issues to be resolved in programs of testing reform in a developing country, and as a reference manual to be consulted selectively at various stages of implementation. At the stage of reviewing a specific testing proposal, Chapters 1, 2, 8, and 9 should provide the most pertinent information; in the construction of the actual test instruments, Chapters 2 through 6 should be the most relevant; and so on, in accordance with the above summary of emphasis and intent.

On the second issue, we decided not to attempt to make the handbook entirely self-sufficient. Basic measurement concepts, such as reliability, are not explained; for adequate definitions of these concepts other sources must be consulted. The appropriate sources are the more widely used textbooks on the essentials of measurement, which we have found to be generally available in the developing countries.

A number of standard techniques (i.e., techniques not affected by cultural variations) are described in the technically oriented chapters, however. This was considered necessary whenever we used a technique that we judge superior but that is not the one most typically used by other practitioners in the field of testing; or when a certain technique is described only in sources that are not readily available in the developing countries. Such discursions from the culture-tied aspects of testing will be found mainly in the Chapter 3 and Chapter 7 discussions.

ACKNOWLEDGMENTS

The full roster of individuals who participate in and contribute to any effort that spans eight years and three continents is virtually endless, and adequate acknowledgement cannot realistically be attempted. But it does seem appropriate to acknowledge the contributions of those who were continuing partners in the research, in the sense of participating over a period of years in two or more of the four phases, and in two or more of the cooperating countries.

Among the many local specialists who were especially active partners in this continuing sense, four deserve special mention. These were Dr. Thomas A. Lambo, Chief S. O. Awokoya, John W. Deakin, and Dr. Claude G. Fontaine. The contributions of the scores of others who also made significant contributions are acknowledged in the separate project reports.

The officials of the Agency for International Development who assisted us at many times and locations include Dr. Samuel C. Adams, M. F. B. Adler, Dr. Joel M. Bernstein, Samuel E. Fuhr, Dr. Robert Jacobs, Dr. Robert Johnson, Arbon Lang, William Lawless, Dr. Clifford S. Liddle, Burnie Merson, W. Haven North, the late Dr. Adam C. Skapski, Dr. Edwin A. Treathaway, Dr. Robert Van Duyn, and Joseph White. And there were, of course, countless others who provided assistance or ideas of critical importance.

Among the AIR staff members, the outstanding contribution to the research reported in this handbook was made by Daryl G. Nichols, who was responsible for much of the original test development during Phase II, and who subsequently directed the projects in Liberia and Malawi. Also important to the development of the methodology were the contributions of my wife, Jacqueline M. Schwarz, who constituted my entire staff during Phase I and remained a member of the research team throughout Phase II; of Richard A. Cohen, who participated in the field research of Phase II and provided supportive services to many of the activities thereafter; and of Dr. Harold M. Chapman, who served on the Phase II Nigeria team and directed the project in Ghana. The primary contributions to our institution-building efforts were made by Dr. Richard R. Rowe, who guided the evolution of the Nigerian testing project into a permanent professional center, and by Dr. Dan H. Jones, who performed a comparable function in Korea. Much of the Phase IV generalizability research was carried out by Dr. Ann

Angell in Brazil, Dr. Joel B. Aronson in Thailand, and Dr. Sam C. Cho in Korea. The visual aids and related materials were designed by Jack K. Greenberg of the home office staff.

Dr. Robert E. Krug directed the home office activities, including a sizable training program, during Phase II and Phase IV of the study; prepared Part II of the handbook; and made numerous contributions to other chapters. Dr. David A. Angell was the director of the project in Brazil, and Dr. Arthur H. Hill directed the project in Thailand. Both made important contributions to the preparation of this handbook by distilling the mass of available information and data to manageable proportions.

Finally, I would reassure the specialist reader who has learned to associate a certain distinguished name with innovation in testing that this project is not the exception. The accomplishments of the research very much reflect the eight years of personal supervision that John C. Flanagan gave this project, and the fourteen memorable years he gave its director.

CONTENTS

Chapter Page

PART II: TECHNIQUES OF TEST ADAPTATION

Chapter Page

PART IV: DEVELOPING LOCAL TESTING RESOURCES

LIST OF TABLES

LIST OF FIGURES

PART I

BASIC ISSUES

CHAPTER

1

THE IMPORTANCE OF "CULTURAL" FACTORS IN TESTING

Most of the topics discussed in this handbook are addressed to the methodological questions of how tests can be adapted for use in a developing country. For it has been in the design of suitable testing procedures that the AID/AIR research has made the most significant advances, and can offer the most useful suggestions. Principles, techniques, and practical applications all are discussed in detail.

Yet, the how issue is only one of the questions that arises when a new test development project is being considered. Even more fundamental is whether the testing that is to be done actually calls for especially adapted procedures, and whether (if in theory it does) the practical gains will in fact justify the necessary investment. The first decision that has to be made is whether a proposed test development project is worth doing at all.

Part I of the handbook is addressed to these basic whether questions. Chapter 1 examines the legitimate reasons for test adaptation; Chapter 2, the related cost-effectiveness implications.

SOME EXTREME VIEWS ON TEST ADAPTATION

Many of the educators and personnel officers who operate testing programs in the developing countries hold widely divergent views on the merits of test adaptation. At the one extreme there are those who look mainly at the vast environmental differences between the developing countries and the highly industrialized nations, and conclude that any test designed for the one ipso facto cannot serve the other. At the other extreme there are those who attach greater importance to the fact that the skills needed in both developed and developing countries are exactly the same, and who fear that "simplified" tests will hamper them in producing equally high levels of skill in their own populations. The former would exclude practically all of the classic testing procedures from use in a developing country, since they were clearly designed in and for the Western cultures; the latter would oppose the use of anything else, since this would be a tacit acceptance of lower performance standards.

Neither view, of course, is correct; but it may be useful to elaborate them in the context of specific examples, to clarify the major issues involved. Both of the following examples occurred during the course of the project.

At a meeting of the national committee for English language examinations, one of the members strongly objected to the continued use of a single test based on United Kingdom specifications. This test, he claimed, was grossly unfair because students from different parts of the country who spoke different native languages had quite different language learning problems; and the existing test did not take these differences into account. The need was for a series of different English tests, each designed to be fair to a certain indigenous language structure, so that each student could sit for the one test of this series that took account of the peculiarities of his own native tongue. Though the test development costs would be high, external assistance almost certainly could be obtained; and he moved that such assistance be sought.

Most of the other members objected. The purpose of an English examination, they insisted, is simply to determine whether or not the student has mastered the language to an acceptable degree. His background is irrelevant to this objective, and special tests should not be developed. The appropriate approach, these members felt, was to retain the U.K. standard of what constitutes "acceptable" English, and to continue testing English proficiency in the same way as before.

The counter to this was that "acceptable" English has to be defined in terms of the individual student; and that the proposed series of tests would all reflect equivalent levels of "acceptability," while at the same time taking account of the country's sizable interstudent variation. The proposal was simply a way of adapting U.K. testing practices to local conditions.

The debate lasted until adjournment, with neither side budging from its original position.

The second example is more complex, in that there was not just one but a wide range of possible modifications to be considered.

The manager of the local branch of a large American firm was trying to recruit trainees for advanced technical positions critical to his company's operations. He asked one of the American professors teaching at the local university for help; and the professor obliged by recommending fourteen students whom he considered exceptionally well-suited for these positions. Each of the students came in for an interview; each was given the firm's standard selection test; each failed the test; and each was rejected.

In the postmortem discussions, the professor took strong exception to the selection procedure, and pointed out three specific shortcomings in the approach that had been used. The first was that certain parts of the company's test included problems of a type unknown in the local setting and therefore not suitable for local use; these should have been dropped. The second was that in the rest of the problems, not even the most obvious of cultural adaptations had been attempted. The mathematical exercises involving dollars and cents, for example, clearly should have been changed to the local currency that his students used. And the third was that evaluating the applicants' scores on the basis of American norms (which had indeed been the procedure) was completely absurd. Given the huge differences in the backgrounds of American and local examinees, no single standard could possibly serve as a meaningful yardstick for both sets of scores.

The branch manager disagreed. The job to be performed in this country, he said, is identical in all respects to the job that the company's American employees are performing in the United States. Exactly the same kinds of abilities and skills are required in both locations. And, since the company's test had been designed to measure precisely these kinds of skills, it is as appropriate for selection here as it is there. He was prepared to believe that the requisite skills are less highly developed here than in the United States, but this meant only that an unusually large number of applicants would have to be tested to find people qualified for the job. Changing the test or adjusting the norms would, he agreed, simplify his present recruiting problems, but would result in the employment of people who subsequently could not make the grade, and was therefore short-sighted.

And so the students were not employed, and the company continued testing. The number of people affected by the company's decision in this example was small. But exactly the same issues arise in many large testing programs, which are similarly debated.

The admission of foreign students to American universities is another, perhaps more familiar illustration. Should one argue that the foreign student will be expected to perform at the same level as his American classmates, and therefore use the university's standard admission procedures? Or should one consider the differences in the backgrounds of the foreign applicants, and try to make suitable adaptations? And if one does decide to adapt the test, how much adaptation is needed? Which aspects of the testing process are most affected by intercultural variations?

In considering these issues, it is convenient to divide the testing process into its three major components, and to examine their separate (and quite different) implications. These components are 1) the test rationale, 2) the specific test content, and 3) the testing mechanics. Each is discussed at a semitechnical level here and elaborated in greater technical detail in the later chapters.

THE TEST RATIONALE

When one develops a test for a specified purpose, he obviously does not pick the test problems at random, but tries to select those that he thinks will be particularly effective. He constructs the test exercises so that they will have a certain logical relationship to the real-life skill that the test is to measure. And this logical relationship is called the test rationale.

If he wants to select trainees for a carpentry course, for example, he begins by analyzing the job of a carpenter to find out which types of skills might make certain individuals more proficient than others. He might conclude that certain skilled muscle movements are especially important; so, he would design a test that duplicates these movements as closely as possible, and he would measure individual differences in this skill as one part of the selection procedure. The relationship between the muscle movements programmed into the test and the muscle movements involved in the job would constitute the underlying test rationale.

If the test turns out to be effective, the test constructor can reasonably conclude that the rationale was indeed sound—that the logical relationship he posited really is valid. He assumes, even though he may not be able to prove it, that the rationale explains _why_ the test was effective. In the above example, he would say that the test is a good selection device _because_ it measures the muscle movements that skilled carpentry requires. And he would not hesitate to try the same test again for other jobs that seem to require similar kinds of physical manipulations.

Thus, the "standard" American or European tests for a given purpose have not only a statistical pedigree but also a rational explanation. The first question that must be asked from the point of view of test adaptation is whether these rationales are equally sound in a developing country. For, if they are not—i.e., if using a certain type of test cannot be justified on rational grounds—it would clearly be wasteful to examine the appropriateness of its content or other specific details. The need would be not for adaptation but for an entirely different approach.

On this point, the AID/AIR findings are reasonably conclusive. Most of the standard test rationales are equally valid in a developing country. Each of the I-D tests is based on a standard test rationale, and each is effective for the specific applications for which this rationale is intended. Though many of the physical characteristics of the standard tests had to be changed to fit local conditions, the underlying rationales remained the same. If a test of ability A was known to predict success in curriculum X in the United States, an appropriately adapted test of ability A would consistently provide comparable results for curriculum X in an entirely different cultural setting.

This finding has important implications for the testing specialist, in that it permits him to apply the vast literature of testing to his work, irrespective of the cultural setting. By beginning with what is already known, as elaborated in Chapter 3, he can often effect a substantial saving. The wheel does not have to be reinvented.

For the administrator or funder of test development programs, there are similar implications. In accordance with this general finding, he can appropriately use the degree to which a proposed project builds on established test rationales as one criterion for evaluation. Projects that would pioneer new rationales before checking the validity of standard approaches generally should not be undertaken.

In the early days of crosscultural testing, especially in tropical Africa, much research was based on tests of unproved merit which were used mainly because they were easy to administer to naïve examinees. And this is perhaps the main reason that this substantial effort had so few tangible results. Beginning with excellent rationales and then trying to solve the difficulties in applying them is likely to be much more productive.

Similarly, low priority should be assigned to a project that would analyze a standard job or curriculum to determine the specific abilities that it requires in a particular country. If the component skills have already been identified in studies elsewhere, any local differences that may be found by repeating these studies will probably not justify the time and effort required.* The standard findings should be applied, at least for the first set of trial testing procedures.

Exceptions to the universal applicability of the established test rationales occur rarely. But the errors that can result from the use of an inappropriate rationale are so sizable that the logic of each proposed rationale should nevertheless be double-checked before it is used, to ensure its suitability in the local situation.

The use of achievement in earlier school courses as a predictor of performance in more advanced courses is one case in point. In the educational systems of most developing countries, the most crucial selection decisions are made at the transition from primary to secondary school, which is the make-or-break hurdle for most of the country's youngsters. And, typically, language and arithmetic achievement tests are used as the major indexes for these admission decisions. Is this an effective procedure?

Looking at the results of American testing experiences, one finds that predictors of scholastic success better than achievement tests have not yet been discovered. For most applications, the use of achievement measures is one of the indicated selection procedures. But a second look will show also that this experience has been based largely on the testing of high school students for college admission, since selection for secondary schools is not important in the American system. And so, before investing in these types of tests, it is necessary to ask whether the rationale for using achievement tests, however thoroughly validated for university admission in the United States, is logically generalizable to secondary school admission in a developing county.

The rationale for achievement tests as scholastic predictors is based on three major assumptions. The test constructor reasons that—

---

*One type of difference that does arise is in skill requirements that need not be tested with American applicants (e.g., being able to communicate in English), but do have to be checked for certain jobs in other countries. Such skills can usually be identified without special studies, however.

1. _if_ the educational experiences that the applicants were provided by their past schooling have been approximately the same;

2. _if_ the differences in the applicants' relative achievement, given these equivalent experiences, were the result of certain differences in their individual abilities and characteristics;

and

3. _if_ the advanced courses for which they are applying will require the same abilities and characteristics;

then the applicants should continue to achieve at different levels, just as before. Having through these assumptions established a link between their past performance and their future potential, he can logically select the highest achievers for admission to the advanced courses.

The second and third assumptions are as reasonable in a developing country as in the United States. But the first assumption is not. For as heterogeneous as the American high schools are in the quality of their instruction—and this has, in fact, been the major concern in U.S. admission procedures—the primary schools of the developing countries are much more heterogeneous still. In many countries, the use of achievement tests can be expected to select _not_ the students with the highest potential, but those who happened to attend the better primary schools. Many of the country's most talented youngsters may well be denied admission if this "standard" procedure is the one adopted.

Similar anomalies can be found in a number of other traditional rationales when applied in different cultures. It can easily be deduced, for example, that the very high predictive power that can normally be expected from English vocabulary tests will be greatly reduced when English is the second language of the examinees; that abstract reasoning tests will probably not measure "intelligence" in settings in which this skill is not practiced in preschool days; and that cross-cultural comparisons of mental ability simply cannot be made.[1] Checking the applicability of the test rationale to local conditions is always worthwhile.

Yet, even when such anomalies are discovered, the principle of beginning with models of excellence should continue to be applied. If one of the established test rationales does not fit, there is probably another that can be applied.

Thus, having ruled out achievement tests as predictors of performance at the secondary school level, one should consider the alternative approaches that have proved useful, to see if any of these are better suited to local conditions. In this particular instance, he will in fact find two suitable rationales that, used in tandem, provide a highly effective selection procedure.

The first is the rationale for screening tests, which are designed to eliminate unfit applicants rather than to identify those who are especially able. Here, the test constructor reasons that—

1. if students in a given cirriculum must have acquired certain basic knowledge and skills in order to keep up with the instruction,

and

2. if there will be little or no opportunity for remedial learning by students who do not possess these skills when they first enter the course,

then applicants who do not have the necessary background should be rejected. No matter how high their native potential may be, they will fail as a result of their poor preparation.

This rationale clearly can be applied for secondary school selection in any developing country. If the specific items of knowledge and skill that the secondary school course requires can be identified, and if a test that measures these items can be constructed, applicants who have not mastered them to a sufficient degree can and shall be rejected. Such a screening test will turn out, it is true, to be a test of achievement; but it will differ from the achievement tests found wanting above in two important respects. The first is that its content will be based not on the primary school syllabus but on the requirements of the secondary school courses, which will narrow considerably the range of skills being measured. The second is that it will be used not to select the top 10 percent or so of the applicants who should be admitted but to screen out the bottom 30 or 40 percent to whom admission must be denied. These two differences make this type of achievement test suitable, whereas the standard predictive version was not.

After the applicants have been screened with this type of test, it is necessary next to select from those who passed the initial hurdle the one out of each six or seven who will be admitted. For this purpose, the appropriate rationale is that of the scholastic aptitude test, which reasons that—

1. if a student's achievement in a given course depends in part on the kinds of mental operations this course requires,

2. if there are tasks that he already knows how to perform which require essentially the same operations,

and

3. if he has had sufficient practice in these tasks to have reached a fairly stable proficiency level,

then this level should be indicative of the level he will attain in performing the new tasks the course will expect him to master. The prediction is quite simply that those who are able to perform related tasks better now will also perform better in the course for which they are being considered. (It will be noted that the earlier example of selecting trainees for carpentry courses used the identical rationale, except that it was applied to "physical" rather then "mental" operations.)

To apply this rationale in a developing country it is necessary to find related tasks that the examinees already know how to perform, which is a problem that will be discussed at length in later sections. For now, it suffices to say that this can usually be done; and that the above two-stage selection procedure has already been tried in at least one developing country and found highly effective.

This one application has been described in some detail to illustrate the importance of analyzing the rest rationale in project evaluation. It is not expected that the administrator will himself carry out this analysis in the depth necessary for meaningful conclusions; but he should require that it be done by the specialists who prepare the project proposal. Specifically, he should ask for the following:

1. A written statement of the rationale that will be followed in developing the proposed testing procedures;

2. A review of the prior applications of this rationale in other locations, and of its effectiveness relative to other approaches; and

3. An analysis of the suitability of the assumptions made in this rationale in the light of local conditions.

This will usually provide him with a sound basis for judging the technical merits of the proposed undertaking; and, as a by-product of the additional thinking that will have been done at the specialist level, result in generally better proposals.

THE SPECIFIC TEST CONTENT

The above conclusions bear directly on the fundamental disagreement noted at the beginning of this chapter, between those who look mainly at the similarities in the job requirements and those who give more weight to cultural variations. In almost all cases, the treatment of the standard test rationales should follow the view of the former. The jobs are largely the same, do encompass the same kinds of skill, and do call for the same _types_ of testing procedures.

When these same rationales are used to generate the specific _content_ of the actual test exercises, however, the approach must shift to the opposite point of view. For the effective application of each rationale depends very much on local conditions. The "best" application of the identical rationale in each of two different locations can (and sometimes does) result in two quite different sets of test questions. And, it is important to note, _both sets can be equally effective_ in the respective settings for which they were developed.

One of the clearest illustrations of this point is afforded by the studies that Michael Cole carried out with Kpelle adults.[2] Cole was interested in the ability of "estimation," which has been used for a variety of selection purposes and which consists of accurately judging the dimensions or measurements of something by sight. He found that the Kpelle scored far below American norms on all of the standard problems of estimation that are normally used in the American culture. But, when given a locally appropriate problem—estimating how many cups of rice there are in a bowl—illiterate Kpelle were ten times as accurate as a comparison sample of U.S. adults.

If a certain job requires this type of ability, therefore, one _might_ find that he can select the best of a group of American applicants with a test based on the length of straight lines, and the best of a group of Kpelle applicants with a test based on the volume of rice in a bowl. In both instances, the test rationale would be based on the identical assumption—that the estimation task posed by the test is similar to the estimation tasks involved in the actual job operations. But the specific test exercises used in the two locations would not be the same.

The general principle that underlies this example follows directly from the basic rationale for aptitude tests described in the preceding discussion. In accordance with the three assumptions of this rationale, an appropriate test problem is one 1) that duplicates operations important to the course or job for which the applicants are being selected, 2) that the applicants are already able to perform at the time they are tested, 3) that the applicants have practiced sufficiently to have reached stable proficiency levels, and 4) that results in individual applicant scores that are sufficiently different to permit selection. Clearly, the tasks that best meet these specifications for groups with totally different backgrounds are unlikely to be the same; and clearly the tasks appropriate to Group A cannot be considered to be intrinsically "inferior" or of a "lesser standard" than those appropriate to Group B. Adaptation of the test content need not at all reduce the accuracy of selection that has traditionally been associated with a given test rationale.

Whether a given task actually meets the above specifications—whether estimating bowls of rice is in fact an effective predictor—is an empirical question. Until the test is actually tried, it is seldom wise to prejudge the results. In the estimation example, it may be that estimating volume is too different from the kinds of estimation involved in the actual job to meet the first of the requirements for an effective predictor. Or it may be that the fourth requirement would not be met because this skill is so highly practiced in the Kpelle culture that all applicants would earn the same score. In the absence of actual tryout data, there is no way of telling. But it does follow that rice problems or any other novel exercises <u>should not be dismissed out of hand</u>—so long as the rationale is sound—<u>just because</u> they do not conform to the "standard" exercises used in the American culture. And that is the first crucial point to be made about specific test adaptations.

The second point is an important corollary or qualification. Before embarking on an adaptation project, one should be quite sure that the backgrounds of the local applicants <u>really are sufficiently different to require different test items</u>. The backgrounds of Kpelle applicants apparently are, at least when estimation exercises are to be used. But, until this was shown, it could <u>not</u> be taken for granted.

The AID/AIR findings suggest that primary school students usually do require tests substantially different from the traditional versions. But at progressively higher educational levels, the differences are progressively smaller; at the university level, some (but not all) standard tests can safely be used without modification. Unless the need for adaptation is self-evident, the administrator should ask for data showing that the standard versions cannot be applied. He should understand, in accordance with the above principle, that adaptation will not necessarily degrade a test, and, in accordance with this corollary, that it will not necessarily improve a test, either.

The third point concerns the amount of background research that must be done to pinpoint the kinds of adaptations required. It is clear on the one hand that some research or experimentation is almost always essential. Without some studies of the type that Cole carried out in the Kpelle example, an effective estimation test probably could not be constructed. But it is also true that background research is one of the most costly steps in test construction, and the one that results in the longest delays before a test ready for use finally is completed. From the administrator's point of view, doing too much research is in many ways even more debilitating than not doing enough.

The two general guidelines for background research that were adopted for purposes of the AID/AIR project proved serviceable, and are recommended for other applied test development programs. The first was to do only such preliminary research as would produce specific content material for the test exercises that were to be written. The underlying dynamics of human behavior, however fascinating, would not be explored. The second was that as soon as there were sufficient test exercises to match the level of accuracy that similar tests provide in the United States, the preparatory research would stop. Further refinements would be left to the later follow-up studies, and the more basic research effort would be shifted to other tests.

The development of the I-D Verbal Analogies Test in Nigeria illustrates this approach. The objective was to design a scholastic aptitude test based on a skill of "verbal reasoning" or "concept formation." Each item was to contain an underlying concept or relationship that the examinee would have to discover, much as he has to be able to see relationships in the materials he studies in school. Thus, in an item such as

coconut and climb

cassava and ___?___

( ) eat

( ) cook

( ) dig

( ) earth

the concept of how one goes about getting this object would be the relationship to be discovered.

There were two major technical problems in writing suitable test exercises of this general type. One was to identify a sufficient number of concepts that were at the right level of difficulty for twelve-year-old Nigerian students. In a skill such as concept formation, there probably are wide intercultural variations. The other was to ensure that the test did measure individual differences in concept formation, and not in the students' relative command of the English vocabulary that solving these problems requires. Knowledge of a second language learned mainly in school would surely be influenced by the irrelevant differences in the quality of the primary schools that were noted in the earlier discussion of achievement tests as predictors.

With respect to the first of these problems, it was decided not to invest in elaborate preparatory research. A study of the development of concepts in the Nigerian culture would have been interesting, but was not necessary to the design of the test. Simply writing down concepts that came to mind as potentially appropriate, and then trying them out was far more expedient; and this is the approach that was adopted.

The second problem, however, presented additional complications. For there is no easy way of looking at the results of this type of test, and determining the extent to which vocabulary affected the scores. And so it was decided to invest in the development of an empirical list of the English words that virtually all students know, to use as source material in writing these and other verbal test items.

The procedure was to collect a sample of English themes from primary schools in different geographic locations, and to tabulate how many students used various words at least once in their papers.[3] At first, all of the words used were tabulated, and for a few dozen themes an accurate count was obtained. But after that point, a short-cut approach was applied. Whenever it became clear that a certain word was either so frequently used as to be sure to be near the head of the list, or so infrequent that it could not possibly catch up with the leaders, it was not counted in the subsequent tabulation. And when the tally reached the point at which a few hundred words far outstripped all the others, the study was stopped. The specific information that was needed to write forty test exercises had been assembled.

Had this been a study of the use of English in Nigeria, the procedure used would have had to be considered seriously deficient. It ignored much of the data, and only partially analyzed most of the rest. It did not establish the relative frequencies of the more common words at all precisely. It did not even consider the many additional words that might be in the passive vocabulary of the Nigerian student.

Its contribution to the professional literature on English usage was virtually nil.

In the development of a similar test in Thailand, moreover, it was decided not to repeat even this fragmentary research procedure, for in Thailand the second-language problem does not exist.* An appropriate verbal analogy test in this country can and should be written in Thai. Accordingly, the Thai version was developed by trial and error, with no background research whatsoever.

Despite all of these apparent shortcomings, however, this approach did produce operational tests fairly quickly; and these tests did turn out to be highly effective predictors. And this should be the overriding concern of the test constructor working against time to meet urgent operational needs in a developing country. For, although basic research surely is vitally important, it is more appropriately carried out in contexts other than that of an applied test development effort.

The spatial and perceptual tests described in later chapters will afford additional illustrations. For the developmental procedure used for these types of tests might well be described as trouble-shooting rather than as research. Each experimental study was addressed specifically and wholly to the perceptual difficulties that the examinees were having in coping with the particular set of test exercises then being adapted. In addition, each was addressed solely to a practical solution of these difficulties, not to an explication of the principles or dynamics involved.

This ultrapragmatic approach is understandably distasteful to most properly schooled researchers. And herein lies the major implication for the administrator evaluating the project design. Often it will have to be he who must ask whether a study suggested is really really necessary to the job to be done. Differentiating the necessary from the "instructive" is a third important consideration in planning the developmental procedure.

---

*In theory, the native languages of the Nigerian students could also have been used for this type of test. But because there are several hundred distinct languages in Nigeria, this was an impractical approach. English is the official language and the lingua franca throughout the country.

A fourth and final point is that effectively adapted testing procedures may in and of themselves not be enough to ensure the success of the students or trainees being selected. The course may have to be similarly adapted. Even though the test may be highly effective in selecting the most able of the applicant group, these very able individuals may nevertheless not be ready to profit from the standard course of instruction. The more the test content has had to be adapted, in fact, the less ready they are likely to be.

This difference between ability and readiness is shown perhaps most clearly in the case of the I-D Mechanical Information Test, which was one of the most successful of the AID/AIR test adaptations. It was developed as a means of selecting applicants for technical training institutions in West African countries. And the problem of test adaptation, of course, was to measure mechanical aptitude in individuals who had little prior experience with modern mechanical devices.

The adaptation process began, as always, with a standard test rationale. It was assumed that—

1. if certain mechanical and scientific phenomena are readily observable in each applicant's everyday surroundings,

2. if certain of the applicants have learned more than others from the incidental learning opportunities that these phenomena provide,

and

3. if the reason for this unequal learning lies in the applicants' unequal interests and inclinations,

then a test of familiarity with these phenomena should identify the applicants who are most inclined toward technical careers. The task was to find technical phenomena that are readily observable in rural Africa, since the gadgets used in the American applications of this rationale obviously would not do.

Finding and validating an adequate number of suitable test items took nearly a year.[4] But the resulting test was highly effective for a wide variety of applications in Africa and, with some further modifications, in other parts of the developing world. Its validity in selecting technical trainees was consistently as high or higher than that being attained by the standard version in the United States, as will be seen from the data presented in later chapters. The test clearly accomplished its mission of picking out the best of those who apply.

How the best of the African applicants, as identified by this test, compare in ability with the best of the American applicants, as identified by the standard test, cannot readily be determined. They might be the same, or poorer, or better with respect to potential. But it was clear that the best African applicants were considerably less ready than the best of the American trainees. For while an African who can answer a test question about an oil lamp may show as much basic aptitude as an American who can answer a question about an electric light, he will operate under a considerable handicap when he enters a course in which electricity is the topic of instruction. An individual who has not the background to answer questions about electricity (or gears or pulleys) when they appear on a test paper will have similar difficulties when he encounters them in a textbook or lecture.

Put another way, the content of the standard mechanical test is much closer to the content of the curriculum than is the content of the adapted version. And the very fact that the I-D tests had to move further away from the actual curriculum to be equally effective shows that the African examinee is less well prepared for the course than an American youngster of equivalent ability and potential. Selecting him with a test appropriate to his background and then subjecting him to an imported curriculum geared to the background of Americans does not make sense. And yet this is frequently done.

The implication is that the administrator evaluating a testing proposal should also consider the suitability of the course for which the test is to be used. If the plan is to use an imported curriculum with standard instructional materials at the established rate of speed, the development of culturally appropriate ability tests may well be a waste of time.

In summary, then, four major points have been made about specific test adaptations. The first was that changes of content do not cheapen or degrade a standard test, and do not imply that less able applicants will be selected. Often, adapting a test is the only way of identifying people as able as those selected in other countries with the traditional versions. The second was that although adaptation is normally required in a developing country, there can be exceptions; and the need for adaptation should be verified before the project proceeds. The third was that elaborate background research is seldom necessary to produce effective tests and should not be programmed when there is an immediate need for operational testing procedures. And the fourth was that training failures can as easily result from deficiencies in the course as deficiencies in testing, and that a project which would cure only the ills of the tests may therefore not yield the improvements desired.

THE TESTING MECHANICS

In the early planning of the AID/AIR research, an important decision was made about the mechanics of the tests to be developed. The objective would be to develop tests that could be administered to large groups of applicants by people with little or no background in testing; that cost no more than a few pennies each; and that were suited to rapid scoring by hand or machine. Tests that would have to be administered individually, that would use apparatus, or that would require professional testers were rejected as too costly for use in most developing countries.

This decision led to the intensive studies of the mechanics of testing that dominated the early months of the research. For it was soon found that taking a test is a highly skilled procedure that an examinee unaccustomed to objective testing cannot possibly master on the basis of the instructions typically provided. However adequate the standard test forms might be for the test-wise American or European youngster, they posed an impossible challenge for examinees who had not had this highly specialized training. Not infrequently, the skilled operations that the examinees had to learn to comply with the mechanics of the test exceeded in number and difficulty the operations involved in the specific skill the test was to measure.

Accordingly, it was necessary to change the format of the test paper, the manner in which instructions are given, the protocol for demonstration and practice sessions, the procedures for enforcing time limits, and other special conventions; nearly all aspects of modern test practice had to be reengineered. The exact nature of these changes will be described in Chapters 4 and 5, and therefore need not be elaborated further in this discussion. For the present purpose, it suffices to note that all this had to be done, at least at the primary school level, and that when done, the resulting tests did meet the criteria of economy and efficiency that had been established at the beginning of the research.

One implication of these findings relates directly to the earlier suggestion that the adequacy of standard test exercises should be checked before extensive adaptation studies are undertaken. To find out whether certain content material is suitable in the local situation, it clearly is necessary first to ensure that the mechanics used in presenting it are not themselves the source of the difficulties that may be noted when it is tried. Otherwise, entirely suitable material may be ruled out because of trivial mechanical malfunctions. Casting the standard exercises into the format recommended in Chapter 5, and then evaluating their suitability will provide a much sharper guide to the need for content revisions. Even when the examinees are reasonably sophisticated, the administrator should require such editing of the mechanics as a prerequisite to content evaluation.

A second implication is that proposals for the development of apparatus tests or individually administered procedures should generally be rejected. Except for a few high-risk applications (such as the selection of airline pilots or the certification of physicians, for example), the cumbersomeness and expense of such tests should be avoided. It is almost always possible to devise a mass-administered test of the same ability, using pencil and paper alone.

RECONCILING THE VIEWS ON TEST ADAPTATION

With this general background, it may be useful to reexamine the two examples that began this discussion. If the above criteria had been applied in these instances, what would have been the administrator's decision?

In the case of the English proficiency test, analysis would have shown that this issue was not really a testing problem. For the rationale of a proficiency test is that—

1. _if_ a given skill has been defined as consisting of certain specific items of knowledge and of certain specified skilled operations,

2. _if_ a test is constructed that measures an adequate sample of this knowledge and these operations,

and

3. _if_ the students do not know in advance which items will be included in the sample actually measured,

then the test will provide an accurate estimate of the degree to which mastery of the total set of component items has been achieved. The task of the test constructor is simply to select an adequate sample of the specific items of skill that the people who developed the curriculum decided to include in the course as appropriate teaching objectives. In this straightforward sampling procedure, issues of culture or background do not arise.

The development of different proficiency tests for different parts of a country, therefore, is not a methodological test adaptation. What it would in fact do would be to establish a different teaching objective for each different geographic location. Asking the educational system to define and teach a set of different "Englishes" throughout the country can hardly be considered an effective solution to the problem of interstudent variation.

The indicated solution—if the problem is indeed serious enough to warrant remedial action—is to use different curricula and instructional methods as appropriate for these different language groups, and thereby enable them all to attain the established teaching objective. A proposal for changing either the test or the objective on the grounds of background differences alone should be rejected.

Yet, it should also be noted that under somewhat different circumstances the objections to the traditional test that were raised in this example would be well founded. Were this same test being used as an ability test to select students for advanced education, the differences in their respective backgrounds would be vitally important. For now the applicable rationale would be that of the aptitude test, which does assume that the observed differences in achievement are the result of the applicants' individual learning skills rather than other factors. And the extraneous differences in their linguistic backgrounds might therefore rule out the use of this test, as did the differences in quality of prior instruction in the earlier discussion of secondary school selection procedures.

Thus, the reconciliation of the extreme views expressed in this situation depends entirely on the intended test application. If the purpose is simply to assess each student's present status with respect to the knowledge and skills the test actually measures, differences in background should not be considered. If the intent is to use these assessments to infer something about the respective abilities of the higher and lower achievers, and to generalize this to their future learning potential, their backgrounds somehow must be equated. Neither view is always right or always wrong, as is usually the case when extreme positions are being debated.

In the case of the American firm's employment practices, there was again some justification for both positions. The manager's focus on the equivalence of the job requirements at any and all locations was sound, but should have been directed at the test rationale rather than the individual test questions. He should have insisted that the same types of skills be evaluated in this country as had been found to be predictive in the United States, but should have realized as well that appropriate content modifications would not necessarily reduce the test's accuracy of prediction. An adapted form might well have been even more accurate in this country than the standard version is in the United States.

The professor's basic thesis, therefore, was sound. But his specific suggestions were somewhat misguided. The exercises that were not familiar to the examinees should not have been dropped entirely; rather, they should have been replaced with alternative measures of the same type of skill. And such "obvious" anomalies as the use of dollars and cents should not be corrected unless and until their inappropriateness has been demonstrated in empirical studies. Cosmetic changes of this general type usually have little effect, and may actually be harmful when there is an underlying skill—in this instance, working with decimals—that is more or less universal.

The mechanics of the test should have received special attention along the lines suggested above. And the need for adaptations of the standard training course for this job should also have been considered. All of the above suggestions, in fact, should have been applied in this situation, which encompasses in miniature the full range of testing problems encountered in a developing country.

This, at least, is the indicated approach from the technical point of view. A proposal for adapting the company's test in this manner would pass technical muster. But whether the gains would justify the fairly sizable costs inherent in the indicated procedure is a separate issue that the administrator must also examine. And this is the issue to be considered in the following chapter.

A SUMMARY CHECKLIST OF TECHNICAL CONSIDERATIONS

The preceding discussion suggested eight major questions that the administrator should ask when evaluating a test adaptation proposal. These are summarized below in a somewhat different order, to reflect the sequence in which they normally would be considered:

1. What is the rationale for using the proposed test for this particular testing problem?

2. Has this rationale been effective in meeting similar needs in other locations? Are there alternative rationales that have been found to be even better?

3. Are the specific assumptions that are inherent in this rationale consistent with local conditions?

4. Have the test items that are traditionally used in applications of this rationale actually been tried in this country to verify that they are deficient?

5. Is it certain that the deficiencies noted in the traditional items are attributable to the test content rather than to the testing mechanics?

6. Will all of the background studies being proposed contribute directly to the content of the new exercises to be prepared? Are there any nonessential aspects of this research that can be deferred?

7. Will the resulting test meet the practical constraints on costs, examiners, and logistics? Are there alternative formats that are more economical or efficient?

8. Is the curriculum for which the examinees are being selected sufficiently attuned to local conditions to make superior selection practices truly worthwhile?

The answers to many of these questions, it may have been noted, do not depend on "cultural" issues at all, if this term is used narrowly to refer only to a people's habits, skills, and traditions. Differences in the development of educational systems, for example, are seldom attributable to cultural variations among the countries being compared. But this is the term that has generally been used in the context of test adaptation, and it will continue to be used in this very broad sense throughout the handbook to refer to all of the special needs of the developing countries.

NOTES

1. For a fuller discussion of these points, see P. A. Schwarz, "Prediction Instruments for Educational Outcomes," in R. L. Thorndike, Educational Measurement (Washington, D.C.: American Council on Education, 1971).

2. Michael Cole, "The Puzzle of Primitive People," Psychology Today (March, 1968), 48-49.

3. We are grateful to Barry Eisenberg of the Peace Corps for collecting these themes, and to Joan Kontos for designing and supervising the tabulation procedure.

4. Much of this work was done by Professor Frank Scott of Western Michigan University as part of his doctoral dissertation.

CHAPTER

2

TESTING REFORM AS AN INVESTMENT

Having determined that a proposed test development program is sound from a technical point of view, the administrator next must try to assess its priority relative to the many other projects that usually are pending. For in most developing countries, it is impossible to fund and staff more than a small fraction of the programs that clearly are "sound" and that clearly are "urgent"; and the administrator has in effect to decide which of the programs that cannot possibly wait shall be put off still further. The relative payoff of the proposed investment is a second crucial consideration.

Computing the benefits of a program in terms of its overall contributions to "national development" has proved to be a most difficult proposition. Even for apparently straightforward economic investments, no one has yet been able to do this precisely. In such a field as testing it is hopelessly unrealistic.[1] How much a test development program would contribute relative to, say, an expansion of the facilities for teacher training simply cannot be reduced to numbers. Yet, the administrator can and should be provided with as much data on the anticipated payoffs and the projected costs as can be assembled. Especially when the costs will be high or when external aid will be required, such information is essential to what often becomes a most difficult tradeoff decision.

This chapter describes the types of cost-effectiveness data that can be assembled when the aim of the proposed project is limited to the improvement of the actual testing procedures. For the present, it will be assumed that the facilities and institutional infrastructure necessary to implement the program already exist, and that the trained personnel the project requires are already on hand. Whether to invest money and time in the development of new and hopefully better methods will be the only consideration. Then, Chapter 8 will extend the discussion to the more typical situation in which the necessary capabilities and institutions also must be created.

THE PAYOFF POTENTIAL

The net payoff of a change in the present testing procedure depends on three major factors. On the positive side, there are 1) the improvements that will result in the accuracy of the decisions that are being made on the basis of the candidates' scores, and 2) the reductions of the present logistic difficulties of testing that will be effected. On the negative side, there are 3) the new problems that will arise as a result of change in the established procedure. Generally, all three factors should be considered.

Improvements in the Accuracy of Test-Based Decisions

After the new tests have been developed, the gains in accuracy that they provide can be measured fairly precisely.* But when their development is still at the stage of a pending proposal, their eventual accuracy obviously cannot be determined; only circumstantial evidence can be assembled.

Such circumstantial evidence can be collected at three levels of effort, in accordance with the nature of the problem and the magnitude of the proposed investment. At the simplest level, the data are limited to the seriousness of the operational problems that have arisen because of inadequate testing procedures. If the present situation is intolerable, or if the proposed investment is modest, estimates of the exact magnitude of the improvement likely to be achieved may not be required. If the situation is less critical or if the investment is substantially higher, some quantification of the expected gains should be attempted.

---

*An important limitation in the accuracy of such after-the-fact measures is that the criteria for assessing an examinee's later performance in school or on the job are generally deficient. None of the criteria typically used—grades, ratings, production records, etc.—provides an entirely satisfactory, index of the quality of performance. The development of more adequate criteria continues to be the single most important need of educational and occupational testing.

At the intermediate level of effort, the accuracy of the present procedures is computed and compared with the results typically obtained in other countries. The assumption is that similar results will be obtained here once suitable tests have been constructed. At the highest level, this assumption is put to the test by carrying out an actual pilot study, using tests similar to those to be constructed. But this can be done only, of course, when reasonably suitable tests are available for experimentation.

To illustrate these approaches, examples will be cited from studies of vocational selection tests and of secondary school admission procedures, which were the two applications most fully discussed from the technical point of view in the preceding chapter. Again, each example is an event that was actually observed during the course of the study.

Accuracy of Vocational Selection Tests

It seems appropriate to begin with vocational selection because this is how the AID/AIR project itself began.

A senior official of the International Cooperation Administration (the predecessor of AID) made an inspection tour of the technical training institutes in Sub-Saharan Africa that the U.S. government was supporting. He found that in terms of facilities and equipment and teaching staff these were all first-class institutions, but that their output generally was appalling. The numbers of trainees enrolled were far below the capacities for which these institutions had been designed; and the proficiency of even these few trainees was lower than had been expected. The central program objective was not being achieved.

The specialists he consulted attributed much of the blame to the lack of selection methods appropriate to the African culture. Suitable tests, they felt sure, would do much to resolve the difficulties that he had noted. But they pointed out also that the development of tests for another culture was a highly risky proposition, and that an investment in testing might well result in no tangible returns.

Still, the magnitude of the U.S. investment in technical training was so very much higher than the costs of the testing project suggested that he decided this was a risk worth taking. Any measurable improvement, translated into U.S. training dollars, would represent a handsome return.[2]

Thus, in the case of the initial AID/AIR project, it was the first of the above approaches that was applied. The judgment of high payoff potential was based not on an estimate of the degree to which the accuracy of selection would be upgraded, but on an assessment of the value of each increment in accuracy that might be achieved, which was in this instance the overriding consideration. And this criterion is generally adequate when the present methods entail losses that the administrator cannot afford to ignore.

When the magnitude of the losses is less compelling, an estimate of the probable gain is usually necessary for an adequate project appraisal. This was the case in the AIR survey of testing needs in Malawi, which (though directed at institution-building rather than at reform of any one testing procedure) affords a convenient example of both the second and third of the above approaches.

One of the specific test applications examined during a first and highly preliminary survey was the selection program of the Malawi Polytechnic, which is the country's premier vocational and technical training institution. Special attention was given to the Basic Technology Course because it was at this junior level that the most serious problems had been reported.

The records showed that the present class of 60 trainees had been selected from a group of 1,350 applicants by a three-stage selection procedure. The first had been to obtain ratings on their character, scholastic ability, and attendance from the primary schools that they had attended, and to eliminate all applicants who had less than straight-A ratings on these three characteristics. This left 200 of the original applicant group. The second stage had been to submit the application forms of these 200 to a central review panel, which selected the 120 who seemed best on paper. And the third had been to give this further reduced group English and arithmetic tests, and to have each applicant interviewed by an experienced instructor as the final admission hurdle.

Yet, despite this methodical procedure fully a third of the entrants had been found to be unsatisfactory even before the first term was completed. Five had been dismissed, six had been placed on probation, and nine others were being given one last chance before formal action was taken.

In view of the very favorable selection ratio (22 applicants per trainee admitted), and in light of the much better results that had been consistently obtained in West African with similar groups, it was concluded that the selection procedure was indeed deficient. And it seemed safe to predict that the introduction of suitable aptitude tests would lead to substantial improvements at or about the level of the West Africa findings.

Given the limited objective of the preliminary survey—to determine whether the situation was sufficiently promising to warrant a feasibility study in depth—this midlevel approach of drawing on experience elsewhere provided an entirely adequate basis for estimating the payoff potential. Had the focus of the survey been limited to the Malawi Polytechnic alone, it would in fact have provided an adequate basis for even the final decision of whether the development of new tests for this institution should or should not be undertaken.

But because of the high cost of the professional and institutional development that would have to be carried out in Malawi to provide the necessary infrastructure for testing, this and the other preliminary findings justified only a more intensive feasibility check. And for this purpose, the highest of the three levels of evaluation approaches was judged to be the appropriate procedure.

In the second study, the survey team administered a set of the I-D vocational aptitude tests to this same class of Polytechnic trainees (at this point only 49 of the original 60 remained), and compared their scores with the grades they had been given by their class and shopwork instructors. It was found that the test scores and grades were indeed highly related, as measured by a standard coefficient of correlation.

Then, this purely statistical relationship was translated into more meaningful operational terms. First, it was assumed that the 25 trainees who had the highest overall grades in class and shop were generally successful and represented "good" selection decisions, and that the 35 lower performers (including the 11 dismissals) were not up to par and represented selection "misses." Then the statistical findings obtained for the I-D aptitude tests were converted into the numbers of selection successes and misses that would probably have occurred if these tests had been included in the selection procedure.

The results showed that if the original pool of 1,350 applicants contained a sufficient number of potentially successful trainees—and experience elsewhere suggested that it almost certainly did—use of the I-D tests would probably have resulted in 59 "good" selection decisions; the one "miss" would probably not have been so poor a performer as to warrant dismissal. Or, stated a bit more precisely, the results indicated that 59 of the trainees would have attained the level of proficiency that was presently being achieved by only the top 25. An additional 34 would have been "good" performers.[3]

Selecting the top 25 as the yardstick for comparison was, of course, an arbitrary decision. The top 20 or 30 or any other similar number could have been used instead. The point was to report the results to the administrator in a form such as "number of trainees who will attain a significantly higher proficiency level," and thereby to enable him to assess the magnitude of the gain in terms of the tangible improvements to be expected. This is the relatively high degree of quantification that is always available from the third of the above assessment approaches. It will be described and illustrated further in Part III of this handbook, in the review of past I-D test applications.

Accuracy of Secondary School Admission Procedures

Each of these three assessment approaches can be applied to school admissions in a manner exactly analogous to that described above for vocational selection. One can look at the high cost of failures or at the accuracy that is being achieved here relative to that obtained at other locations, or actually compute the magnitude of the improvement likely to be effected. The vocational selection examples illustrate the standard approaches that are appropriate for all types of test applications.

The following examples illustrate some of the possible variations in the ways in which these three methods can be applied. The first is an example of one of the many criteria other than student performance that may lead an administrator to decide that the present situation must be corrected.

When the results of the secondary school admission tests were announced, one part of the country obtained far less than its "fair share" of the available places relative to its proportion of the country's total population. This happened also to be the region that had the poorest quality of primary schools in the country, and deliberate discrimination was charged. The tests used, it was claimed, were designed to deny admission to students from these disadvantaged primary schools so as to perpetuate the dominant position of the ethnic-political group in power.

The affair quickly became a major political issue, debated at parliament level. Action had to be taken.

In this situation, a proposal that on technical grounds promised to mitigate or resolve this problem would almost certainly have received immediate attention. Because of the high value of each unit of payoff, quantification of the total payoff anticipated would probably not . have been required.

Had the same type of deficiency been uncovered by the professional community, however, or had there not been such severe political repercussions, a more precise assessment would have been necessary to justify an investment in testing. The following three examples, based on a manifestation of the same problem in another location, illustrate the successively higher levels of quantification that can be attempted.

The principal of a government secondary school in northern Nigeria maintained records of the scores that all of his entering students students had earned on the admission examination. After a period of several years he systematically compared these scores with the students' subsequent academic performance.

He found that during their first year of secondary schooling, the students with the top scores on the entrance test did indeed perform much better than the students who barely qualified for admission. But during the second year, the relative superiority of these high-scoring students was greatly reduced. By the fourth year, the scores on the students' admission tests and the indexes of their scholastic performance had no apparent relationship whatsoever. Students with low entrance test scores performed as well and in many cases better than those who at the time of admission had scored much higher.

He concluded that the present admission procedure selected not the students with the highest potential, but those with the best preparation. They started out as apparently superior students simply because they had learned more at the primary school level and therefore could keep ahead of those who in fact had greater ability and potential. Their actual abilities did not emerge until sufficient time had elapsed to overcome these differences in initial preparation. And he reasoned that if the students' actual abilities are not being measured as the criterion for secondary school admission, much of the talent available in northern Nigeria is no doubt being wasted.

This analysis is entirely consistent with the earlier discussion of the rationale for using achievement tests as predictors, and is persuasive from a technical point of view. But for the decision the administrator must make, such findings are not sufficient. They indicate neither the magnitude of the loss nor the generalizability of the data throughout the region. Nor do they even demonstrate that a problem exists. If the students admitted were all at sufficiently high ability levels, differences in motivation alone would offer an alternate explanation for the phenomenon the principal had observed.

Thus, more information was needed. But extending the above approach to a larger sample would have entailed a wait of four additional years and thus was unrealistic. It was decided instead to analyze the results of the preceding admission test, using a variant of the second of the above evaluation procedures.

The first step was to obtain ratings from the Inspectorate of the Ministry of Education on the quality of the primary schools in the various portions of the Northern Region. This made it possible to identify "advantaged" and "disadvantaged" locations with respect to the quality of primary schooling.

The second step was to compare the admission test scores of a sample of students from these advantaged and disadvantaged locations. When this had been done, it was found that the two distributions were almost nonoverlapping. That is, the highest scores of the disadvantaged set were about the same as the lowest scores of the advantaged sample. If students from the two groups were competing for admission to the same institution, the latter would inevitably be selected.

That such large differences could result wholly or largely from differences in student potential seemed highly unlikely, on the basis of experience in the United States and other countries. To the extent that students from the disadvantaged areas were being denied admission to the secondary schools, talent surely was being wasted. And, by making certain assumptions about the actual distribution of ability, and about its relationship with academic performance (again drawing on experience elsewhere), it was possible to estimate the probable amount of loss from the students' scores on the preceding examination.

Here, the comparisons with the findings in other countries were far more complex than in the preceding examples. But the analysis did provide an immediate estimate which, however crude, was preferable to waiting for the results of a proper follow-up study.

Had there been no potentially suitable aptitude tests to use for further experimentation, moreover, the evaluation could not have proceeded beyond this midlevel assessment. These findings would have had to serve as the basis for the administrator's decision. Further, whether they would have been adequate to prompt testing reform would have depended mainly on the magnitude of the necessary investment.

But because scholastic aptitude tests validated for use in Nigeria were by this time already at hand, it was feasible to proceed to the next higher level.

Arrangements were made to administer a set of I-D scholastic aptitude tests to a sample of last-year primary school students in both advantaged and disadvantaged locations, shortly before the next secondary school admission tests were to be given. Then, after the administration of the admission tests had been completed, the scores on these two types of tests were compared.

Comparative data were available for approximately 500 students. On the admission tests the differences between the advantaged and disadvantaged samples were as large as before. But on the aptitude tests, the average scores of the two groups were almost exactly the same.

This confirmed the earlier hypotheses about the deficiencies in the existing procedures; even more importantly, it showed that aptitude tests relatively unaffected by variations in school quality actually can be constructed. Realistic estimates of the improvements likely to be effected in northern Nigeria, therefore, could now be computed.

In the absence of high attrition rates for strong political pressure, this more detailed analysis was the appropriate level of justification for an investment in improved admission procedures.

The purpose of these and the earlier examples has been to suggest a variety of approaches to the evaluation of qualitative payoff potential. The important implications for the administrator are as follows:

1. Estimates of the improvements that are likely to be realized from testing reform can and usually should be developed.

2. The comprehensiveness of such estimates can and should be scaled to the magnitude of the proposed investment, using one of three basic evaluation approaches.

3. Reasonably accurate estimates can sometimes be obtained quite economically by using the appropriate tests of the I-D series.

The provision of widely applicable tests for use in such advance appraisals has turned out to be an important by-product of the early African studies.

Improvements in Testing Logistics

This discussion of expected procedural improvements is being treated as a topic coordinate with the above discussion of quality gains to emphasize their importance. In most of the developing countries, logistic difficulties are far more serious than they are in the highly industrialized nations, and warrant proportionately more careful attention. Not infrequently, the procedural simplifications that may result from a test development project will be regarded as a payoff equal to or greater than that provided by substantive content revisions.

The approaches that may be used to evaluate this type of payoff are similar to those already described for assessing the probable gains in the accuracy of the decision to which the test will be applied. Again, the evaluation may be based on considerations of the severity of the problem alone, or augmented by actual measures of the improvements likely to be effected.

The most straightforward situation is one in which logistic changes are absolutely essential. The problem described in the following example is not at all unusual in a developing country.

Because of the rapid expansion of the country's primary schools, the number of candidates for admission to secondary school would rise from 30,000 to 70,000 within a few years. Traditionally, a set of essay tests had been used as the secondary school admission procedure. But even at the present level of only 30,000 applicants, the Examination Division was hard pressed to complete the marking of the papers by the time the results had to be ready for use. The projected increase in papers represented a physically impossible task, and a change to objective tests was recommended.

Further quantification in this context clearly should not, and in fact could not, have been attempted. If the situation was indeed impossible, change could not be avoided.

When the consequences of the logistic difficulties are less apparent, additional data may be required. The following examples, illustrative of these kinds of less dramatic problems, were observed in a number of different countries.

In one country the Ministry of Education was trying to upgrade the quality of its secondary school teachers by offering special teacher-improvement courses during the school vacation. But because most of the teachers had to devote this time to the marking of the admission tests, they could not attend these improvement courses.

At another location that also mobilized its teachers as scorers, the volume of testing had already risen to the point at which the teachers could no longer keep up with the numbers of papers to be corrected. It was discovered that one overworked teacher had given half of the papers to his eleven-year-old nephew to grade, and a national scandal resulted.

At still another location, the marking of the admission tests could not be completed until several months after the school term had started. A fairly large number of students who had been admitted provisionally pending the scoring of the examination had later to be expelled, leading to the predictable repercussions.

Problems of these types might be considered sufficiently serious to trigger reform, or they might not, depending on the investment and on specific local conditions.

When additional information is needed, a more precise appraisal of the magnitude of the problem is frequently the indicated approach. Especially when there are only isolated symptoms of trouble, as in the example of the eleven-year-old scorer, a systematic check of the extent to which these problems occur nationwide will clearly provide a better basis for deciding on the urgency of reform. Such further explorations of the problem itself are variants of the first of the above evaluation approaches.

The midlevel approach of drawing on experience elsewhere also can be applied to the evaluation of procedural modifications. In the last of the above examples, knowing that the marking that is taking so many months here is being accomplished in one week in a neighboring country (as it actually was) provides a highly convenient yardstick for estimating the magnitude of the improvement that probably will be effected. Unlike major substantive changes, the efficacy of mechanical and procedural routines is seldom a function of specific cultural factors, and the results obtained at one location can be generalized with considerable assurance to any other.

So accurate are these generalizations, in fact, that local tryouts are rarely required. It is only when there is a specific reason for thinking that the suggested procedure will not work that pilot studies should be undertaken. This happens most often on issues that have more of an emotional than a factual basis, such as the relative merit of composition exercises and objective tests.[4] If a large number of educators believe that objective tests at least as accurate as the present essay tests cannot be constructed, a demonstration project may have to be carried out as part of the evaluation procedure.

A final point on logistic improvements is that the very process of changing the testing mechanics frequently results in improvements of the test content as well. When a test is being closely inspected—whether it was substance or form that actually led to the study—deficiencies of both types are often discovered. And, inasmuch as the test is to be reprinted in any event, all of the indicated improvements are made. Revisions that result in changes of form or content alone are the exception.

The implications for assessing a test's total payoff potential, therefore, are two:

1. The assessment of logistic improvements can be carried out in much the same way as the evaluation of the benefits attributable to substantive revisions.

2. Estimates of the probable payoff of testing reform should always encompass both qualitative and procedural gains, irrespective of which happens to be the major developmental objective.

The Negative Consequences of Testing Reform

When the expected benefits have been tabulated and seem impressive, the possibility of negative side-effects should be explored. Any new problems that are created by change in the established order will either reduce the net value of payoff that has been projected or require special corrective action that will increase the projected cost. Either way, the estimate of cost-effectiveness will be affected.

Negative consequences follow mainly from procedural changes, since these are more visible than the esoteric content revisions. The following example was noted during one of the feasibility studies.

The decision to be made was whether or not automatic data processing, including test-scoring machines, was a sound investment for this particular country. And, on the basis of an initial appraisal, the advantages seemed overwhelming. The teachers who had traditionally been used as scorers clearly could not keep up with the rapidly mounting volume of testing, and most of the logistic problems noted above were already being encountered. On qualitative and procedural grounds, the use of machines was the indicated solution.

Yet it was also discovered that the traditional method served another important function. Under the terms of the government's austerity program, the salaries of the country's teachers could not be increased; the extra pay they received for marking the tests was intended in part as a device for raising their income to a reasonable subsistence level. Introducing machines would lead in effect to a sizable cut in the salaries of the large number of teachers affected. Any computation of the payoff of automatic data processing that did not take this negative by-product into account would have been seriously misleading.

A quite different class of consequences is the phenomenon that is usually called the backwash effect. When the educational system is geared to a set of external examinations, the teachers will naturally tend to give the greatest emphasis to the topics that they expect the examinations to cover. Topics that appear frequently are taught intently; topics that are rarely included are taught superficially or not at all.

Thus it can happen that a conversion from essay tests to objective questions provides vastly superior measures from a statistical point of view but pedagogically leads to a marked drop in the teaching of composition in all of the country's language classes. This may well be regarded as an intolerable by-product that offsets all of the positive payoffs expected. Using a combination of objective tests and composition exercises, though much more costly, may prove on balance to be the better procedure.*

---

*A useful compromise that was developed in one country was to administer both objective and essay tests, but to score and use the essay tests for only the "short list" of finalists who were selected from the much-larger pool of applicants on the basis of the objective tests only. This procedure was not publicized, however, to avoid backwash effects.

Nor is the impact of drastic changes in testing limited to the teaching profession. Negative reactions may arise also among students, parents, alumni, or any other group accustomed to and comfortable with the traditional procedure. Often, an extensive public information program, carried out in advance of the change, is another necessary investment.

Overall, the varieties and intensities of potentially negative outcomes can seldom be accurately predicted. Unanticipated consequences almost always occur. But an attempt at identifying as many of these side-effects as practicable should nevertheless be included as an explicit step of the evaluation procedure.

Quantifying the Total Payoff Potential

Throughout this discussion of payoff potential a wide range of payoff categories has been considered. They have spanned the effects of testing on investments in new technical training centers, on political stability within the country, on wastage of potentially productive human resources, on the effectiveness of teacher improvement courses, on teacher salaries, on teaching methods, and on several types of public reaction. What are the implications of this list for the quantification of a test's total payoff potential?

The first implication is that the degree of quantification that can be achieved depends not only on the sophistication of the assessment method applied, but also on the <u>basic nature of the problems</u> that the new test is to resolve. Such problems as "loss of training investments" are inherently more quantifiable than any problem of "adverse public reaction," no matter how much or how little data may be collected. The definition of the problem itself imposes a ceiling on the degree of quantification that can be expected.

The second is that even for the most quantifiable of the above payoffs, entirely <u>adequate metrics of value do not exist</u>. In the Malawi Polytechnic example, the estimate of "34 substantially more proficient trainees" that was obtained is as quantified a payoff as can be provided for improvements in testing. But the actual worth of each proficient technician to Malawi's development is unknown; and the benefits of improved testing relative to other investments can therefore not be computed.

The third is that the various payoffs that a single test may provide <u>cannot be combined into one overall measure</u>. Although it is possible to impose a common denominator on the different categories of payoffs—such as their respective financial implications—the tortured assumptions that are necessary to translate each payoff to a common base make such efforts unrealistic. And because testing reform usually does have two or more separate payoffs, this is another problem in quantifying the total potential.

Accordingly, the procedure that seems most consistent with the present state of the art in payoff assessment is as follows:

1. Identify each of the anticipated categories of payoff that is likely to result from the proposed change in testing procedure;

2. Treat each category separately in determining the appropriate type and degree of quantification (if any) that should be attempted; and

3. Report the results in the form of a "profile" of payoffs, each of which is described qualitatively, and some of which are also reduced to numbers.

The synthesis of this profile into an overall payoff assessment must necessarily be left to the judgment of the administrator who will decide on the project's implementation.

COSTS AND COST REDUCTION

The cost of a new testing program consists of the capital investment that is necessary to develop an instrument ready for use and the recurrent expenses that will be incurred each time it is applied. The major capital costs include the preparation of the trial tests; the conduct of one or more of the developmental sequences of tryout, analysis and revision; and the collection of the statistical information that will be needed to interpret the scores when the tests are eventually given. The recurrent expenses consist of the printing, storage, and distribution of the various test papers; the administration of the tests at one or more field locations; the scoring, analysis, and reporting procedures; and the periodic revisions that must be made to change, update, or improve the tests for future administrations. And sometimes there are certain additional categories of expenditures, such as examiner training or public information programs, that also must be included.

Because the discussions of these items in the standard literature of testing are equally applicable in a developing country, they need not be reviewed in detail.[5] Rather, the focus will be on the few items that are especially susceptible to distortion; and on the savings in cost that often can be effected.

The Capital Investment

Estimates of the developmental costs of producing a new test are necessarily approximations. It is difficult to judge the amount of research that will be required to prepare a form ready for trial, to predict the number of cycles of tryout and revision that will be necessary to produce the operational version, and to anticipate all of the contingencies that will arise. Especially when the test is of a type never before used in this country, or when it will have to meet stringent statistical specifications, the risk of appreciable errors of estimate cannot be avoided.

There is a second category of even larger errors that can and should be avoided, however. These are the errors that arise from the inclusion of developmental procedures which are not truly essential and thereby inflate the budget beyond the amount that actually must be expended. The extravagance of background research that does not contribute directly to the content of the test exercises, already discussed in Chapter 1, is one common example.

A second example, perhaps even more prevalent, is the heavy investment in test norms that has been made in a number of countries. Though it is one of the shibboleths of testing that every test should have adequate "reliability, validity, and normative data" before it is put into use, there are in fact many situations in which norms are superfluous; and these situations are the more numerous in a developing country.

Basically, the purpose of normative data is to permit a reasonable interpretation of an individual's test score when he is the only one being tested or when the decision to be made about him does not depend on his performance relative to that of the other candidates who are taking the test at the same time (as would be the case, for example, if all of them could be admitted). In these situations, it is important to know whether a score of "38 out of 50 correct" is good enough for admission, poor enough to warrant rejection, or in-between enough to suggest putting off a decision until more applicants have been invited to come in for testing. Such judgments are possible only when a large and representative sample of individuals has already been tested and has provided the norms (or distributions of typical scores) with which this particular score can be compared.

When there is a fixed number of applicants for a fixed number of places, however, such external yardsticks are not required. The applicant with a test score of 38 is accepted if his competitors earn lower scores, rejected if they score higher. Information on his performance relative to the general population of nonapplicants is not pertinent to the decision.

In the developing countries situations of both types arise. But usually it is only the huge testing programs for which an investment in original test development is at all realistic, and most of these are of the competitive type for which normative data are not required. The inclusion of normative studies in the design of projects addressed to these situations will seriously distort the cost-effectiveness appraisal, since norming a test is by far the most costly of the preparatory data-collection procedures.

Similar though less serious distortions can also be introduced in the design of the other data-collection activities that are part of test construction. The most frequent is the use of larger samples of examinees than necessary for the tryout of the preliminary versions. Especially in the first tryout, more can often be learned by giving the test individually to half a dozen examinees and asking them to explain their answers than can be learned from the full-scale analysis of a large number of scores. Even in the final reliability checks only a modest sample is necessary to determine whether or not the test is ready to use, which is generally the only function these checks are to serve. Accurate reliability estimates are useful only when these estimates will actually be used to adjust or weight the test scores, and it is wasteful to invest in the large sample that a more precise estimate requires when such adjustments are not intended.

Thus, the criterion for evaluating a proposed capital investment in testing should focus less on the accuracy of the estimates that have been made than on the relevance of the items that have been included. And the cost items related to background research and to experimental tryouts should be given especially careful attention.

The Recurrent Costs

The costs of using the test once it has been developed can be estimated much more accurately than the developmental expenses. If a step-by-step scenario is prepared of the entire process that will be followed from the preparation of the copy for printing to the reporting of the results, the necessary items of cost can be systematically listed and, being essentially logistic routines, costed fairly precisely. In estimates of the recurrent costs, problems seldom arise.

The interpretation of the completed estimate frequently does raise problems, however. The evaluation of the recurrent costs is generally based not on the absolute amount that will be required, but on the cost of the proposed test relative to that of the present procedure. In many situations it is difficult or impossible to obtain an estimate of the present costs that is truly comparable to the recurrent costs of the proposed modification.

One type of difficulty is the strictly mechanical one of extracting the information from the budgets and records on file. Usually, the office responsible for the conduct of the testing program has other responsibilities as well, and separate records of its expenses for each different type of activity are rarely maintained. There are single-line items for all salaries, all travel, and all printing combined; prorating these costs introduces errors of perhaps sizable proportions.

A second difficulty is that the present procedure may not include certain steps that properly should be included to make it effective, and that the costs actually being incurred therefore do not give an accurate picture of the true cost of this approach. If the tests are currently being scored manually, for example, but the check-scoring that should be done to ensure reasonable accuracy is being omitted, comparisons with a proposed machine-scoring procedure that is known to be 98 percent accurate clearly will be misleading. However, there is no entirely satisfactory adjustment that can be made. Computing the present cost on the basis of what it "should" be introduces an element of the hypothetical that may cast doubt on the reliability of the entire costing procedure. And the alternative approach of taking account of this difference by simply including improved accuracy among the benefits of the new program does not give sufficient weight to the present problem of scoring errors that (in the absence of check-scoring) is probably not known to exist.

Similar difficulties arise also in trying to attach cost figures to expenditures that do not have direct monetary implications. If the manual scoring of the test papers in the above example is currently being done by salaried teachers without extra pay, the present scoring operation may be regarded in one sense as free. But, in another sense, the time that these teachers might otherwise be able to devote to study and course preparation is not free at all. Yet, what cost figure is a fair representation of this expense? The problem here is the same as that typically encountered in trying to quantify the payoffs expected, and approaches for satisfactorily resolving it do not exist.

For these reasons, even the hardest of cost data will usually be found to be much less clear-cut than the bare figures at first suggest. As much judgment may be required in the interpretation of the recurrent costs as in the evaluation of the apparently softer payoff projections.

Cost Reduction

Assessing the cost-effectiveness of a program makes sense, of course, only when the absolute amount of the costs could in fact be provided within the total budget that the administrator has at his disposal. If the costs are excessive on absolute grounds, the proposal must be rejected irrespective of its payoff potential.

This happens infrequently when the proposal reform is limited to the testing procedures, as has been assumed throughout this discussion; the costs of substantive and procedural revisions alone are seldom so high as to be considered excessive. But when this does happen to be the case, an alternative approach must be sought that permits the necessary reductions in the capital or the recurrent costs or both to be effected.

The most feasible way of accomplishing this is to find ways of sharing the costs among a larger number of users, so that the investment that each one must make is trimmed to manageable proportions. The following procedure, first used in Liberia, illustrates an approach that is generally useful when it is the low volume of testing that makes the costs prohibitive for any single consumer.

The manager of a local commercial establishment was dissatisfied with the performance of a certain specialized clerical function, and wanted to upgrade the selection procedure. But his annual rate of employment for these specialized positions was too low to justify either the capital or the recurrent cost of introducing a custom-made testing program.

But there were numerous other small employers who were also experiencing difficulties in recruiting competent staff for other types of essentially clerical positions. It was thought that a series of basic clerical tests—though perhaps less effective than tests addressed specifically to the requirements of each position—might offer substantial improvements for all of these spearate employment decisions. Accordingly, a series of "general office worker" tests was developed for use with a wide variety of clerical positions; experimental tryouts confirmed that it was indeed generally effective. This solved the problem of the excessive capital cost that would have been required to develop a separate testing program for each employer.

The problem with respect to the recurrent costs was that applicants for these positions were recruited one or two at a time, and administering the tests to such small groups was far too expensive. Yet, no employer could expect to "hold" his applicants for two or three months while waiting for the group to build up to the thirty or more that were needed to conduct an economical testing session. The solution was to hold a regularly scheduled testing session for office workers "every other Monday" at the central testing center, and to invite all employers to send their applicants to these regular sessions. Some Mondays, there were only a few; some Mondays the room was crowded. But the average per capita cost was sufficiently low so that an extremely modest fee met all of the recurrent expenses.

In a developing country, where there are generally large numbers of small employers, and where it is seldom possible to purchase suitable "off-the-shelf" tests from publishing houses, this is an effective compromise, and one that can be used for public as well as private employers.

In this example, the solution depended on the existence of a central testing center. And, as will be noted also in the subsequent chapters on institution-building, this is generally a prerequisite for significant cost reduction.

A SUMMARY CHECKLIST OF COST-EFFECTIVENESS CONSIDERATIONS

The preceding discussion was addressed to the many issues that arise in evaluating the cost-effectiveness of a proposed change in an existing testing procedure. The following eight lines of inquiry were suggested:

1. Are the operational problems for which the new tests will be addressed so serious that quantifying the anticipated improvements is not really necessary to a fair project appraisal? Or should some quantification of the probable payoffs be undertaken?

2. If quantification is necessary, is it sufficient to compare the situation here with the related findings in other countries? Or does the magnitude of the investment require onsite pilot studies?

3. If a pilot study has been completed, have the statistical findings been translated into a measure of the tangible improvements that would be effected?

4. Does the payoff assessment include all of the different categories of payoff, in quality and in logistics, that can reasonably be expected?

5. Have the potentially negative consequences of a change in the traditional procedure been adequately considered?

6. Are all of the developmental steps that comprise the proposed capital investment really essential? Are the scope and scale of the experimental tryouts consistent with the applications that will in fact be made of the data to be collected?

7. Is the estimate of the recurrent cost of the present approach truly comparable to the estimate of the recurrent costs of the new procedure? Are there important qualitative differences that should also be taken into account?

8. Are there other similar test needs in the country that could also be met within the scope of this project, so as to reduce the magnitute of the per capita investment?

These questions and the ones listed at the end of the preceding chapter are cumulative, in that both sets must be applied in an overall assessment of a proposed change in established testing procedures. Similarly, the checklist of institutional issues in Chapter 8 is to be added to these two for a comprehensive evaluation of an institutional development proposal.

NOTES

1. This comment applies to such global criteria as "national development" only. The cost-effectiveness of a test in terms of its contributions to a specific selection program generally can be computed. See L. Cronbach and G. Gleser, Psychological Tests and Personnel Decisions (Urbana: University of Illinois Press, 1957).

2. This official was John K. Meskimen of the Office of Labor Affairs, whose central role in initiating the research should be specifically acknowledged.

3. A more complete description of the studies at the Malawi Polytechnic is given in C. Langmuir and D. Nichols, Educational and Occupational Testing in Malawi: Needs and Recommendations (Pittsburgh: American Institutes for Research, August 10, 1965).

4. One of the reasons for the low regard in which objective tests are held in many developing countries is that the local educators are most familiar with "true-false" forms and other elementary approaches, and have not been exposed to the more sophisticated techniques later developed. We found it helpful to distribute copies of the excellent summary of objective test formats that is provided by B. Bloom et al., Taxonomy of Educational Objectives. Handbook I: Cognitive Domain (New York: David McKay, 1956).

5. An especially comprehensive account of the individual steps in test construction is given in E. Lindquist, Educational Measurement (Washington, D.C.: American Council on Education, 1951).

PART II

TECHNIQUES OF TEST ADAPTATION

CHAPTER

3

THE ABILITIES TO BE MEASURED

In this and the following chapters, the focus of the discussion shifts from the evaluation of a testing proposal to the development of actual testing procedures—from the concern of the administrator to that of the practicing test constructor. The culture-tied problems previewed in Chapter 1 will be reexamined in greater detail and specific guidelines for resolving them will be suggested.

The first step, as before, is to examine the basic question of what it is that the test should measure. Given a group of applicants with specified background characteristics, given a course or job in which certain types of skilled performance will be expected, and given a total of perhaps two or three hours that can be devoted to aptitude testing, what kinds of test exercises should be developed? What set of skills, measurable within these practical limitations, is likely to be maximally predictive?

To develop the full range of issues that are pertinent to this question, the discussion begins with a review of the general methodology for developing suitable test specifications for a course or job for which adequate tests have not previously been constructed—with the basic steps to be followed in all original test construction. Then, this methodology will be reexamined for the special case of generalizing tests already developed to new geographic locations, to identify the steps that can be skipped and those that must be repeated.

DEVELOPING TESTS FOR NEW APPLICATIONS

As already noted in Chapter 1, the context of an aptitude test cannot be taken directly from the course syllabus, as is done in the design of achievement and proficiency tests. Only skills that the applicants have already acquired at the time of admission can be assessed. The test constructor must therefore develop a strategy or "rationale" for selecting from the many dozens of specific skills in the applicants' present repertoire the few that will best predict their mastery of the new skills the course will require.

The development of a complete test rationale is a three-stage procedure.[1] The first is to obtain an accurate description of the skilled performance that the applicants will be expected to master. The second is to analyze the characteristics of this performance, to determine the kinds of abilities that it will require. And the third is to decide on the nature of the test exercises that will reliably measure these kinds of abilities in the population of applicants to which the test will be applied. If the resulting instrument is effective, the test constructor can assume that the many inferences involved in this process were made reasonably correctly. If not, he must look for flaws in his logic and repeat part or all of the developmental procedure.

Description of the Performance Expected

The two major requirements for an adequate description of the performance to be predicted are 1) that it describe this performance objectively, in terms of the specific activities required, and 2) that it indicate the relative importance of these activities to the overall criterion of successful performance that will be applied. Detailed descriptions of the actual activities are superior to the more generalized statements that are typically obtained when an administrator or teacher is simply asked to describe the outcomes expected, since such generalizations as may be appropriate are better made by the test constructor, who is more familiar with their measurement implications. Priorities are important because all of the component activities can usually not be incorporated in a practical testing program, and those most critical to success must be determined.

For the design of educational admission programs, therefore, a course syllabus is less adequate as a comprehensive description than are lesson plans that show the step-by-step learning process that the students will be expected to follow. And copies of typical examination papers are less useful as an index of the relative importance of the various skills taught in the course than are records of the students' answers to each of these questions. For, from the latter the deficiencies in present student performance—which are presumably what an improved admission procedure is to correct—can be quite specifically determined.

Descriptive data for occupational selection programs are more difficult to obtain because job descriptions as detailed as lesson plans and assessment procedures as objective as final exams do not exist in most job situations. Usually, the test constructor himself must develop the highly specific descriptions that are required. One approach is simply to observe the job being performed, which will result in statements such as those in the following example.

When he receives each sales receipt, he copies the sales price of each item the customer bought in one of the twelve columns on the ledger sheet, according to the category of merchandise that this item represents. (Every item in the inventory has been assigned to one of twelve categories of merchandise, and for these categories separate records are kept.) At the end of the day, he totals each of the twelve columns of four-digit and five-digit numbers (there is an average of about six hundred receipts and 1,800 items processed per day), and writes the category total at the foot of each column. Then he adds these subtotals to obtain the grand total of sales, which is checked against the total obtained by adding the daily sales that each of the five salesmen reported. Any discrepancy in these two totals must be rectified before the books can be closed for the day. From such an action-oriented description, a very precise account of this part of the job is obtained. And some gross judgments of priority also can be made on the basis of the data presented. It can quite reasonably be assumed, for example, that accuracy in copying the entries of the sales slip onto the ledgers is more important than accuracy in adding the entries together, since the additions can be much more rapidly checked than the transcriptions when a discrepancy is discovered.

Whether such reasonable assumptions about the priorities are in fact applicable in this particular situation, however, cannot be determined without further study. It may be that transcription mistakes have occurred so rarely that they are in reality less important than the more frequent addition errors, because these have too often required the salesmen to stay after hours and caused employee dissension; or than the errors made in entering the figures in the correct columns, which have necessitated costly audits when the sales and inventories are cross-checked at the end of each quarter. Or it may be that the employees the firm prizes most highly are those who, however careless in any of these clerical operations, are alert to subtle changes in the pattern of sales, and call them to the manager's attention. Clear-cut priorities can seldom be established on the basis of straightforward observational data.

For this reason, and for greater economy in data collection, many test constructors prefer to use a more narrowly focused approach that considers only the extremes of very good and very poor employee performance. They have concluded, on the basis of considerable experience, that in virtually every job much time has to be spent on routine activities that contribute little if anything to the over-all quality of the employee's performance; and that data on everything that the employee does is neither necessary or appropriate for test construction. As an alternative to the observational approach, they interview the supervisors of the employees or a sample of other individuals directly involved in the job, and ask these to recall actual instances in which an employee's actions led to clearly favorable or clearly unfavorable results in the past. From a large number of such specific examples, the "critical requirements" of the job then are inferred.[2] For the above clerical example, a list of positive actions, such as

1. Noted that salesman had charged incorrect price for an item;

2. Reported that sales in a usually popular category seemed to be slipping;

and a second list of negative actions, such as

1. Transposed digits when copying sales price for receipt onto ledger;

2. Was unable to keep up with the increased volume of receipts during the Christmas season;

would be developed. Each would represent a contribution or deficiency that is known actually to occur in the job, and would for this reason be an appropriate target for the selection procedure.

The applicability of this technique, or of the approaches earlier mentioned, is entirely independent of cultural variations, as should be apparent from the examples. At this first stage in the development of a test rationale, any of the standard methods of job description are equally appropriate in a developing country. Cultural factors need _not_ be considered.

Identification of the Abilities Required

In some instances it is possible to devise suitable tests on the basis of the job description alone, without trying to identify the kinds of abilities that this performance requires. In the job illustrated above, for example, it would be possible to give each of the applicants a stack of receipts, a code book, and ledger, and (after suitable explanations) to measure his proficiency in performing the actual function. Since the entire task is one that the applicants should be able to perform without specialized training, it can simply be replicated as a whole in the test situation, and the question of component abilities never arises.

Yet, for three major reasons, such direct job-sample tests have limited utility as selection procedures. The first is that sufficiently stable measures of performance are seldom obtained from the examinees' initial attempt at carrying out actual job operations. After a month or more on the job, the relative proficiency of the applicants might be totally different, perhaps because the ability to remember the more frequent codes without looking them up (which is not tested in the examinees' initial attempt) is more important than skill in copying or addition. The second is that certain of the critical job operations—such as noticing sales trends in this example—are not amenable at all to testing by the direct job-sample approach, and must be ignored completely when the selection procedure consists of job samples only. And the third is that using unique tests for each position is generally inefficient. Even within a single firm, the skills necessary for clerical operations in the sales department almost certainly overlap with those required for purchasing, accounting, and inventory control operations; and the use of separate tests for each position would be extravagantly expensive.

Thus, the identification of the more general abilities that lead to success in the specific operations desired is the necessary second step in the development of rationales for most practical applications. From the job description he has obtained or developed, the test constructor must infer the nature of the major ability components that are involved in these operations, trying to define them in such a way that

1. The components identified are sufficiently distinct to warrant the construction of that many separate aptitude measures, and

2. Each of the individual definitions strikes the proper balance between the specificity to this one job that is necessary for accuracy in this one application, and the generality that will lead to a more widely applicable selection procedure.

A more broadly applicable definition is desirable not only because of the greater utility of the new instrument that may be developed from this rationale, but also because a more general statement may suggest tests already developed for other purposes that can be applied, saving the costs of new test construction.

The task of writing definitions that meet these two criteria is perhaps the most difficult in the entire field of aptitude testing, for many basic questions arise that the present state of the art in psychology cannot fully answer.

What, for example, are the distinct ability factors involved in the above clerical operation? Is the "attention to detail" that is necessary in transcribing digits correctly the same as the "attention to detail" that is involved in entering them in the proper column? Is "memory" for a classification system similar to "memory" for normal patterns of sales? Is "speed" in coding related to "speed" in adding numbers? Can the performance of a task that involves all three of these components simultaneously be predicted adequately by a composite of three separate ability tests, or does the complexity of the whole introduce an additional dimension not measured by the sum of the parts? The test constructor can find much relevant information on these kinds of issues in the literature of past testing research, but will have to rely also on many enlightened guesses in picking out the distinct ability factors.

In deciding on the appropriate level of specificity, similar problems arise. The memory component that is involved in learning the coding system, for example, should probably not be defined as a more or less "pure" memory factor, because the classification of the various items into the twelve merchandise categories is a rational procedure based on certain item characteristics, and rote learning is not really what is required. "Memory" alone is too general a definition. But a definition such as "ability to remember a classification system in which consumer goods are assigned to twelve categories on the basis of the purpose for which they are used" is needlessly specific. An appropriate definition somewhere between these extremes must be developed, and this step again requires considerable insight on the part of the test constructor.

The data on which he may draw have come from two separate but related fields of research. Both grew out of the tests of general intelligence that began to be constructed around the turn of the century, and both have generated a vast literature of pertinent information

The first of these efforts has been directed at the development of a detailed inventory of the domain of human abilities, in which all of the separate abilities that exist would be listed. Each of the component abilities would be defined operationally by the content of a test that measures it (but no others), and the inventory would be considered complete when tests that measure something not already measured by the existing set could no longer be constructed. Although much theoretical speculation about the organization of human abilities has guided and also resulted from this research, the development of a set of independent and exhaustive ability tests has in fact been the operational objective.

To develop such tests, one straightforward approach is to administer a large number of different test items to a large number of people, and then analyze the patterns of overlap in each examinee's scores to identify the unique components. And, using the techniques of factor analysis as the statistical vehicle, this mainly empirical procedure has been the one generally applied.[3] The research began with Spearman's discovery that the various kinds of intelligence tests seemed to consist of one common factor (presumably the "general intelligence" component) and one specific factor peculiar to the nature of the test items; and then took another giant step forward when Thurstone identified six "primary mental abilities" that seemed to explain the major differences in examinee performance on 56 different ability tests. His list included verbal, number, spatial, word fluency, memory, and reasoning skills, and this terminology has profoundly influenced the ways in which tests have been labeled in the thirty years since it was first developed.

More recently, Guilford and his associates have developed a new model of the "structure of intellect" on the basis of a long series of studies. According to this model, intellectual tasks differ from each other along three major dimensions: the mental operations that it requires (memory, recognition, evaluation, etc.), the nature of the content material to which this operation is to be applied (figures, language, symbols, etc.), and the product or result (relations, transformations, implications, etc.) that is to be achieved. Overall, there are five separate operations, four different areas of content, and six kinds of possible results, leading to a total of 120 unique combinations. Each of these combinations should logically represent a different ability component, and a total of 120 separate tests therefore should be required to represent the entire domain of mental skills. To date, the proponents of this model have developed about half this number, mainly for purposes of further research.

In most of these studies the practical utility of the resulting tests for educational or occupational selection has not been the major concern. The objective has been a complete explanation of human mental behavior. But clearly, the attainment of this objective would also solve any practical prediction problem, since the task of the test constructor would thereafter consist of simply selecting an appropriate subset of tests from an inventory that is all-inclusive. And even today, the extensive data concerning the interrelationships among different kinds of test items that have been compiled through such research is a highly important resource for the test constructor when he encounters practical questions like the above in the development of a test rationale.

The second line of inquiry into these issues has been the related research of practitioners concerned with specific selection problems. Here the basic objectives have been to identify the abilities that are most important to success in the major kinds of educational programs and occupations and to devise tests that will measure these abilities most effectively from the point of view of prediction. As in the factor analytic approach, a conscious effort was made to minimize the overlap among tests that would be used jointly, since overlap is wasteful of testing time. But limiting each test to a single, relatively pure skill was not necessary for purposes of prediction because most job operations require the application of skills in certain combinations or clusters. And it was therefore logical in this research to use definitions of ability such as "mechanical aptitude" or "clerical accuracy," even though these might be composites of theoretically separable aptitude factors.

This approach to the definition of abilities has resulted in statements less general than the basic Thurstone dimensions but not so specific as those of the Guilford structure, and provides yet another set of constructs that the test constructor can use in the preparation of a new rationale. The findings obtained from such multipurpose test series as the Flanagan Aptitude Classification Tests, which tries to encompass all of the vocational decisions likely to be faced by an American high school student with a set of 21 basic job-element tests; or the General Aptitude Test Battery, which is used for the many hundreds of jobs filled by the United States Employment Service, are particularly instructive.

Comparable data on the structure of abilities (however defined) have not yet been amassed in any developing country. But it seems reasonable to assume that the dimensions of skilled human performance are the same everywhere in the world, and that well-documented findings from one location can be generalized safely to any other. For this second step in the development of a test rationale, as for the first, it seems safe to assume that cultural differences need not be considered.

Item Specification

The third step is to decide on the exact content and format of the text exercises that will be used to measure the abilities that have been identified as important. The major objectives here are three:

1. To devise problems that will provide maximally reliable measures of these abilities, given the background of the examinees for which the test is intended;

2. To minimize the number of operations extraneous to these abilities that the examinees will have to perform, so that irrelevant ability factors are not inadvertently tested; and

3. To design the overall testing mechanics of maximum efficiency in administration, scoring, and related logistic procedures.

Although certain compromises will frequently be required, notably in the tradeoff between higher reliability and greater efficiency, all three of these factors should be explicitly considered in the development of item specifications.

In the context of the above clerical job, for example, one of the abilities to be measured might be "speed in classifying objects in accordance with a logical system of classification." To write suitable items, the text constructor will first have to ensure that the classification system used in the test is in fact logical for the applicants to be tested. For, in addition to the fact that the applicants will generally not have the specialized knowledge about the firm's line of products to permit the use of the actual products in the test items, there is also the possibility that they will not even have sufficient knowledge about the presumably more familiar classes of objects that the test constructor may decide to use instead of the actual products to eliminate the need for specialized information. However familiar they may seem to the test constructor, the classification concepts or the essential nature of the objects or the vocabulary used to describe them may in fact not be uniformly well understood; if this is the case, the first objective of reliable measures will probably not be attained by the resulting tests. Further simplification may well be required. But from the point of view of the second objective, any extreme simplifications that would seem to avoid the above difficulties, such as using pictures of objects rather than verbal descriptions, or requiring a simple match of colors and numbers, may also be inappropriate, since these clearly entail extraneous operations. Pictorial representations may introduce a requirement for speed in recognizing objects from drawings, which is an ability irrelevant to the job; the use of colors may inappropriately eliminate examinees who happen to be color-blind but are potentially excellent clerical workers. And in evaluating all of these options, purely administrative implications—such as the costs of printing in color—also must be considered.

In seeking guidance on these kinds of issues from the literature of past research, the test constructor will find much less pertinent information than is available on the other components of the test rationale. For explicit written rationales addressed to these points have in actuality been the exception in past test construction, and it is difficult to infer why a certain test was designed as it was from the bare reliability and validity coefficients that typically are the only findings reported. For each of the major ability factors, a wide variety of different test items has been developed, but their relative advantages and limitations for different types of applicant groups have not been adequately explored. Whether it would be best to measure three-dimensional visualization for a specified application with a task that requires visualization skills in counting blocks, for example, or in fitting solid objects together, folding a pattern to form a shape, rotating a figure in certain directions, or performing any of the other operations used in the many available tests of this ability, cannot readily be determined from the results published to date.

Certain more general issues, such as the degree to which an examinee's socioeconomic status or sex influences the scores on various tests, have been studied more fully; these findings have proved useful in avoiding a number of mistakes commonly made in the earlier days of testing. But controlled experimental studies of the effects of specific item characteristics are rare.

For rationales prepared in the developing countries, this problem is compounded by the fact that not even such limited information as has been assembled is readily generalizable to other cultures. At this third stage of the development of a test rationale, the background of the examinees is all-important; and the background of the vast majority of the examinees who generated the standard literature of testing is not at all typical of that normally acquired in a developing country. Many of the specific characteristics of the test and of the testing procedure may have to deviate from standard practice, as will be described in the two following chapters.

Overall, then, the test constructor in a developing country can follow standard procedures in identifying the critical requirements of a job, and in deducing from these the major types of abilities that ought to be measured. But he is very much on his own in deciding on the specific test exercises that will best measure these abilities in the particular situation in which he is working.

APPLYING OLD RATIONALES IN NEW LOCATIONS

Theoretically, rationales for a given job should be developed separately for each organization, even within the same cultural setting, for, as a result of differences in the specific job situations, some variation in the critical requirements should be expected. The relative importance of the standard elements of the job will generally not be the same in all organizations, and this should (at least in theory) affect the choice of abilities measured.

But in practice, the actual effects of these differences on the resulting test instruments are usually too small to warrant an investment in new rationales. As will be recalled from the preceding discussion, the test constructor's task in defining the abilities to be measured is to strike an appropriate balance between the specificity of the job description and the generality of the underlying ability factors; and, in this process of generalization, most of the specific situational differences among separate organizations are likely to disappear. Although the descriptions of the job developed in the first part of the rationale may vary in certain respects, the abilities selected for measurement in the second part will normally be highly similar if not exactly the same. It has therefore been only when the results obtained from the established rationales were considered inadequate or when certain aspects of the performance expected were obviously quite different from the standard requirements that organizations in the same cultural setting have invested in new rationales.

For generalizations of established rationales to different cultures, the AID/AIR findings suggest that exactly the same principle should be applied; i.e., that insofar as the indentification of the abilities that are most important to a certain job is concerned, the difference in geography should be largely ignored. Because the interorganization differences in the specific requirements of a job within a single country (e.g., within Nigeria, within Thailand, or within the United States) are larger by far than the corresponding differences among these countries, cultural variations are in and of themselves minor considerations. Unless certain practices of the firm itself seem to require a new analysis of such jobs as bank teller, draftsman, or computer programmer, the results of past critical requirement studies can be applied irrespective of the firm's geographic location. Job analyses made in the United States should be applicable to Nigeria and Thailand, and vice versa.

For the vast majority of test applications, therefore, the test constructor need be concerned only with the third step of writing suitable item specifications. As already noted in Chapter 1, the decision as to which abilities are the appropriate ones to measure for a given job can and should be based on the findings of past studies of this job, here or in other locations.

Operationally, the development of culturally appropriate item specifications can proceed in one of two separate ways. The first way is to begin with the test rationales that have been prepared for this type of practical application, to retain the description and analysis portions, and then to write new item specifications consistent with this analysis and with the characteristics of the local applicant group. The second way is to begin with the actual test items that have proved effective in other locations, to retain those features that are equally suitable here, and then to modify those that are inapplicable to this cultural setting. Each way has advantages and limitations.

The major advantage of beginning with the rationale is that this does not automatically predispose the resulting test to a certain format, and permits the test constructor to exercise maximum ingenuity in devising suitable items—perhaps resulting in the discovery of items that are inherently better than the traditional ones for all locations. The disadvantages are that relatively few rationales have been published in concise written form, and that to generate new items from scratch, the test constructor may need more complete information on the background of the examinees than is available in most developing countries.

The major advantage of beginning with actual test items is that the significant differences in the background of the local examinees need not be known in advance, but can be determined through systematic trial and error by using the results obtained when these items are administered to local examinees to diagnose why they are ineffective. The disadvantage is that any inherent (i.e., noncultural) limitations in the specific test format selected for experimentation will probably not be overcome as a result of the research. A radically new and possibly far superior approach is much less likely to be discovered through this method than through a fresh look at the basic test rationale.

In the case of the AID/AIR research, it was necessary to begin with the second approach of experimenting with standard test items, because at that time too little was known about the nature of the background differences that are important to deduce suitable item specifications. From a careful analysis of the ability described in the rationale, it might have been possible to determine the type of task that would provide a reasonable measure of this ability in the local culture; but to answer the many strictly mechanical questions that arise in trying to portray any task so determined in the form of a pencil-and-paper item, experimentation was clearly essential. And, therefore, the approach that was adopted was to select a wide range of standard test items and to try, as a first step, to convert these into locally suitable forms through repeated trial and error.[4]

Once guidelines for generally appropriate testing mechanics had been developed, it was feasible to use also the other approach of working directly from the test rationale rather than from a set of actual items. The Mechanical Information Test described earlier was one of the instruments constructed in this manner. Questions appropriate for this test were deduced from the rationale, applied to local environmental conditions, and then converted to pencil-and-paper items in accordance with the general guidelines developed in the earlier experimental research.

Thus, as one practical result of the AID/AIR studies, the development of a new test rationale or the application of a standard rationale in a developing country is today as feasible an approach as the traditional method of adapting the actual items used in other locations. By applying the procedural guidelines described in the following chapters, the test constructor may apply any of these three approaches, in accordance with the pros and cons developed above.

SUMMARY OF MAJOR SUGGESTIONS

The major points that have been made about the preparation of test specifications for a given practical application may be summarized as follows:

1. Test construction should begin with the development (or adoption) of an explicit rationale that links the test items with the actual performance to be predicted.

2. The first part of this rationale should consist of a detailed description of the performance to be predicted, written in behavioral

terms and focused on the activities that are most critical in terms of the performance standards expected.

3. The second part of the rationale should specify the abilities that the successful performance of these critical activities is thought to require. The definition of these abilities should be sufficiently specific to the performance that has been described to permit accurate prediction, but not so specific as to preclude the use of the resulting test for other similar application.

4. The third and final part of the rationale should consist of detailed specifications for the individual test items to be developed. These specifications must be consistent both with the abilities defined as important and with the examinees' background characteristics.

5. New rationales should be developed only when those available have not provided acceptable results, or when the performance expected differs significantly from that normally required in this type of position. In all other instances, including applications to new cultural settings, established rationales should be adopted.

6. When an established rationale is adopted for use in a developing country, the description and analysis sections may be retained, but the item specifications must be revised in accordance with local conditions. This can be done either by deducing new specifications from the initial parts of the rationale, or by evaluating the original test items experimentally, to determine the specific changes required.

7. In the preparation of item specifications, either for an established or for a new rationale, the guidelines of Chapters 4 and 5 should be applied. These have proved useful for a wide range of tests, and will usually avoid confounding the evaluation of the substantive merits of the rationale with the strictly mechanical deficiencies that can be introduced in the overall design of the test or testing procedure.

NOTES

1. A more detailed description is given in J.C. Flanagan "The Use of Comprehensive Rationales in Test Development," *Educational and Psychological Measurement*, XI, 1 (Spring, 1951), 151-5. Flanagan has been the foremost advocate of detailed written rationales as the basis for all test construction.

2. This approach, commonly termed the "Critical Incident Technique," was also developed by Flanagan; and has since been applied in more than four hundred job analysis studies. A description of the basic steps to be followed may be found in J. C. Flanagan, "The Critical Incident Technique," Psychological Bulletin, LI, 4 (1954), 327-58.

3. Factor analysis is a method of analyzing a set of intertest correlations to determine the number of independent variables that seem to be affecting the scores. Each of these variables is called a "factor," and by examining the characteristics of the items that led to its identification it may be given a "name." Thus, a variable based on the interrelationship of a group of items that are all measures of language skills may be called a "verbal factor"; one based on items that all measure visual form relationships may be called a "spatial factor"; etc. Having identified these factors, the test constructor may then try to devise a new test that measures only the verbal factor, and one that measures only the spatial factor, and so on, to generate a smaller number of more independent tests than were in the set with which he began. For a detailed mathematical discussion, such texts as H. Harman, Modern Factor Analysis (2nd ed., rev.; University of Chicago Press, 1967) may be consulted.

4 At the time the AID/AIR research began, a national census of the aptitudes of American high school students, termed Project TALENT, was being begun; we selected items for experimental tryout largely on the basis of the skills that had been identified as most appropriate for this census by the large panel of experts who served as Project TALENT consultants. Additional samples of items were drawn from the Flanagan Aptitude Classification Tests, the General Aptitude Test Battery, and other widely used series of ability tests.

CHAPTER

4

THE DESIGN OF SUITABLE TESTS

This and the following chapter summarize the specific guidelines for test construction that were developed as a result of the AID/AIR studies. This chapter focuses on the design of the test paper itself; Chapter 5, on the administrative and mechanical procedures for conducting the testing session. In both of these components of the testing process a number of features different from standard testing practices had to be introduced.

CONTENT OF THE TEST ITEMS

Three basic requirements relevant to the content of the individual test items were developed in the preceding discussions. The first was that the specific skill required to solve the problem is one that the examinees have already had an opportunity to acquire. This requirement is, of course, fundamental. The second was that all of the information that the item is supposed to communicate to the examinee about the nature of the problem and the desired solution—i.e., about the "givens" with which he is to begin—is presented in a form that he will in fact be able to interpret correctly. And the third was that neither the interpretation of this information nor the solution of the problem requires additional skills that are irrelevant to the intent of the items, but that have nevertheless crept into the test and distort the examinees' scores. When test items designed for American or European examinees are used without modification to test examinees in a developing country, one or more of these requirements will generally not be fulfilled.

One common reason for this breakdown is that an examinee who grows up in a developing country has not acquired certain of the specific items of knowledge that can be taken for granted in the American culture, and is unable to cope with problems in which such prior knowledge has been assumed by the test constructor. A second and even more common reason is that the examinee in the developing country is less proficient in extracting the "givens" of the test problem from the particular words or drawings that the test constructor has used as the medium of communication, and is unable to solve problems he actually has the ability to solve simply because of the way in which they are presented. In adapting a standard test or in preparing a new test directly from the specifications of the test rationale, the first step is to ensure that the knowledge, language, and perceptual skills the items require are consistent with the background and experiences of local examinees.

Knowledge Factors

That the specific items of knowledge available to an examinee vary greatly as a function of his environment has been recognized in most of the past efforts at test adaptation, and does not warrant extensive discussion. No one would seriously consider using a test item based on vacuum cleaners in rural Africa, for example, or fail to chuckle at the study that used a test based on ships at a site nowhere near a body of water. Even in developing tests for use within a single familiar country, test constructors have grown increasingly sensitive to the differences in the knowledge of the intracountry subcultures, such as the black and the white, the rich and the poor, or the urban and the rural sections of the American population.

Still, there are two major points to be made about the use of test content that is consistent with the knowledge available in a particular cultural setting. The first is that there are few instances in which the nature of the knowledge elements that should be included is immediately "obvious" and can be determined without special study. The residue of what is left of a standard test after the inappropriate elements have been eliminated is generally not an adequate basis for a reliable ability measure. A more systematic procedure for generating suitable test content usually must be developed. The second related point is that the knowledge elements of a standard test that in fact are inappropriate in this cultural setting may not be at all "obvious." Some elements, though strange to the examinee, may in actuality not affect his performance at all because they are not central to the problem he is to solve; and changing such elements willy-nilly simply because they are strange may be a needless extravagance in situations in which economy in test development is all-important.

With respect to the first point of selecting content that will lead to reliable measures, the key limitation is that direct observation of the local scene seldom suffices. If the test constructor relies solely on the observations of the available information sources from which the examinees could learn, he will invariably include some that have in reality had no impact on the examinees whatsoever, and miss many other less obvious sources that have had a substantially greater effect. In the early African studies, it was somewhat surprising to find that the typical Nigerian student in those days knew much less about the trees or flowers that grew all around him than did the American staff members' wives, and less about the history of his country in precolonial days than the staff members themselves had learned in their orientation courses. As a function of his inherited educational system, his knowledge of European flora and history was in actuality considerably higher. With the growing spread of transistor radios and television, the knowledge of youth anywhere in the world is almost certain today to hold many even stranger surprises.

To identify the categories of information suitable for use in a test more systematically, one of the following three approaches can generally be applied:

1. The first and safest is to compile examples of materials the examinees themselves have produced that indicate the kinds of knowledge they actively use in nontest situations. This is the approach that was used to determine knowledge of words as the basis for designing the Verbal Analogies Test, as described in Chapter 1. Only when examinee-produced materials relevant to the test (i.e., themes in the Analogies example) are not readily available should less positive indications of knowledge be used.

2. Second best is to examine the content of relevant information sources that the examinees have been actively encouraged or instructed to use. Textbooks are one such source (applied in the I-D Reading Comprehension Tests); the daily newspapers (used for the I-D World Information Test) are another.* Such sources offer fewer guarantees than those that show the actual acquisition of certain ideas or knowledge, but do generally result in items that require only limited post-tryout revisions.

---

*All tests cited in this chapter are discussed fully in Chapter 6, where the developmental procedure that was followed is also described.

3. Least satisfying, from the point of view of the amount of research required, is to identify stimuli from which the examinees might have learned (though nothing was done to encourage such learning), and then to determine empirically to which of these they have responded. This approach will usually require many sequences of tryout and revision, but for some tests (such as the I-D Mechanical Information Test) other good options do not exist. Whichever technique is applied, the important principle is to use an empirical approach in generating the knowledge elements suitable for a given ability test in a given cultural setting.

The second related point applies to those cases in which the task is not to generate new items, but to adapt those of an existing version. Here the important first step is to ensure that solving the test problems really does require adequate knowledge about a certain "unfamiliar" component before work to adapt that component is undertaken. The I-D Checking Test affords a convenient illustration of one common situation in which this issue of "to adapt or not to adapt" logically arises. The task in this test is to inspect the five objects that are portrayed in each item, and to pick out the one that is defective. Five gears might be shown, for example, one of which has a single tooth missing. The question that had to be asked was whether or not to replace such items with drawings of different objects that are more familiar than gears in the African setting. Arguing against adaptation was the fact that the basic task in solving these problems consists only of picking out the one drawing that is "different" from the others, and that this can clearly be done whether or not the examinee has any knowledge at all about the nature of the objects presented. Arguing for adaptation was the fact that this type of test must be speeded to be effective, and that the requirement for speed might give an edge unrelated to the purposes of the item to the examinees who do happen to know about gears, and can therefore pick out the "defects" more quickly. To resolve this issue, empirical data were needed.

Accordingly, experimental test forms that contained both familiar and unfamiliar objects were administered to several classes of sixth-grade students, and the results were compared item by item. The finding was that there were no systematic differences in performance whatever, Items based on esoteric objects had the same properties as those based on objects from everyday life. Specific knowledge of the drawings was not an important consideration in selecting content for this particular test, and this had the very important practical advantage—in light of the limited facilities for precision printing—of permitting a selection based mainly on the ease of mechanical reproduction. To the casual observer, many items in this test may seem obviously inappropriate to the African culture, but they are nevertheless fully effective.

A second and somewhat different concern about the use of non-indigenous test content has been that even if the examinees have the knowledge to solve the problems, they will recognize the test as being a "foreign" one intended for other countries and not put forth the effort required. Because of the apparent difficulty or unfairness or irrelevance of the test, their motivation might suffer. And so the test constructor must ask whether a sketch of a house that has a roof different from local practice in house construction should be redrawn even though the examinees will almost certainly recognize the house as being a house from the original drawing; or whether an English passage that spells "colour" as "color" should be reprinted, even though the examinees should have no problems at all in reading the passage correctly. Do cultural anomalies that are incidental to the solution of the problem itself affect the examinees' performance adversely?

In the AID/AIR studies, no adverse effects of this type were noted. The results on the original and the modified versions typically were the same. But because most teachers and administrators are understandably reluctant to institutionalize materials that someone sooner or later will question, the following compromise approach was adopted:

1. Throughout the feasibility and early developmental studies, the original version is used, without any of these "cosmetic" adaptations (e.g., the African version is used in Thailand). So long as there are no substantive changes that have to be made before the test can even be tried in a country, cosmetic change is deferred.

2. Then, at the point at which operational test forms are to be printed, the cosmetic changes are made as part of the preparation of copy for printing. Since a number of substantive changes normally have to be made at this stage in any event, little additional cost is incurred.

Reprinting a test for the sake of appearances before its basic utility has been verified through tryout studies may well entail needless expense.

Language Factors

In some of the developing countries the language component of test construction poses few if any unusual problems. The local language is used, the standard techniques are applied, and a culturally appropriate test sooner or later emerges. Methodologically, the process in an advanced country like England and in a developing country such as Korea can and should be the same.

But this ready generalizability is not universal. In many countries, such a Nigeria, Mali, or Bolivia, the English, French, or Spanish that must be used for nation-wide testing is not the first language of the examinees; nor is it the language in which they have done much of their thinking and learning. The task here is to test youngsters in a language that has served more as a subject to study in school than as a tool for normal communication; this is so radically different from the standard test situation that much of the standard approach to language in testing must be adapted.

This chapter describes the adaptation of the content of the test items for second language examinee groups, first for tests of verbal abilities, and then for the other kinds of aptitude measures. The many additional adaptations that must be made in the administration of the test will be taken up in the following chapter.

The Language Content of Verbal Ability Measures

Tests of verbal abilities (reasoning, comprehension, and expression) have traditionally been the most widely used of all aptitude measures. They are the best single index of an individual's overall learning potential, and for situations that require learning ability, such as admission to school, they have consistently proved superior to all other aptitude tests in predicting future performance. In the advanced countries a comprehensive testing program that does not include verbal aptitude tests would be an unthinkable proposition.

Yet it has also been recognized that for groups who have not attained a certain level of language proficiency, tests of this type will result in a greatly distorted picture of learning potential. And considerable effort has been devoted to the construction of tests that will measure the general mental capacity of an individual without the use of any language content whatever. As a replacement for words, abstract shapes, drawings, mazes, and numerous other essentially spatial configurations have been applied, and a wide variety of entirely nonverbal tests, including all of the so-called culture-fair measures, has by now been developed.

Thus, the first and most basic decision the test constructor in a multilingual country must make about general ability measures is which of these two different routes to follow. Should he begin with the rationale of the verbal aptitude test and try to devise language items that will be effective despite the verbal handicaps of the groups with which he is working? Or should he select the nonverbal approach and develop abstract and spatial items? Or must he invest in both and defer the decision until comparative data for this particular group have been assembled? At the time the African studies began, these issues were being widely debated.

At the extremes of the educational spectrum, there was no disagreement, of course. For students at or above the secondary school level, verbal tests were the indicated procedure; for illiterates, the nonverbal approach was the only recourse. The question centered on the "gray zone" of examinees who had perhaps four to six years of primary school education, and whose language skills (in English or French) were far below those of their counterparts in the industrialized countries. Because this group included the examinees at the critical secondary school entrance level, the resolution of these issues was deemed highly important.

The design of the African research did not permit the controlled experimentation that would firmly and finally lay this issue to rest. But, for a variety of logical and empirical reasons, it was eventually concluded that the initial investment for partially educated examinees should always be in verbal tests, and that in most practical situations effective verbal tests can in fact be constructed. The nonverbal approach to "intelligence" testing, at least in the context of pencil-and-paper tests, is likely to be much less effective.

The basic reason for this probably inherent in the rationales of the two approaches. In virtually every learning situation, language is the essential medium whereby new information is acquired, and a verbal test replicates this process more closely than will ever be possible with a nonverbal procedure. Even when the language skills of the examinees are rudimentary, a closer match to the critical requirements of the criterion performance can be achieved. Verbal items also are grounded more firmly in skills the examinees have practiced before than are the essentially artificial tasks that comprise most of the nonverbal approaches. A test that is fair to all cultures by being equally irrelevant to the important activities to every culture is not likely to yield a meaningful ability measure.

A second, more practical reason for chosing verbal tests is that the substitution of pictures or symbols for words frequently increases rather than eases the problems of test adaptation. None of the abstract reasoning tests tried in Africa survived even the early trials, and the one nonverbal test that eventually was developed (i.e., the Similarities Test) has been only partly effective. Probably as a function of the education methods and materials to which these examinees had been exposed, words were a generally more effective medium for testing than were symbols or pictures.

And a third reason is that the adapted verbal ability tests did turn out to be highly accurate selection procedures. Although the development costs were in each case substantial, the cost-effectiveness of the Verbal Analogies and Reading Comprehension tests are perhaps the highest of the I-D test series.

The nature of the adaptations required for examinees with limited language skills is best illustrated by the Reading Comprehension Test, described more fully in Chapter 6. The first problem was to find paragraphs that are so simple that most of the examinees can understand the basic information presented, but that despite this simplicity permit some degree of inference and interpretation, so that "verbal reasoning" items could be constructed. The second problem was to determine which of the contextual clues of written English that are normally used as the basis for interpretative test questions with native speakers of English could also be used with examinees who have had only a few years of English instruction, and which of these clues were too subtle to be applied. An extensive series of tryouts and item analyses was required and, as will be seen in Chapter 6, the tolerance limits for this type of test were found to be exceptionally narrow, in that a change in a single word could turn an unusable test item into one that is fully effective.

For applications in other languages and other countries, it will almost certainly be necessary to repeat this entire developmental procedure. Because the subsequent studies in Brazil, Thailand, and Korea were limited to examinees who were native speakers of the languages used, general guidelines for second-language could not be developed. And, indeed, cross-cultural principles for the construction of these types of tests may not even exist. The one important and hopefully generalizable conclusion of the AID/AIR research on verbal ability tests is that they can be adapted for use with marginally qualified groups and that such adaptations should be attempted in a much broader range of situations than had been suspected.

The Language Content of Other Ability Measures

The other types of ability tests that have a significant language component are those in which the nature of the operation the examinee is to perform changes from item to item, so that he has to be told as part of each item what it is that he is to do. In the I-D Mechanical Information Test, for example, the 56 problems are in effect 56 separate tests, and as the examinee reaches each one, he must be asked the appropriate question. A sizable language component, encompassing at least 56 separate sentences, has to be introduced.

The danger is that so large a verbal component will dilute the accuracy of the test by turning it into a measure of language skills as well as of the strictly mechanical aptitude that was intended. The examinees who have somewhat greater or lesser skills in language comprehension might earn inappropriately higher or lower test scores, and so might those who read a little faster or slower. Even when the testing is being conducted in the first language of the examinees, suitable precautions have to be taken.

The normal precautions are to pretest the questions from the point of view of examinee understanding, and to rephrase or replace them as necessary to achieve uniformly high levels of comprehension. And, in the advanced countries, this can almost always be done. But when a second language has to be used with examinees who have only a primary school education, such editing typically is not enough. The individual differences in language skills are so large that a sizable verbal factor continues to confound the ability the test is to measure.

The I-D solution is to change the medium of communication from printed to oral questions, so that skills in reading (which had been found to be the largest source of inter-examinee variation) are not involved. The test paper contains only the problems, represented in the case of the Mechanical Information Test by appropriate sketches; and the associated questions are presented by the examiner, who reads them out loud. The normal precaution of pre-testing the questions is still necessary because the specific words used remain highly important; but it is the basic change from a written to an oral approach that is the key to obtaining the high levels of comprehension required.

As a by-product of this technique, it provided also a vehicle for explaining the sketches and for pacing the test, as will later be noted. It was one of the most useful of the I-D testing approaches;

and, though designed mainly for use in second-language contexts, may in fact have general utility in most cultural settings. In Thailand, administrations of the Mechanical Information Test with printed rather than oral questions significantly increased its correlation with general academic performance, suggesting an unduly high verbal loading, even though the examinees' first language was the medium used. And it may well be that an oral approach can profitably be applied in all countries to reduce the verbal component of a variety of specific ability measures.

This approach is by no means a panacea, however. It cannot be applied to complex verbal problems, such as those of a mathematical reasoning test, because the examinees cannot absorb the pertinent information from an oral presentation alone. To reduce the huge verbal loading of this type of test, an entirely new kind of item that does not rely on "word problems" at all probably must be developed. But the attempts that were made to concoct such items have so far been unsuccessful.

Perceptual Factors

If one compares any tangible object with a faithful sketch of the same object on paper, he will be able to find dozens of specific characteristics that are far from the same. Certain aspects of the object have been ignored, others have been distorted, and still others have been represented by special conventions that the artist has used as a sort of a code. And yet, most American youngsters could glance at the sketch, and immediately name the object portrayed.

The reason for this, of course, is that objects are sketched in accordance with certain set rules that the American youngster has learned to interpret. The thousands of visual representations to which he has been exposed have so conditioned his responses that he not only looks at the sketch and "sees" the object, but is actually hard-pressed to identify the discrepancies between the two without careful concentration.

Individuals who have not had this specialized training, however, will generally not have developed these special responses, and will see in a sketch what is actually there rather than what is intended. A sphere will look flat; a mouse in the foreground of a drawing will seem larger than an elephant on the horizon; a column of smoke will be a meaningless blur. Wherever visual representations are rare, these kinds of "more natural" responses are the more likely, and appropriate adaptations of every pictorial test item will probably have to be made.

The nature of these adaptations varies from test to test in accordance with the kind of perceptual skill the items require. Certain approaches are most useful for adapting test items in which the examinee has to recognize the object portrayed in a drawing in order to answer the question, certain others for adapting items that are based on abstract configurations.

Drawings and Sketches

In some tests, such as the Checking Test described in an earlier example, it will be found that the examinee can work the items without recognizing the objects that are represented, and that adaptation of the perceptual content is not required. But in numerous other tests—such as the Similarities or Mechanical Information Tests of the I-D series—the items are based on the characteristics of the objects portrayed, and the correct interpretation of each sketch is absolutely essential. In the early African studies, the fact that many examinees did not recognize even simple objects from the drawings used in standard aptitude tests was one of the first major hurdles encountered.

One possible approach to this problem was to try to develop a core set of drawings that nearly everyone could interpret correctly, and that could then be used and reused for all pictorial tests. And to this end, a large set of trial sketches was assembled, and shown one at a time to two classes of sixth-grade students whose task was to identify the objects portrayed. Each student was interviewed individually, and could use either English or his own language to name the object or to describe its function. Then, the percentage of students who identified each object correctly was used as an index of the relative suitability of these drawings for use in a test.

As a result of this study, some progress was made. It was found, first—as one so many other occasions—that the apparent cultural relevance of an object is a poor basis for predicting the interpretability of a sketch. All of the examinees recognized the sketch of the airplane, for example, but very few recognized the banana, probably because of the former's much more distinctive characteristics. And it was found also that certain objects which are not recognized from one type of visual representation can sometimes be made recognizable by simply changing the sketch, such as replacing a head-on view of an elephant with a less complex profile drawing. With care, a small set of generally recognized drawings probably could be assembled.

But the findings showed also that many of the objects that would be most appropriate for use in an aptitude test could not be made recognizable by stylistic changes alone. Each time an object that is not normally seen in isolation was shown—such as one eye, for example—very few of the examinees were able to identify it correctly. And the same was true of all of the sketches that had necessarily to make use of special conventions, such as drawings of the sun, lightning, or fire. None of these very common and therefore very desirable phenomena could be used in a straightforward pictorial test.

The solution that was eventually developed was based on the fact that in both of the I-D pictorial tests the questions are presented orally by the examiner, for the reasons noted in the discussion of language factors above. It was entirely feasible, therefore, to have him name the objects shown in each item as part of the oral question; and this method of visual-plus-verbal presentation was found to be fully effective. It solved the problems of object recognition not only for items that are based on discrete objects, such as those of the Similarities Test, but also for items that show more complex scenes or actions, as a number of the Mechanical Information questions require.

In some of the developing countries these difficulties are less acute, and naming the objects shown in simple sketches is not essential. But when a test is to be presented orally in any event, this technique may still be a worthwhile addition, as an economical fail-safe procedure.

Size, Shape, and Spatial Orientation

In a number of perceptual aptitude tests, the examinee has to perform operations that depend on the dimensions or attitudes of abstract configurations. The essential concept is that two or more shapes must be absolutely identical with respect to these characteristics, and the problem that arises at many locations is that the concepts of geometric identity or congruence or not adequately developed.

In the I-D series, this problem arose in the Figures Test, in which the examinee is to find which one of five given shapes is "hidden" in each of a set of larger and more complex drawings. For examinees in the industrialized countries, this is a relatively simple task, and it is mainly the difference in the rates of speed at which they can solve the problems that accounts for the variance in their scores. But the initial tryouts in Africa showed that many examinees could not solve standard items of this type at all. And most of those who did grasp the concept had to spend much more time than could be allowed for the entire test to solve even a few of the problems.

To adapt this type of test, it seemed clear that the basic approach of relating the items more closely to the prior experiences of the examinees (which is the indicated adaptation procedure for most of the less abstract aptitude tests) could not be applied. Apparently, the examinees had few if any prior encounters with geometric congruence, and one type of item would be as novel and therefore as difficult as any other. The only feasible approach was to try to teach this skill to the examinees as part of the testing process, hoping that they could fairly quickly reach at least the minimum level of proficiency that is necessary for reliable test scores.

The steps that were necessary to develop an effective teaching approach are described in detail in the discussion of the Figures Test in Chapter 6. Basically, they consisted of the following:

1. Eliminating a number of the complexities of the standard test problems, to reduce the task to be learned to essentials;

2. Developing an instructional sequence to teach this task as part of the testing session; and

3. Providing the examinees with opportunities to practice these skills, and to obtain feedback on their performance.

To obtain adequate reliability on this novel perceptual task, all three of these steps were essential.

As will be seen in the following chapters, the same technique is applicable to a wide variety of other tests and is in fact used in all of the I-D tests to teach the basic mechanics. Whenever one or more of the skills involved in a test is strange to the examinees, this approach of "testing by teaching" is an exceptionally powerful technique of test adaptation.

Three-Dimensional Visualization

Drawings that show depth relationships are especially difficult for examinees who have had only limited experience with visual representations. Any test item that depends on the perception of what is at the front and what is to the rear of a drawing will generally not be effective.

The reason for this is that, strictly speaking, there is no possible way of faithfully reproducing a three-dimensional image on a piece of paper. Depth as it actually looks in the real world cannot be shown. What are commonly called three-dimensional drawings are in fact two-dimensional representations that suggest the third through a special convention that artist and viewer have agreed to use as a code. A viewer who has not learned this convention will see the image as it actually is—i.e., perfectly flat.

This raises two types of problems for the test constructor who is trying to develop a comprehensive set of aptitude measures. The first is that certain kinds of test questions, such as those of a mechanical aptitude test, are normally communicated to the examinees by three-dimensional sketches; and if he is denied perspective drawings as a medium of communication, these kinds of items cannot be used. The second is that the skill of three-dimensional visualization is itself a highly effective predictor of success in most technical occupations, and if he cannot obtain an index of this skill in the abstract there will be a serious gap in the comprehensiveness of the measures.

With respect to the first problem of using perspective drawings as a vehicle for measuring other ability factors, little if anything can be done. If the test constructor cannot devise an alternative way of framing the question, the item will probably have to be dropped from the test. Many of the principles it had been decided to measure in the Mechanical Information Test could not be included simply because there was no practical way of communicating them to the examinees. And such practical considerations must, of course, override the inherent "cultural" relevance or expected predictive power of a proposed test item.

With respect to the second problem of measuring individual differences in the skill of visualization, adequate solutions can be developed. The effective approach, as in Figures Test, is to devise a task that can be taught to the examinees during the course of the testing session, following the same three-step procedure outlined above. In the I-D Boxes Test, the crucial breakthrough was to reduce the task to a problem that requires visualization of only two cubes, and to use the same two cubes in every item. Teaching even this simple task required a highly elaborate instructional procedure, but the examinees did learn, and the test did prove to be both reliable and predictive.

That tests adapted in this manner measure ability rather than readiness, however, should be explicitly noted. Teaching the examinee a relatively simple version of an important skill is adequate for purposes of the test, but will not prepare him for the more complex versions that may be required in the course for which he is being selected. He could easily earn a top score on the Boxes Test and yet be completely baffled by a normal textbook illustration. As suggested in an earlier chapter, the need for test adaptation usually is symptomatic of a need for comparable revisions in the standard training procedures.

FORMAT OF THE TEST PAPER

The single most important difference between examinees in the advanced and the developing countries lies not in their relative sophistication about the specific content of any one aptitude test, as in the cases described above, but in their relative familiarity with the testing ritual as a whole. The ease of administering tests in the United States tends to obscure how complex a skill effective testmanship has become and how much highly specialized training the standard process of testing requires. In Africa it quickly became apparent that just following the mechanical instructions can be more challenging to an inexperienced examinee than the problems posed in the actual items.

Thus, teaching the examinees the mechanics of each test is an essential part of the testing procedure. And since such teaching takes time, it is clearly desirable to simplify these mechanics as much as possible in the design of the test's physical characteristics. Operations extraneous to the effective use of the test should be avoided.

The problem lies in deciding which steps are extraneous and which are essential. For most of the steps of the standard process were introduced as a means of reducing the costs of testing, and this cost factor cannot be ignored. Appropriate compromises between simplicity and efficiency must be developed.

The format of the I-D test papers reflects the compromises that seemed, on balance, to be the most cost-effective. They were introduced specifically for examinees who have had minimal education and little or no prior experience with aptitude tests; but a number of them may well have more general utility in all countries and at all educational levels.

The Use of Reusable Booklets

A number of the standard aptitude tests which were tried experimentally at the beginning of the research are published in the form of reusable booklets which contain the test questions and the alternative answers. The examinee is to read the question, to select one of the options, and then to mark his choice on a separate sheet that can be scored by machine. This answer sheet is "consumed," but the booklet can be used again in subsequent sessions. And, since one booklet and one answer sheet will accommodate several tests, extremely low material and data processing costs are incurred.

In Africa this highly efficient approach did not survive even the first set of field trials, however. The examinees had great difficulty in finding the place at which each test begins, in determining when to turn or not turn the page, and in coding the answers from the booklet to the separate answer paper. Time limits were nearly impossible to enforce; attempts at proctoring were ineffectual; and so preoccupied were examiner and examinee with the mechanics that the substance of the test was reduced to an incidental. A tightly structured test-taking process that the examiner could control in step-by-step fashion clearly was essential.

To obtain such control, it seemed reasonable to pay any price *except* that of giving up the capability for machine scoring. This led naturally to the idea of printing the test questions directly on machine-scorable answer sheets, using a separate answer sheet for each of the different tests. Each answer sheet would be distributed at the time the examinees were to begin the test, and collected a specified number of minutes thereafter; and this process would be repeated for each of the tests to be administered during the session. At no time would the examinee be working with more than a single sheet of paper, and the problems of starting and stopping, turning pages, and coding responses should be eliminated completely.

Coupled with the administrative procedures describe in the following chapter, this format proved fully effective. It is illustrated in Figure 1, which shows the first half of the I-D Figures Test. The second half is printed on the reverse side of the same sheet, so that all of the items (for this and all of the other I-D tests) require no more than one piece of paper. For manual scoring, two overlay stencils are used; for automatic scoring, the sheet is fed twice through the machine.

This format is somewhat more costly than the conventional approaches, mainly because of the additional costs of processing scores that must be collated from several pieces of paper. But for all except the most experienced examinee groups, its overall cost-effectiveness is likely to be substantially higher.

FIGURE 1

I-D Figures Test

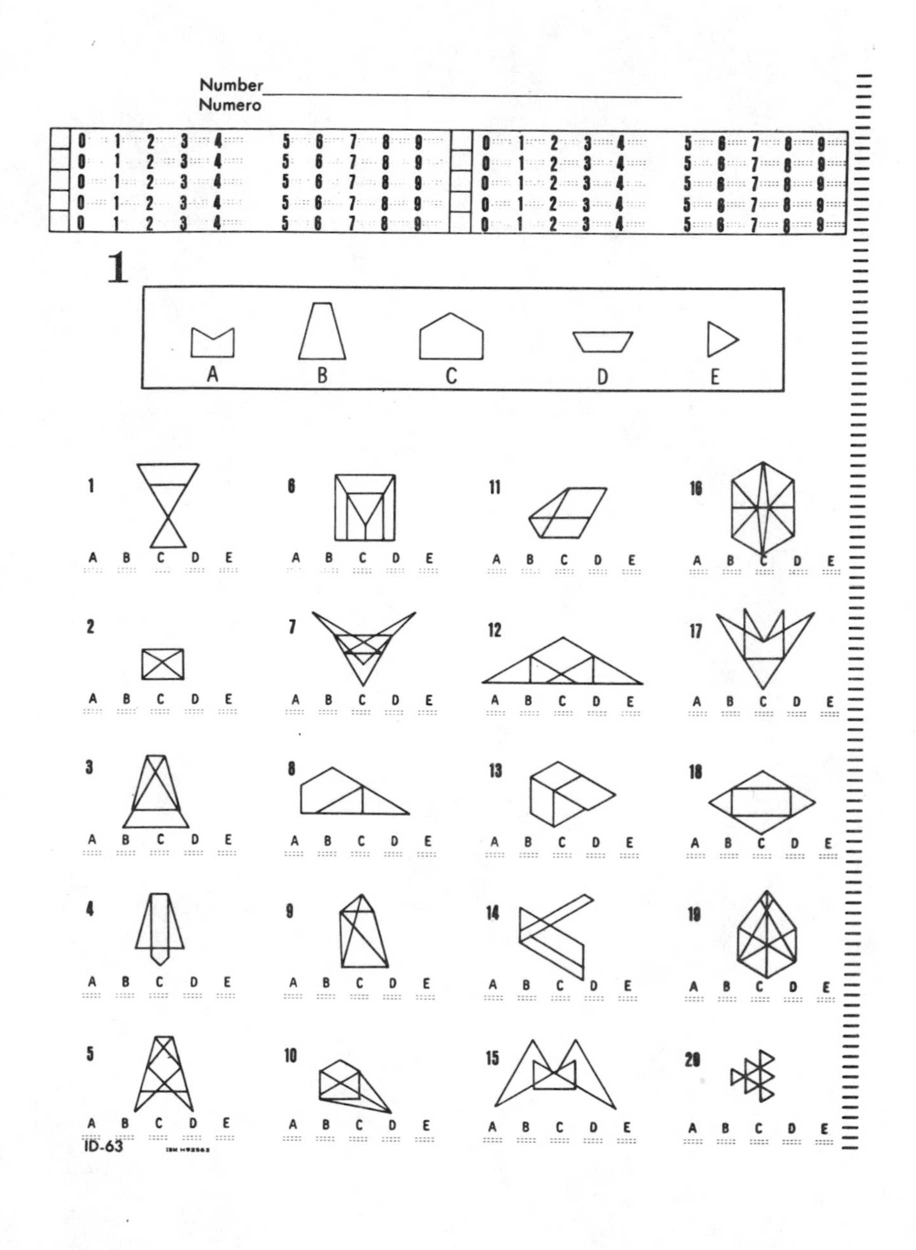

(Cont'd.)

FIGURE 1 Continued

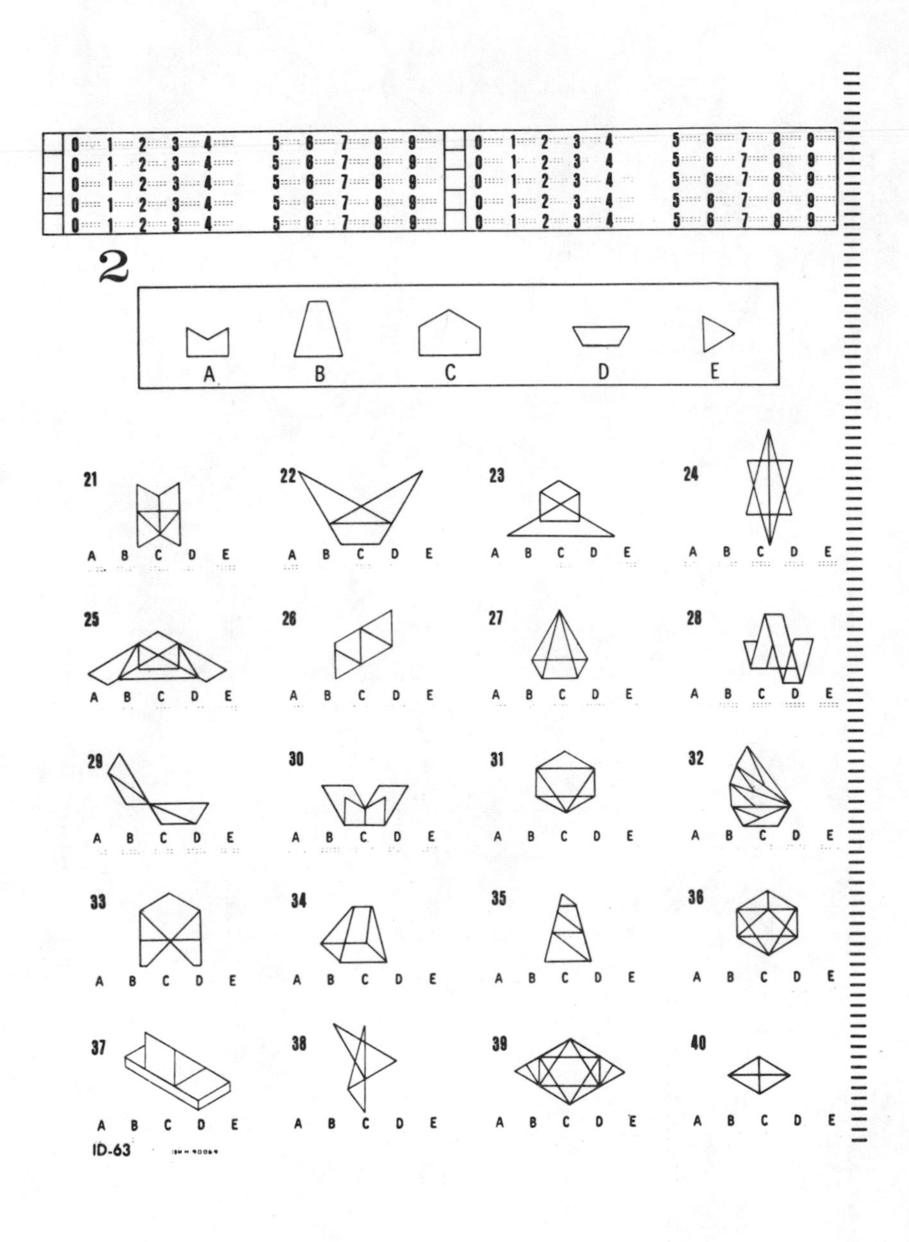

Printed Instructions

Another feature of the I-D test format that will be noted in Figure 1 is the absence of printed instructions. There are no explanations of the task, no sample problems, no "Go on to next column" or "Stop here" directions. The word that indicates where the examinee is to write his identification number is the only printed text on the entire page.

The reason that printed explanations are not used is that these introduce a sizable verbal ability factor into this type of test, as noted in an earlier discussion. All explanations are given orally by the examiner, in accordance with the procedures outlined in Chapter 5. Printed "Stop" or "Go on" directions are not used because these were found to be generally ineffective. Instead, the tests are designed so that the examinee is to work every problem on the page before him without pause in <u>every</u> I-D test; and once the examinees have been taught this rule (which is in any event consistent with their natural inclinations), the need for special directions in the midst of a test never arises.

The sample and practice problems are printed on a separate sheet, distributed and used as part of the pretest explanations. This serves mainly as a means of ensuring that all examinees begin the test at the same time, which had been found to require an excessive number of proctors when the practice problems and test problems are printed on the same piece of paper. Similarly, the printing of Part I on the front and Part II on the reverse side of the sheet simplifies the enforcement of the time limits for these separately timed halves, since one proctor can easily monitor a group of 40 examinees if his task is only to ensure that no one turns over the paper.

Marking of the Responses

Integrating the problems and answer spaces on the same sheet eliminates the coding task inherent in reusable test booklets, as earlier noted. The alternative answers are printed directly below the problem to which they apply, and the common mistake of entering the correct answer in the wrong place is thereby avoided.

In most of the I-D tests, moreover, this task is even simpler than in the Figures example. The items of the Figures Test do require the examinee to relate the answer spaces that are labeled only with capital letters to the key at the top of the page, and this extra step does require additional explanations. In most of the other tests, each of the five answer spaces is printed below the actual answer to which it refers (rather than below a capital letter), and the task is reduced to one of simply underlining the answer.

Such flexibility in positioning answer spaces virtually anywhere on the sheet to fit the format of a particular pictorial, symbolic, or verbal test problem was not possible a few years ago. The sensors of the mark-sensing machines formerly used would not have been able to trace the many different patterns of answer spaces the I-D tests require. But with optical scanners (such as the IBM 1230 or 1231, used in the later African studies) the tolerance limits are broad, and each of the multiple-choice tests of the I-D series could be cast into a format that these machines are able to score. The only important requirement was that a special type of ink had to be used in printing the questions, so that only the marks the examinee makes would register on the machine.

The one desired response that the examinees were <u>not</u> able to make correctly was to code their ten-digit identification numbers into the answer space format at the top of the page, which is necessary whenever the test is to be scored by machine. One problem was that too many errors were made, even after detailed explanations. A second was that coding had to be done on both sides of the paper, which disrupted the examiner's control over the time limits when the examinees ended Part I and begin Part II. Accordingly, this operation was performed by the center's clerical staff before the papers were fed through the machine; or, when rosters of the examinees' names were available in advance of the testing session, the computer was used to preprint the appropriate number on the test papers each examinee would be given.

Uniformity of Separate Tests

Since an examinee usually is given four or five separate tests during the course of a testing session, it is highly desirable to follow the same standard format for every test of the series. Making tests of different abilities identical in appearance is, of course, not feasible in many cases, but inconsistencies in the mechanics common to all tests can and should be avoided. The placement of the answer spaces, for example, should consistently be beneath the answer, or in front of the answer, or after the answer, and not vary from one test to the other. The examinees can learn any rule the test constructor decides to adopt, but sudden changes in a rule that they have already learned are extremely disruptive.

SUMMARY OF SUGGESTED TEST CHARACTERISTICS

Eight major topics related to the content and format of an aptitude test were discussed in this chapter. They may be summarized briefly as follows:

Knowledge Factors

1. The residue of what is left of a standard aptitude test after the culturally inappropriate elements have been eliminated will generally not serve as an adequate ability measure. New content specifically appropriate to this culture should be developed, using one of three methods suggested.

2. Before undertaking such adaptations, however, the inappropriateness of the original content should be verified by empirical studies. Considerable savings can be effected by deferring purely cosmetic changes until the initial tryouts have been completed.

Language Factors

3. As an index of general learning ability, verbal tests are generally superior to culture-fair methods, even for second-language examinees. The development of such tests may be quite costly, however, because of the many highly specific local adaptations that will be required.

4. In tests that use printed language as a vehicle for measuring nonverbal skills this incidental but substantial verbal component may significantly distort the scores. Replacing printed instructions with oral instructions is frequently an effective and economical solution.

Perceptual Factors

5. An oral approach may also be used in pictorial tests when the examinees are unable to interpret the drawings. If the test is paced by the examiner in any event, he can simply name each of the objects portrayed as an integral part of the instructions.

6. In tests that require perceptual skills unfamiliar to the examinees, these skills must be taught as the first step of the testing procedure. This can be done by simplifying the task, developing an appropriate instructional sequence, and providing the examinees with feedback on their performance during a practice session.

Design of the Test Paper

7. When the examinees are not highly experienced in taking tests, the standard format must be revised to reduce the number of mechanical operations they will have to master. Printing the questions directly on a machine-scorable answer sheet will provide most of these necessary mechanical simplifications.

8. Each of the separate tests of the series should be designed to fit (front and back) on a single sheet of paper, so that the examinees will have to manipulate no more than one sheet at a time. This can be done for virtually any type of aptitude test.

As important as the design of the actual test paper is the development of effective administrative procedures. This is the topic of Chapter 5.

CHAPTER

5

THE DESIGN OF EFFECTIVE TESTING PROCEDURES

The instructions that accompany the standard aptitude tests were painstakingly developed, and it would be unfair to characterize them as anything but detailed and complete. The examiner is told exactly what he should do from the time the examinees enter the room; exactly what he should say before, during, and after each test; and exactly how he should respond to the various mishaps that sometimes arise. The examinee is told when, where, and how to enter his name and other biographical data; how to work the problems and mark his responses; and even how to obtain a maximum score. For most groups, the procedure is much more complete than it actually needs to be—a comfortable margin of safety has been provided.

Yet, as was earlier noted, the effectiveness of this process depends on two important characteristics of the examinees for which the standard tests are intended. The first is the examinees' familiarity with the general ritual of modern testing. Except for certain minor differences, the test they are taking today is "like all of the others" they have been given on so many prior occasions. And the second is their facility in understanding and following printed instructions, for the power of the printed word to elicit a desired response has been the key to the efficiency of packaging that has made the testing of many millions of individuals per year routine in the American culture.

For examinees who have neither of these two characteristics, procedures that are still more complete and still more detailed must be developed. The first step is to revise the format of the test so that it _can_ be administered, as described in the preceding chapter. The second is to devise the methods whereby this actually will be done in a "live" testing session.

TEACHING THE TEST OPERATIONS

Even after an aptitude test has been simplified to its barest essentials, it will still require the examinee to perform a fairly large number of skilled operations. Some will be substantive, inherent in the process of solving the problem; some will be strictly mechanical, imposed by the logistic demands of group testing and economical scoring. Both sets of skills must be taught as an integral part of the pretest instructions.

The I-D teaching procedures rely mainly on demonstration, visual aids, and supervised practice sessions. For inexperienced examinees with limited language skills, all three proved essential.

The Demonstration Procedure

The substantive and mechanical operations the examinees must master are best explained by means of a detailed demonstration that encompasses every step of the procedure. Using a large mock-up of the actual test paper, the examiner works a number of sample problems exactly as the examinees are to work them, showing by his actions (and explaining by the oral commentary that accompanies these actions) just what it is that they are to do. As the demonstration proceeds, the examinees are asked to participate more and more actively in the solution; by the time the final sample problem is reached, they are in actuality solving it on their own (or, that at least is the goal at which the development of the demonstration procedure must be directed).

Achieving this goal may require a lengthy trial-and-error process, in which many alternative approaches are tried and discarded; for, in addition to the general guidelines applicable to all demonstrations, most tests present one or more unique explanation problems for which ad hoc solutions must be developed. A number of these special cases will be illustrated in the following review of the principles generally applicable to the pretest demonstration.

Topographical Orientation

The first step of the demonstration should consist of a "guided tour" of the test paper (i.e., the sheet of sample and practice problems) that the examinees have been given. Using the large mock-up of this paper, the examiner should identify each of its major components, distinguishing the "sample problems we shall work now" from the "practice problems we shall work later," and naming all of the test's unique features, such as "the graph that will help us to find the answer." Before the examinees' attention can be focused on any one part of the test, their natural curiosity about its many strange features must be dispelled, and even the briefest of orientations will significantly increase the attentiveness of the group to the subsequent more detailed explanations.

In addition to its utility as a general familiarization device, this initial orientation also serves the highly important function of showing the examinee just what is meant by a "test problem" in this particular test. The radical change in the appearance of the problem-unit to which he is to respond as he goes from one aptitude test to the next is a major source of confusion for an inexperienced examinee. In the I-D tests, for example, a "problem" sometimes consists of five drawings, sometimes of two small squares, sometimes of a path that covers half of the page. If the examinee is not shown explicitly the nature of the units into which each of these tests is divided, the demonstrations will not be fully effective. In this first step of the procedure, defining the problem units is the key teaching objective.

Sequence of Instruction

The sample problems that follow this general orientation should be designed to teach the task in logical chunks, beginning with the essential concept and then adding the others more slowly. The first sample problem is especially important since many examinees will "tune out" if it seems too complex or obscure. For tasks that inherently are complex, ways of reducing this complexity for purposes of the first sample problem may have to be found.

One useful technique is to split the central concept into a number of separate components and to teach these piecemeal, using two or three separate problems. This was the approach used in the I-D Similarities Test, which is intended for semiliterate groups and therefore requires especially simplified explanations. The basic task in this test is to discover the characteristic that is common to four of the five objects shown in each item, and to indicate which one does not belong in the group. The problem encountered was that the examinees, having been told to mark the one that is different, would look for the unique characteristic of the one exception rather than the common characteristic of the similar four, and—because each of the five objects invariably had at least one unique characteristic—would become hopelessly confused. The difference between the operation required to solve the problem (to find the four) and the operation required to mark the answer (to check just one) created a conflict situation that the initial set of sample items did not resolve.

Accordingly, the teaching of the concept was split among several sample items. The first sample problem contains four drawings that are not only similar but identical, and the concept taught is that "four are the same." Then, the second sample extends this concept to the one that is actually desired by showing four pieces of fruit which, though not identical, clearly are "in one way the same." Then, more subtle categories are gradually introduced in the subsequent sample items. The confusion was not completely resolved, but the initial focus on the component of sameness alone did significantly improve the comprehension of at least the more able examinees.

This piecemeal approach is useful also in many tests in which accuracy and speed both are important. In the I-D Manual Dexterity Test, for example, the initial demonstration is limited to the accuracy component alone—the examinees are shown only what is "right" and what constitutes a "mistake." Then, after this aspect of the task is thoroughly understood, the examiner repeats the entire demonstration procedure, this time working at breakneck speed. Trying to teach both requirements in a single demonstration, as was done in the earlier version, was too large a chunk to be effective.

For complex tasks that are not readily split into discrete components, a more general training session in advance of even the first sample problem is often a useful precaution. In the I-D Boxes Test, examinees at the more junior levels had to be shown how a cube looks when drawn on paper before they could follow the demonstration of even the simplest one of these items because the basic ability to "see" the cubes shown in each item is an essential prerequisite to a meaningful demonstration. And in the I-D tests that are based on tables and graphs, a general explanation of these kinds of data displays also proved to be a necessary preliminary to the actual sample items.

Another useful technique is to arrange the order of the four or five tests that the applicants are to be given so that the most difficult to explain will be the last of the session. Because of the overlap in at least the mechanical operations that the various tests require, part of the teaching burden of the more complex tests can in this way be shifted to the earlier demonstrations, permitting both examiner and examinee to concentrate on the more difficult skills that these tests require. In the I-D series, the numbers of the tests are arranged so that this will be done automatically if the tests are administered in numerical order.

Physical Demonstrations

Insofar as possible, the instructional sequence should rely on physical demonstrations—i.e., on visible actions of the examiner—rather than verbal explanations. If the examinees are able to see what they are to do, the instructions will be considerably more effective; the test constructor should try to find ways in which even "mental" tasks can be reduced to actions the examinees can observe.

For some tests, physical demonstrations are the natural mode of explanation, and no special efforts are necessary to reduce the task to one that can be demonstrated concretely. The I-D Dexterity Tests, which are based strictly on the physical action of tracing a path with a pencil are one clear-cut example. But for other tests, considerable trial and error may be required to develop a demonstration procedure from which the examinees will in fact be able to learn. And, interestingly, the solution may turn out to be quite complex—as in the chalk-talk, solid models, and folding patterns that Boxes requires —as in the demonstration based on two fingers that was found most effective for Table Reading.

The descriptions of the tests in Chapter 6 will provide a number of additional illustrations of the kinds of physical demonstrations that can be developed to teach tasks that require primarily mental operations. For inexperienced examinees, the research investment necessary to develop such procedures is highly worthwhile.

Oral Explanations

The ideal role of the examiner's oral commentary is that of a strictly supplementary explanation of procedures taught mainly by physical demonstration. But this ideal is seldom achieved. Certain aspects of a mental ability test simply cannot be shown, and the teaching burden for these aspects must be carried by an oral explanation alone. When this is the case, even more trial-and-error than is necessary for the development of the demonstration techniques typically will be required.

One problem is that the use of a single word or phrase in the course of the commentary can mean the difference between success and failure, especially for second-language examinees. The I-D Coding Test is a case in point. As noted in Chapter 6, the instructions for this test were not fully effective until the examiner began to use two entirely different words to designate the squares that contain the stimulus figures and the (identical) squares in which the examinees are to mark their responses, and taught this two-word vocabulary as the first step of the topographical orientation. And such subtle differences are, of course, difficult to discover.

A second problem is that the basic approach to the explanation—the nature of the bridge that is used to link the concept to ideas with which the examinees are familiar already—appears to be peculiar to each type of test, and must be developed through ad hoc experimentation. Especially instructive in this respect was the problem of trying to explain verbal analogy items. None of the alternative approaches tried was successful, until it was decided to try dropping the explanation completely and letting the examinees develop the concept themselves through induction. The effective technique for explaining this test was to use no explanation whatever; and, as would be expected, it took many successive tryouts to generate so unorthodox an approach.

A third difficulty, perhaps peculiar to the African setting, is that a number of key words had to be changed when the test was used in a different country in which the same language is spoken. Thus, "capital letters" in one country had to become "block letters" in another; "pitcher" had to be changed to "jug," "water glass" to "tumbler." The most numerous differences of this kind naturally were found in changing the Nigerian tests to Liberian versions because of the basic differences in British and American speech; but even among the ex-British countries (e.g., Nigeria and Malawi) many specific changes had to be made. Isolating these needs is, of course, not an especially challenging problem—so long as the test constructor is prepared to take the time to identify them and is aware of this difficulty when he plans the initial research.

Design of the Visual Aids

Throughout the examiner's demonstration, extensive use is made of visual aids and supplementary illustrative items. In the preceding discussion, specific reference was made to the large mock-up of each page of sample problems that is the core of each demonstration, and to a variety of additional props—folding patterns, cut-outs, etc.—that certain aptitude tests also require. In an instructional sequence based largely on physical demonstrations, adequate visual aids are essential.

To be suitable for use in a developing country, these visual aids must meet not only the technical needs of the test but also the practical criteria of serviceability and minimal expense. They must be large enough to be seen, portable enough to be easily and cheaply transported to each testing location, and durable enough to withstand frequent transport and use under unfavorable climatic conditions. They must be reusable, even though the examiner will write on them as part of each demonstration, and they must be fairly cheap to produce. Designing suitable visual aids is itself a quite challenging task of product engineering.

To provide a high degree of reusability at reasonable cost, plastic laminates proved to be by far the most satisfactory approach of those that were tried. The mock-ups are printed on regular paper and then encased in thin plastic sheets by a process similar to that used for such other common laminates as identification cards or credit cards in the United States. The resulting visual is light but sturdy, and the marks that the examiner makes on its surface during the administration of the test can be rubbed off with a cloth after the session. In quantity, the cost of production is low, and each visual can be used for five years or longer with no sign of wear.

To display the visuals, use was made of the "hook 'n' loop" nylon tape that was just then coming into popular use. The display board (which doubles as a carrying case for the visual aids) is covered with the "loop" tape, and to the back of each visual a few strips of the "hook" tape are affixed. When the visual is placed against the board, it stays in place until pulled off by force. This had the advantage not only of simplicity but also of making it possible to cut some of the larger mock-ups into smaller pieces for transportability and then easily to reassemble them on the board.

The use of this tape was first suggested by the requirements of the Boxes Test, in which the examiner must be able to remove the patterns from the display, fold them, and then replace them as an integral part of the demonstration procedure. It continues to serve this purpose, in addition to its more general utility for all other types of aptitude tests.

The visual aids used for the Figures Test are illustrated in Figure 2.

The Supervised Practice Session

The practice session that follows the demonstration is another essential element of the teaching procedure. It should be designed to serve three major functions.

FIGURE 2

Examiner's Instructions for the I-D Figures Test

MATERIALS NEEDED

For each student:
- One Green practice paper number 10
- One Test Paper
- Two pencils and eraser

For the examiner:
- One Timer with bell
- Five Display Sections for the Figures Test
- Five yellow cut-outs
- One Display Board
- Two black or red marking pencils (china marker)

PROCEDURE

1. Set up the display board.
2. Students turn to the green paper number 10.
3. Examiner explains the four sample problems.
4. Group does the four practice problems in one minute.
5. Examiner puts problems 5, 6, 7, and 8 on the display board.
6. Examiner explains and demonstrates the practice problems.
7. Group puts away their green books.
8. Test papers are distributed.
9. Each examinee writes his number on the test paper.
10. Part One is administered in five minutes.
11. Part Two is administered in five minutes.
12. Test papers are collected.

Examiner's Instructions FIGURES TEST

1. DISPLAY BOARD

Set up the display board exactly as shown at the right. Be sure that the display board is placed high enough for everyone to see.

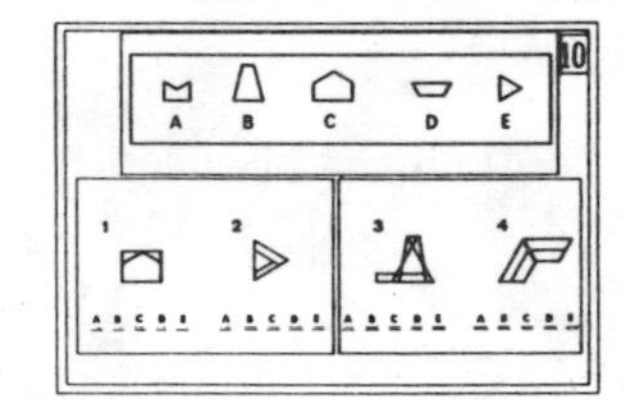

2. INSTRUCTIONS

Everybody take your green book. (Pause) Find paper number 10. It looks like this paper in my hand (Hold up a copy of page 10 for all to see). The front of your paper looks like this (Point to visual).

At the top of the paper are five pictures, A, B, C, D, and E (Point to each). Under the pictures are problems . . . Problem one, Problem two, Problem three, and Problem four (Point to each). These are pictures (Point) and these are the problems (Point).

3. SAMPLE PROBLEMS

Now, look at problem one. (Pause) Inside problem one . . . somewhere inside here (Point) . . . there is hidden . . . there is hidden . . . one of these five pictures (Point to the pictures). Only one. One of these five pictures here (Point) is hidden inside problem one. It is exactly the same size, exactly the same shape, and it has not been turned in any way. It looks exactly the same inside problem one (Point), as it looks up here (Point).

Which picture is hidden inside problem one? Is it A, B, C, D, or E? (Get group response.) All right, let us check. Look at C. (Pick up cut-out and superimpose on C.) It fits exactly inside problem one (Superimpose on problem one). It is exactly the same (Keep moving cut-out from one to the other while talking). It is exactly the same size, exactly the same shape, it has not been turned in any way (Turn figure). Not turned in any way. The answer is C. (Put down cut-out.)

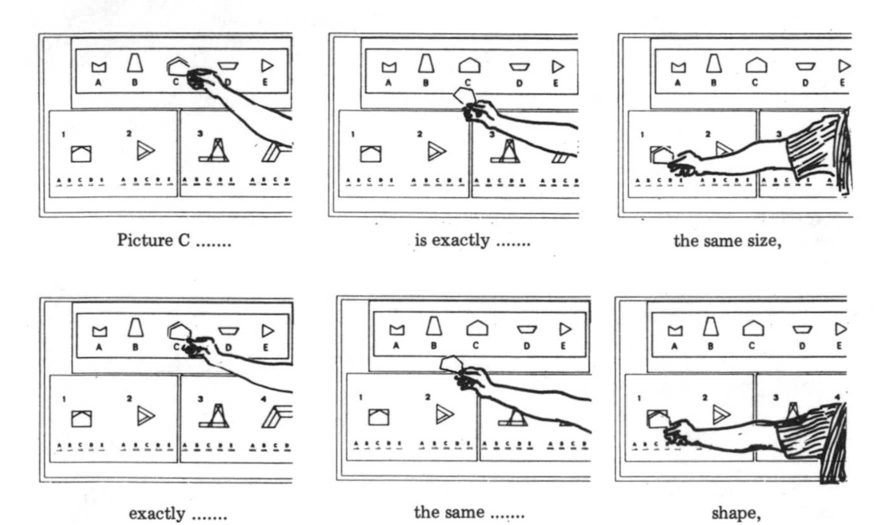

Picture C .... is exactly .... the same size,

exactly .... the same .... shape,

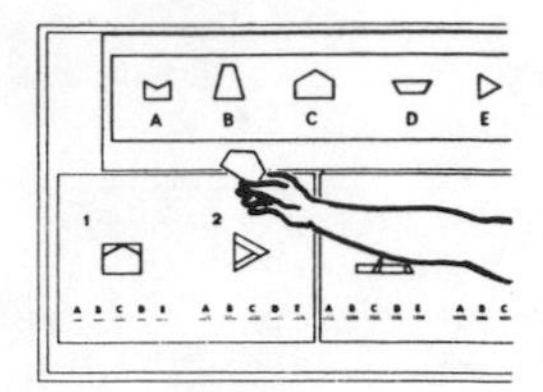

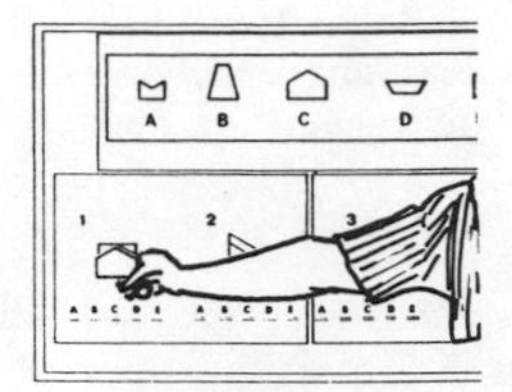

and it is not turned in any way. It fits exactly inside problem one.

To show that C is the right answer. I take my pencil and mark under C. Fill in the two lines under C. (Mark visual.) Everybody, take your pencil and mark under C. (Give proctors time to check.)

Now look at problem two. Look at problem two. The question is the same. Which picture is hidden inside problem two? (Pause) Who can tell me which one? (Get response.) That's right, it is E. (Pick up cut-out and demonstrate.) Remember it must be exactly the same size. Exactly the same shape. It cannot be turned in any way. It must fit exactly. The answer is E. Everybody mark E for number two. (Mark visual.)

Problem three. Which picture is hidden? (Get group response.) That's right, it is picture B. (Demonstrate with cut-out.) It is exactly the same size. Exactly the same shape. It has not been turned in any way. It fits exactly. The answer is B. Everybody mark B for number three. (Mark visual.)

Problem four. Which picture is hidden? (Get group response.) That's right, it is picture D. (Demonstrate with cut-out.) It is exactly the same size. Exactly the same shape. It has not been turned in any way. It fits exactly. Everybody mark D for number four. (Mark visual.)

Put your pencils down!

4. PRACTICE PROBLEMS

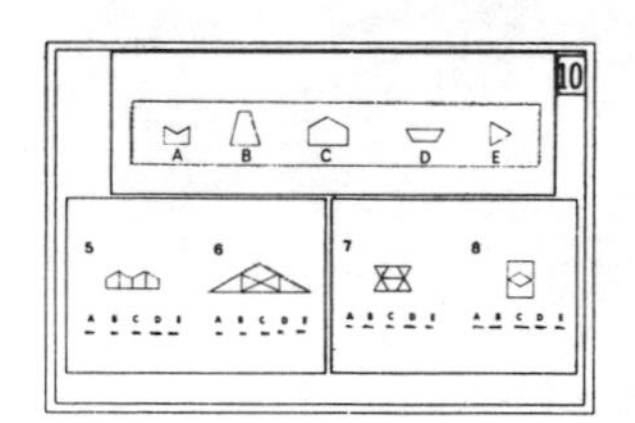

On the bottom of your papers are problems 5, 6, 7, and 8. You will do these problems for practice. You will do these four problems in one minute. Pencils up! Everybody begin! (Start clock.) (While students are working replace the four problems on the visual board with problems 5, 6, 7, and 8.) Allow exactly one minute.

Stop! Put your pencils down!

Let us check on the answers.

Problem 5. Which picture is hidden? (Get group response.) That's correct, it is A. (Demonstrate with cut-out.) It is not C. C will not fit (Demonstrate).

Problem 6. Which picture is hidden? (Get group response.) That's correct, it is C. (Demonstrate with cut-out.) It is not E. E will not fit (Demonstrate).

Problem 7. Which picture is hidden? (Get group response.) That's correct, it is D. (Demonstrate with cut-out.) It is not B (Demonstrate). It is not E (Demonstrate).

Problem 8. Which picture is hidden? (Get group response.) That's correct, it is A. (Demonstrate with cut-out.)

Everybody take your green books and put them under your seat. (Proctors check.)

5. TEST PAPERS

Proctors distribute the correct number of test papers to the first examinee in each row. The first examinee walks down the aisle and gives one paper to each person in his row. Check that papers are being passed quickly.

Does everybody have a test paper that looks like this? (Hold up a copy of the Figures Test for the class to see.)

6. NUMBER

At the top of your paper is the word <u>number</u> (Point). Everybody find the word <u>number</u>. Now take your pencil and write your number on the line next to the word <u>number</u>. (Proctors check) Everybody write your number.

7. PART 1

We will now do Part I of the test. It has 20 problems and five minutes of time. If you finish before the time is up, put your pencils down and wait. You are to do these 20 problems (Point) and no more. Pencils up! Everybody begin! (Start clock.)

Allow exactly five minutes. Check that no one turns his paper over. Pencils up! Everybody stop! (Insure all stop and keep pencils up.) Part I is finished.

8. PART II

We will now do Part II which has 20 problems more. Turn your papers over to the back. You will do these 20 problems and not go back to Part I. Everybody begin. (Start clock. While examinees work, set up visuals for the next test, if any.)

Allow exactly five minutes.

Pencils up! Everybody stop!

Help proctors collect papers quickly.

The first is to give the proctors an opportunity to check each examinee's performance as he works on the practice items and to provide any additional clarification that may be required. Such individual checks are necessary in the developing countries because most inexperienced examinees will not voluntarily admit that they are confused, and the standard approach of ending the explanation by simply asking for questions is seldom effective. Looking at an actual sample of each examinee's work—which an experienced proctor can learn to do at a glance while "patrolling" the aisles during the practice session—is the only realistic way of verifying that the instructions have been understood.

The second is to provide the examinees with feedback on their individual efforts in solving the problems, as a basis for more meaningful follow-up explanations. After the examinees have completed the practice exercises, the examiner should go over these items and explain the answers intended, so that each examinee can identify (and hopefully profit from) the errors that he has made. From a teaching point of view, such feedback on problems the examinee has already tried to solve on his own is an important adjunct to the initial demonstration, in which the problems are worked jointly by the entire group.

The third and perhaps most important function of the practice session is to teach the examinees the rate of speed at which they must work to obtain the best possible score. The timing of the practice exercises should be proportional to the time that will be allotted during the actual test, so that the examinees can actually experience the pace that will be expected. Simply announcing that "you will have five minutes for thirty problems" is a quite meaningless form of guidance for examinees not accustomed to aptitude tests, and so is the standard caution to "work as fast as you can without making mistakes." Here, as at all other stages in the instructional sequence, the examinees have to be shown by concrete demonstrations.

To serve these three functions, the practice session has to be considerably longer than that typically included in standard aptitude tests. One or two practice problems are seldom enough. And, as a result of this extended practice session (and of the detailed demonstration that precedes it), the I-D approach does require more time than the standard testing procedures. But the twenty-four minutes of total testing time that the average I-D test requires is thought to be entirely reasonable for measuring novel skills in populations seldom if ever tested before.

Criteria for Evaluating the Teaching Procedure

A final point on the development of an adequate teaching procedure concerns the criteria by which the effectiveness of a trial procedure can be assessed. In all of the approaches that have been suggested, the test constructor has eventually to put his ideas to the test by trying them in a live testing session and by determining the degree to which they actually communicated the essential concepts and operations to the examinees. The question is: How can he tell? How can he differentiate the examinee errors that are attributable to a faulty teaching procedure from those that reflect deficiencies in the content of the test or in its format or in any of the other structural features considered in Chapter 4? In the standard analyses of the results of a test, the effects of all of these different kinds of shortcomings are intermingled.

In the AID/AIR studies it was found that three separate types of criteria could generally be applied. They are increasingly expensive but provide increasingly sharper results.

At the simplest level, the examiner can rely on the observations that the proctors make during the practice sessions. By noting the frequency of procedural errors, the number of examinees who need special assistance, the amount of hesitation when the starting signal is given, and other symptoms of uncertainty or confusion, experienced proctors can usually make fairly astute judgments about the "readiness" of a procedure and can often pick out the specific elements of the sequence that require further attention. During the early tryouts, when the procedure is still in the preliminary development stages, such proctor judgments are generally sufficient.

As the procedure is developed further, however, additional indexes will be required, for the observations of the proctors are necessarily limited to a small sample of examinee performance and are sensitive mainly to the grosser kinds of mistakes. And, however accurate they may be in identifying deficiencies at the early development stages, they cannot verify that a more polished procedure is in fact ready for use. Whether the desired criterion of examinee comprehension—e.g., that 95 percent of the group members understand the procedure—has or has not been attained is something that a proctor cannot be expected to assess during the course of a live testing session.

Somewhat better for this purpose is a check of the examinees' test scores, using _not_ measures of central tendency but the raw score distribution. When the procedures have not been adequately understood by a part of the group, the shape of the distribution will generally have two humps rather than the one normally expected, for the scores will pile up not only around the mean but also at the chance level at which those who did not understand will perform. And, though there are other kinds of deficiencies that can lead to the same phenomenon, inadequacies in the teaching procedure is by far the most probable explanation in the developing countries.

A more accurate criterion still is an index based on the nature of the examinees' answers to the individual test question—i.e., on the kinds of mistakes that they made. Two examples of such indexes are given in Chapter 6 in the discussions of the Boxes and the Verbal Analogies Tests. The former is based on a certain subset of items that every examinee who has understood the concept should be able to answer correctly, the latter on the one response in each set of five answer options that would logically be selected by an individual who does not understand the basic idea. These kinds of indexes are useful not only during the developmental stages but also in an operational testing program, to monitor the quality of administration at the various field locations.

CONTROLLING PERFORMANCE

Another essential requirement of effective testing is that the conditions under which the various examinees take the test be sufficiently similar to ensure that the relative magnitudes of their scores are in fact a meaningful index of their respective potential. No one should enjoy an unfair advantage; no one should be handicapped by an unfair constraint. In the jargon of test construction, reasonably standardized testing conditions must be maintained.

The unique problems of standardization that arise in the developing countries lie not in ensuring that the examiner and proctors will make the same inputs to all groups at all testing locations. This is a universal problem in all countries, and the same types of precautions (i.e., adequate training, detailed manuals, and statistical checks of the scores) should be applied. Rather, the unique problems lie in adequately "programming" the behavior of the examinees to ensure that all of them will abide by the explicit rules and regulations, and that all or most of them will use roughly the same test-taking tactics in their individual efforts to obtain a maximum score. To attain reasonable uniformity in individual performance, a variety of specific controls usually must be applied.

The Explicit Test Regulations

In all aptitude tests, there are certain explicit rules that all of the examinees are expected to follow. Some of these are general test-taking rules, such as not beginning until the signal is given; not completing Part I when Part II is to be started; or not returning to the incompleted Part I problems later, even when there is time to spare. Others are specific to certain types of items, such as not erasing and changing responses in the case of the Manual Dexterity Test. All such rules must be explained as part of the initial instructions, and then enforced as strictly as possible throughout the session.

The problems in enforcing these basic rules derive mainly from the naïveté of the examinees. Although some deliberate cheating does, of course, also occur, deviations from the rules prescribed for a test are much more often ingenuous errors, resulting from the examinees' failure to understand or to appreciate the importance of a certain procedure. If they are helped to avoid honest mistakes, most of the deviations that typically are noted in the administration of a standard aptitude test—and frequently misconstrued as deliberate cheating—will disappear.

One way of helping the inexperienced examinee is to use _obvious and unambiguous signals_ at the beginning and end of the test. Before each of the I-D tests begins, the examinees are told to hold their pencils up in the air and to wait until the examiner says "Go!" before starting the test. The action of the examinees and the word used by the examiner are the same for every test—and both are practiced at the very start of the session, during the examiner's introductory remarks. Similarly, a darkroom timer (which rings when the preset time has expired) is used instead of a stopwatch in timing the tests; and the examinees are taught to raise their pencils to the starting position at the sound of this ring. At the beginning and end of each part of each test, no "honest" mistakes can be made.

A second type of control is that afforded by the _proctors_, whose primary task once the test is begun is to spot and correct procedural deviations. This task can be greatly simplified, as noted in the preceding chapter, by designing the test in part from the point of view of controlling performance. Printing Parts I and II on opposite sides of the sheet, for example, enables the proctors to listen for as well as to watch for infractions of the rule that prohibits moving on or going back.

A third and especially effective control is to "human engineer" the test or procedure to _make it impossible_ for the examinees to deviate from the prescribed regulation. To enforce the rule against changing answers on the dexterity tests, the most simple solution is to provide the examinees with pens or pencils that have no erasers. To prevent them from consulting their practice papers after the actual test is begun, these papers can be collected; or, to save time, the examinees can simply be asked to sit on these papers—as is actually done in the I-D testing procedures. Many ideas for improved controls will occur to the examiner who actively looks for deviations during each testing session, and then asks "How can these be prevented?"

Tactical Variations

Some of the individual differences in test-taking behavior are virtually impossible to control. If an examinee decides to work the last problem in the array first or to do the array in horizontal rather than vertical order, the chances that this will be discovered and corrected in time are essentially nil. Monitoring performance at the level of the individual test items is simply not practical in a group testing session.

What the test constructor can and should do, however, is to ensure that the tactics which are taught as the "normal" test-taking procedure are in fact those that are likely to result in a maximum score. If the tryouts show that certain of the examinees found a better approach and thereby obtained inflated scores, the test should be revised either to preclude these tactics or to adopt them as the normal test-taking procedure; for, even though this will not guarantee uniformity, the number of examinees who will deviate from the optimum tactics is likely to be appreciably lower.

A case in point is the I-D Arithmetic Test, which is based on simple addition, subtraction, multiplication, and division problems. The initial version that was prepared presented these four kinds of problems in scrambled order, so that the score would reflect a sample of performance on all four operations for every examinee, including those who completed only a small number of items. But in the tryouts the proctors noted that many examinees skipped the harder problems and worked the problems based on the easier operations first rather than following the numerical sequence that was intended. And even though these examinees did not necessarily earn higher scores—the data on this were not clear—it seemed desirable to try to reduce this large individual variation by unscrambling the test and presenting the four kinds of problems in four separate groups. The more "natural" sequence of addition first, subtraction second, multiplication third, and division last was followed in subsequent versions; and the large differences in examinee tactics that were initially noted no longer occur.

To a considerable extent, of course, this difficulty can be attributed to the test constructors for adopting an unnatural sequence for less than compelling reasons. Herein lies perhaps the key principle in controlling these kinds of variations in test-taking behavior. If the test constructor consistently uses the pattern of presentation that affords the most natural, straightforward approach to each type of problem, and foregoes the niceties of measurement that are not truly essential, relatively few deviations in examinee performance will be encountered in the developing countries. One of the advantages of testing inexperienced examinees is that they tend to be docile as well as naïve.

For a second major source of tactical variations, so simple a remedy cannot be prescribed. Individual differences in the management of time limits—which are substantial even in groups of highly experienced examinees—are magnified many times over in the developing countries; a number of special measures must be introduced to obtain comparable scores. If one examinee races through the test in half the allotted time while another checks and double-checks his answer to each problem before trying the next, their relative aptitudes cannot be determined.

The nature of the appropriate controls varies in accordance with the mix of speed and accuracy that a particular test requires. Speed tests, power tests, and time-limit tests are the three major categories to be considered.

Speed Tests

Strictly speaking, a speed test is one in which every examinee would get every item right if adequate time were provided. The examinees' scores are different only because the time limit is set so that no examinee can possibly complete all of the items, giving those who can work them more quickly the higher test scores.

In practice, few tests are so devoid of skills other than speed to meet this strict definition; and the term is used more broadly to include all tests that depend so greatly on speed that mistakes rarely if ever occur. Thus, the speed tests of the I-D series include not only the Marking Test (which is a pure speed test in the classical sense), but also such tests as Coding and Checking, in which counts of the "number of items attempted" and of the "number answered correctly" are almost always the same.

The most effective way of encouraging the examinees to work at the peak pace that will yield the maximum score on these types of tests is to use a greatly exaggerated pace during the demonstrations. If the examiner works the sample exercises at frantic speed, the examinees will immediately get the idea—and the spectacle of a harrassed examiner trying (unsuccessfully) to beat the clock will help considerably also in easing the tensions that typically inhibit all-out performance. From the point of view of uniform test-taking behavior, speed tests require the least demanding controls.

The only caution to be observed with these tests is that they should not be given as the first test of the session. Most groups need the warm-up a more tightly controlled test provides to prepare them for high-speed performance.

Power Tests

A pure power test is at the other extreme of the speed-accuracy continuum in that in this type of test, at least theoretically, time is not important. The differences in the examinees' scores derive strictly from the inherent difficulty of the test items; and, even if infinite time were permitted, the results would presumably still be the same. In practice the term is used more broadly to include all of those tests in which the test constructor wants every examinee to attempt every item, and has made the time limits unusually generous to bring this about.

From the point of view of the cost of testing, "unusually generous" must normally be limited to a maximum of about one minute per item, however, and if the test is to serve its purpose, the examinees must all work at this pace or faster. The normal precaution is to tell the examinees periodically during the course of the test how many minutes remain, to encourage those who have fallen behind to work a little more quickly. And, for certain tests, this standard technique is adequate also in the developing countries. It is fully effective for the Information Tests, probably because of the advanced educational levels at which these are given; and at least satisfactory for the lower-level Reading and Verbal Analogies Tests, perhaps because the simplicity of the language used in these items encourages faster performance.

But for the more novel types of test items—such as those of an abstract reasoning test— these periodic reminders were not sufficient.

The interexaminee differences in number of items attempted within a reasonable time limit were far too large; to reduce these differences too much time had to be given. And it was in part because it proved impossible to devise more effective controls that these tests were eventually dropped from the series.

The less abstract tests that are subject to similar problems, such as the Similarities and Mechanical Information Tests, could be saved because of the way in which these tests are given. As will be remembered from an earlier discussion, the items of these tests are presented orally by the examiner to reduce language and drawing interpretation problems; this approach naturally incorporates an automatic pacing procedure. The examiner reads the questions at fixed intervals, the examinees mark their responses, and the aim of having every examinee attempt every item becomes part of the testing routine. For all power tests that will accommodate it, this method of external pacing is the most effective technique by far for controlling performance.

Time-Limit Tests

Most aptitude tests lie somewhere between the speed and power extremes in that both factors contribute significantly to the differences in the examinees' scores. The aim, like that of the power test, is to measure facility in a certain type of skilled operation, in which speed may or may not be intrinsically important; but the index used to measure facility is, as in the speed test, accomplishment per unit time; the two elements are thereby interwoven. To obtain a maximum score, an appropriate blend of both is required.

The problem in administering such tests is that the "appropriate blend" varies from one examinee to another, and that the examiner therefore cannot establish hard and fast rules that the entire group is to follow. Each examinee must develop the particular strategy that is most consistent with the strengths and weaknesses of his own performance; this, of course, is extremely difficult for examinees who have had at best limited exposure to testing.

Two useful techniques for assisting the examinees in this task have already been noted. One is to use the practice session as a training ground by making the time limits for the practice problems proportional to those that will be applied during the test. The second is to administer these more challenging tests later in the session, after the examinees have had an opportunity to become more familiar with the testing procedure. Both are generally helpful, but for many groups are in themselves not enough. Because the examinees are still learning about the management of time when the test begins, many of them will continue to adjust their performance throughout the test, and not only interexaminee but also intraexaminee differences in tactics may be encountered.

As a further remedy, therefore, experimental studies were made also of the value of statistical corrections that might help to equate the performance of the more conservative and the more reckless examinees, so that their scores could be compared. Using maximum reliability as the criterion, it was found that subtracting the number of mistakes from the number of right answers was the formula that consistently gave the best results in the African studies. This formula has been used since for scoring all time-limit tests, but its utility has not been verified for other locations; this should be done.

STREAMLINING THE TESTING PROCEDURE

Once a fully effective testing procedure has been developed, the test constructor should continue to look for ways to make it more efficient. If he can increase the number of examinees that can be tested in each testing session, reduce the amount of time each session requires, or make do with fewer administrative assistants, substantial savings can be effected.

The major constraint on the size of the group that can be tested is the physical layout of the room in which the tests will be given. In a typical rural classroom—crowded and poorly lighted, the examinees seated at double or triple desks—a group of 35 to 40 examinees is the largest that should be attempted. But in an auditorium with individual seats and broad aisles, as many as 150 to 200 can be tested with comparable results. And it is therefore well worth the effort to make advance arrangements for the best possible testing site at each location. Town halls, cafeterias, churches, and even football fields were used in the African studies to reduce nation-wide testing programs to manageable proportions.

The most significant savings in time that can be effected, at least in the I-D procedures, is in the distribution and collection of the many separate sheets of paper that these tests require. Assembling the four or five practice papers that will be used into a single booklet that the examinees are given at the beginning of the session and do not return till the end is one highly useful procedure. Similarly, the answer sheets—especially when preprinted with the examinees' testing numbers—can be distributed in a folder from which the examinees extract them, one at a time, when the appropriate signal is given. To the maximum extent practicable, all sorting and arranging of the test papers for fast distribution should be done in advance of the session by personnel less costly than the examiner and proctors.

The most feasible way of reducing the number of administrative personnel that are required is to utilize the examiner as a proctor once the demonstration has been completed. This can easily be done for all tests except those in which the examiner has to present the test questions orally, and even here can be accomplished by presenting the questions instead via tape recorder. Another device that is helpful when a minimum number of proctors is used is to provide the examinees with mechanical pencils so as to eliminate broken pencil points as a crisis to which the proctors have to attend.

Even greater savings, of course, would be realized by changing the I-D procedures themselves to make them more comparable to the standard testing procedures. Many of the features that were eliminated —separate answer sheets, printed instructions, etc.—could be reintroduced for groups more advanced than the examinees for which the I-D techniques were originally developed. And some preliminary evidence suggests that in certain situations this can be done with little or no loss in the accuracy of the results. But the more careful research that would be necessary to determine the level of examinee sophistication at which the I-D approaches can in fact be replaced with standard methods has not yet been carried out in any developing country, and ad hoc determinations will have to be made for each situation in which such simplifications are being considered.

SUMMARY OF SUGGESTED TESTING PROCEDURES

Ten major aspects of the administration of an aptitude test were discussed in this chapter. They may be summarized briefly as follows:

1. The most effective method of explaining a test to inexperienced examinees is by an actual demonstration in which the examiner performs every task, substantive and mechanical, that the examinees will be expected to master.

2. The first step of this demonstration should be an overall orientation to the test paper that explains all of its components, and teaches the examinees the nature of the problem-unit to which they are to respond.

3. The explanation of the task itself should be programmed into discrete stages, beginning with the central concept and then adding the others more slowly. This type of sequential approach should also be used in deciding which tests should be given near the beginning and end of each session, so that the examinees can learn the complex tasks more readily by building on what they learned before.

4. To the maximum extent practicable, each operation the examinees are to perform should be reduced to a physical action that the examiner can actually show. Visual aids are especially helpful in reducing "mental" tasks to observable operations.

5. The development of the oral commentary that accompanies the demonstration may require extensive trial and error. In certain tests, the choice of a single word can be critical to the effectiveness of the procedure.

6. The final step of the instructional sequence should be a supervised practice session in which each examinee gets feedback on his performance. The time limit for the practice exercises should be proportional to that used during the actual test.

7. To evaluate the effectiveness of the teaching procedure the test constructor may rely on the proctors' evaluations, on analyses of the distribution of scores, or on special indexes based on the nature of the examinees' mistakes. The last of these will usually provide the most accurate indication.

8. To assist the examinees in understanding and following the "rules" of the test, the most effective approach is to design the procedure so that it is physically impossible for them to make a mistake. Unambiguous and consistent signals and the effective use of proctors are also important.

9. The major source of interexaminee differences in test-taking behavior is the variability in individual tactics that time limits permit. To obtain comparable performance samples from the more conservative and the more reckless examinees, special controls, training, and statistical corrections may be required.

10. The efficiency of the I-D testing procedures—with respect to capacity, time, and personnel requirements—can be increased by making appropriate arrangements in advance of the testing session. For certain groups, some of the more time-consuming features of this approach can be replaced with conventional testing procedures.

To illustrate the entire I-D process, the examiner's instructions for the Figures Test are shown in Figure 2 exactly as they appear in the I-D Examiner's Manual. The detailed guidance that these instructions provide the examiner, so as to promote uniform testing procedures at all locations, should also be noted.

PART III

PRACTICAL TEST APPLICATIONS

CHAPTER 6 THE I-D APTITUDE TESTS

Each of the techniques described in the preceding chapter was applied in the development of one or more of the tests in the I-D Aptitude Series. This chapter describes nineteen of these tests, both as an illustration of the adaptation techniques and as an introduction to the following chapter on practical test applications.

Each description begins with a summary of the special features of the test, as it was originally developed for use in West Africa, and then notes the ways in which this original version had to be modified for use in other countries. It will be seen that relatively few modifications had to be made in either the test content or the testing mechanics, and that the approach to test adaptation suggested in the preceding chapter appears to be safely generalizable to a variety of cultural settings. This was the major finding of the "generalizability phase" of the AID/AIR research.

REASONING TESTS

Five of the I-D tests measure skills in working with concepts and logical relations, and are in this way similar to the instruments popularly called "intelligence" tests. They are based on three different types of test items, and are intended for use with examinees at different levels of education.

The Similarities Test is entirely pictorial and is intended for use with illiterate or semiliterate groups, or with examinees who are functionally illiterate in the second language in which the testing program must be conducted. The Verbal Analogies Test (Low) and the Verbal Analogies Test (High) use printed words rather than pictures, and the Reading Comprehension Test (Low) and the Reading Comprehension Test (High) are based on paragraph-long descriptions and explanations. The Low forms of these tests are of approximately equal difficulty and are intended for examinees who have the equivalent of a primary school education. The High form of the Verbal Analogies Test is of intermediate difficulty and is intended for examinees with a few years of postprimary education or training. The High form of the Reading Comprehension Test is more difficult still and extends the range to the university level.

I-D Test 1: Similarities

Most of the developmental work on the Similarities Test was done in the very early days of the research, when the identification of talent in semiliterate groups was regarded as an important project objective. But as the rapid expansion of primary education throughout most African countries began to produce an ever-larger surplus of job seekers with at least minimal literacy qualifications, the need for this type of test was reduced; its development thus was not fully completed. Accordingly, the Similarities Test is useful chiefly as a model of the methods of adaptation that can be used in testing individuals with little or no education. In its present form, it is considered suitable for only limited practical use.

General Description

The Similarities Test contains two types of items, as shown in Figure 3. All but eight of the 30 test items are of the "four of these are in one way the same" type, however. The administration time is approximately 35 minutes, including the fairly lengthy explanation and demonstration procedure. Answers are marked directly on the test paper, so that scoring could be done by machine; but a machine-scorable version has not been prepared.

The Adaptation Procedure

The major problem in developing this kind of test is that it is virtually impossible to devise a test item that has only one logical solution. Invariably there are a number of concepts that can be applied, and the trick is to try to develop items in which one concept is clearly "more logical" than all the rest, but yet not so obviously logical that every examinee will solve the problem correctly.

Thus, in the first sample item in Figure 3, the intended answer is "trunk" because all of the other objects are open rather than shut.

FIGURE 3

Sample Items of the I-D Similarities Test

When the examinees reach this item, the examiner says: "Number Five: Tin-Trunk-Book-Lock-Chest of Drawers. Four of these are in one way the same. Mark the ONE that is different."

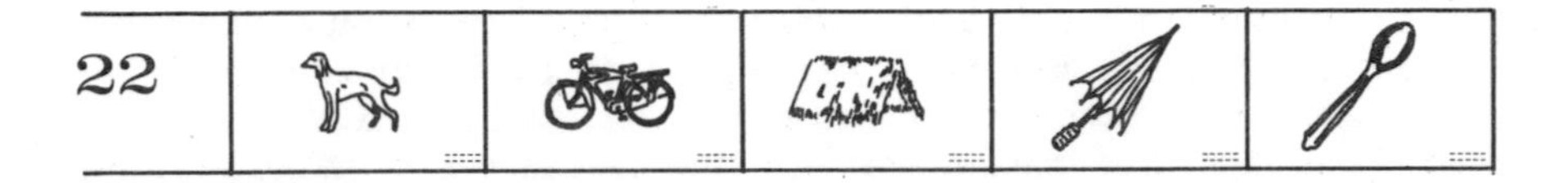

When the examinees reach this item, the examiner says: "Number Twenty-two: Dog-Bicycle-Roof-Umbrella-Spoon. Two of these things are in one way the same. Mark the TWO that are the same and be sure to mark TWO."

But it could also be argued that the right answer is "tin" because all of the others are reusable while this one is not. And in the second item, the intended answer of "roof and umbrella" competes with "dog and bicycle," using the concept of mobility rather than the intended concept of shelter.

Whether the intended concept is sufficiently more logical than the others to provide a usable test item is not a rational but an empirical question. If analysis of the item's difficulty, reliability, and predictive validity show it to be effective, it can safely be kept; if the statistical findings are poor, it must be revised or rejected. The opinion of the test constructor is not particularly important.

Where the test constructor's insights do matter, however, is in the preparation of the trial items, since the number of empirical tryouts that will be required depends mainly on the adequacy of the first trial form. Here it is likely that knowledge of the examinees' first language is probably the most important single requirement for effective test construction. For even though this does appear to be a nonverbal test, the relationships that are logical in a given cultural setting are closely linked with the local language structure. The concept of "open" in the first sample item is viable in English only because English speakers use the same word for tins, trucks, books, locks, and chests of drawers. In another language, where different words are used to describe the openness of different types of objects, this concept may not be a logical one at all.

For this reason, extensive use was made of the technique of asking examinees to explain their answers, as was earlier suggested, and of repeated item analysis studies. But even this was not sufficient. The present version of the Similarities Test is the product of seven cycles of item analysis and revision, and still is not so effective as the other tests of the I-D series. Tests of this type should be developed by local specialists, not by an outsider.

In addition to this basic substantive problem, most of the procedural difficulties described in the preceding chapter were also encountered, and the format of the Similarities Test illustrates the solutions that have been suggested. The test is paced by the examiner, who reads the questions one at a time, to avoid the large variations in test-taking strategy that proved to be an especially serious problem with illiterate examinees. Each of the objects portrayed in the item is named by the examiner before he asks the question, to ensure that the examinees will interpret the drawings correctly. The pacing of the initial practice items is slow, to permit the proctors to verify that each examinee has understood the marking procedure. The pacing of the later practice items is at the same rate of speed as that of the actual test items, to acquaint the examinees with the amount of time they will be given. The standard I-D demonstration procedure, using visual aids and separate practice papers, is followed in giving the pretest instructions and explanations.

All of the features of the Similarities Test but one are thought to be necessary for the testing of groups at the level for which this test is intended. The exception is the intermingling of two types of test items, which was done to ensure that the examinees would work at the pace at which the examiner reads the questions. Since the examinees would have to listen to each question to determine the type of answer required, it was thought that they would neither linger nor race ahead; this desired result is in fact effected. But the examinees might well keep pace even without this feature, simply to hear the examiner identify the five objects by name. The greater simplicity of administering and scoring a test based on only one type of item suggests that this be attempted.

Intercountry Modifications

The one change that was made as a matter of course in all of the countries outside Africa in which the Similarities Test was evaluated was to replace the drawings that are peculiar to the African scene. Some of these changes were strictly stylistic, such as replacing the typically African roof in the second sample item with the type of roof most commonly seen in these other countries. Some were a little more substantive, such as replacing the tropical fruits portrayed in a number of the African items with fruits better known in a country such as Korea. In making these latter changes it was necessary to find substitutes that had all of the characteristics of the original important to the concept underlying the item but that did not have additional properties which would introduce a second "right" answer as logical as the one desired.

Culture-tied changes in the concepts themselves did not seem to be required, at least to match the effectiveness of the original version. In Brazil and Thailand, the original concepts were used with no modification whatever, and the statistical findings were essentially the same as those obtained in the African countries. Whereas a number of changes were made in Korea after the item analysis of the original version, these were straightforward technical improvements that had no cultural connotations.

These findings suggest that the concepts which survived the many tryouts that were carried out in West Africa during the initial development of the test are reasonably generalizeable across different cultures. But it is virtually certain that further research would generate concepts more effective than these for use in this type of test, and it is possible that the "very best items" for each location would indeed vary from country to country.

Typical Results

The reliability estimates typically obtained for the Similarities Test are summarized in Table 1. It is interesting to note that the reliability of the test was highest for the young adults tested in Thailand, since this sample is most nearly representative of the types of groups for which it is intended. For primary school students, reliabilities in the range of .50-.60 are the best that can be expected. Lengthening the test by ten or so additional items would raise these figures to more acceptable levels.

TABLE 1

Typical Reliability Estimates of the 1-D Similarities Test

Country	Group	Education	Number	r*
West Africa	Primary school students	6-7 years	5,189	0.56
Thailand	Young adults (16-22 years)	4 years or less	150	0.68
Brazil	Primary school students	5 years	140	0.51

*Since all examinees try each item, KR-20 coefficients were used.

The validity of the Similarities Test in the study of the young Thai adults, who were students at a rural vocational training center, was .41 against the criterion of grades in the center's courses. Elsewhere, validities in predicting course grades, instructor ratings, or other performance evaluations have generally ranged from .25 to .40; and for planning purposes an estimate of .30 is a reasonable projection. When the examinees are primary school dropouts who have been out of school for five to ten years, the results tend to be better than with groups at younger ages.

Overall, the major advantage of the Similarities Test is that it can be administered to nonliterate groups of all ages in any language by an untrained examiner, and can identify with reasonable accuracy at least the 10 percent or so of the examinees who have the highest potential. Its chief limitation is that its accuracy drops sharply when a larger percentage of the examinees are to be selected, and further revisions are necessary to ready the test for such applications.

I-D Tests 2 and 3: Verbal Analogies

The development of the Verbal Analogies Test was described in Chapter 1 as part of the discussion of the background research that some tests require. The Low form has become one of the most widely used of the I-D tests, and is generally included in the selection procedure for any application in which examinees with six to eight years of formal education are to be tested. The High form is used less often because individuals with nine to ten years of education are "in between" the major selection decisions made in most countries; above this level the High form of the Reading Comprehension Test has been found more effective.

General Description

Each form of the Verbal Analogies Test contains forty items of the type shown in Figure 4. There are twenty items of approximately equal difficulty on each side of the test paper, and these two sets of problems are administered as two separate parts. Nearly all of the examinees complete the test in the allotted time, which is ten minutes and seven-and-a-half minutes per part, respectively, for the Low and the High forms. The total administration time is approximately 30 minutes, and the test can be scored by machine.

The Adaptation Procedure

The major problem encountered in the development of this test was that the concept of an "analogy" proved to be extremely difficult to explain. All of the initial attempts—such as "these two things are alike in a certain way, and these two are alike in the same way"—led mainly to mass confusion; the research never did produce a satisfactory explanation to use with twelve-year-old African students.

FIGURE 4

Sample Items of the I-D Verbal Analogies Test

(Low Form)

17. bicycle and wheel
boy and ___?___

foot ride girl road father

(High Form)

9. scale and pound
clock and ___?___

hands hour run watch measure

The approach that did prove effective was the simple one of not trying to explain the concept at all. The examiner merely points out that the last word is missing in the first demonstration item, and reads this item aloud to the examinees: "Mother and daughter, father and. . . ." He asks for the missing word, and most of the group in unison reply, "Son." Then he goes through seven additional samples, each time explaining the relationship after the group has responded; later, he explains each of the six practice problems that the examinees work individually on their own practice papers. At the end of this session, the group understands what is required, even though none of them may be able to explain the analogy concept in the abstract. The test itself can then be given.

At each stage of the development of this procedure, the effectiveness of the instructions was judged not by the numbers of test problems that the examinees answered correctly, but by the nature of their mistakes. In the first sample problem of Figure 4, for example, an examinee who does not understand the analogy concept will tend to ignore the top line of the problem completely and select "girl" as the answer, because "boy-girl" is a more logical pair than "boy-foot," "boy-ride," or the other possible combinations. By counting the number of examinees who consistently chose such logical pairs, it was possible to estimate the number who did not understand the instructions. The revision and rephrasing of the instructions was continued until these error counts showed that the goal of 95 percent comprehension had been achieved.

The content of the test evolved through a series of straightforward item analysis studies, in which no unusual problems were noted. Nor were there any difficulties with the testing mechanics, which follow the standard I-D procedures.

Intercountry Modifications

The Low form of the Verbal Analogies Test was translated into Portuguese and Thai, the High form into Thai only. In translating the Low form it proved possible to retain all forty of the original problems in both countries, with only such minor modifications as the change from "pound" to "kilogram" in the second sample item of Figure 5. In the Thai translation of the High form, a number of the original items had to be replaced; and eight new items were added to the test (as was done in Thailand in the case of the Low form as well) to produce a 48-item version.

The basic reason for the replacement of a number of the original concepts was that the Thai language would not accomodate certain word-pairs that in English are suitable for use in analogy items. Thus, the item "school and study; office and __?__," in which "work" is the intended answer, would in Thai be written as "building-for-learning and learn; place-for-work and __?__," in which the answer would be indicated by the word structure. The item "school and principal; army and __?__" was used instead. But this was the only type of modification that was at all attributable to cultural factors. The rest were straightforward technical improvements based on item analysis data.

In Korea it was decided not to attempt to translate the original version, and a totally new 48-item test was developed. As a result, the generalizability data from the Korean studies show only that the analogy <u>format</u> is suitable in also this country; they provide no information about the transferability of the original items.

In Thailand, administrations of the Verbal Analogies Test with printed rather than oral instructions were also attempted, and they gave generally comparable results at the seventh-grade level. The reasons that this approach was feasible in Thailand but not in West Africa are probably that in Thailand the examinees' first language could be used for the instructions and that proportionately fewer Thai than Africans reach the last grade of primary school, making this a more highly select examinee group. One possible advantage of giving this test with printed instructions is that since it is used mainly for school selection, the examinees' relative proficiency in understanding written explanations may itself be predictive of their success in advanced academic courses.

Overall, the Verbal Analogies Test proved highly generalizable to at least two of these other countries. Not only the basic approach but also the vast majority of the specific test items were equally effective.

Typical Results

The reliability estimates typically obtained for the Verbal Analogies Test are summarized in Table 2. It will be seen that the estimates for the Low form are virtually identical at all locations, and that the reliability of the High form is somewhat lower. But all of these figures are adequate for operational use.

Most of the validity data so far compiled on the Verbal Analogies Test are based on students who had already been admitted to the higher-level institution, and who therefore are not representative of the unselected applicant pool to which the test actually would be applied. In these studies, validity coefficients in the range of .40-.45 typically have been obtained against the criterion of end-of-term grades. In a study of 669 Thai seventh-grade students, in which current course marks were used as the criterion, the coefficients were in the range of .60-.65, which are probably higher than would be obtained from follow-up studies based on grades in secondary school courses. For planning purposes, a figure of approximately .50 is a reasonable projection.

I-D Tests 4 and 5: Reading Comprehension

The Low form of the Reading Comprehension Test has been used in two ways. The first has been as an alternative to the Verbal Analogies Test for secondary school selection, when it seemed desirable to obtain evidence of the candidate's reading proficiency as a by-product of the measurement of his overall ability level. The second has been as an initial screening device for secondary school applicants, to reduce the numbers to a "short list" of finalists who are then given a more comprehensive series of tests, including Verbal Analogies and three or four others. It has proved effective for both of these applications.

TABLE 2

Typical Reliability Estimates of the I-D Verbal Analogies Test

Form	Country	Group	Education	Number	r*
Low (40 items)	West Africa	Primary students	6-7 years	374	0.87
Low (40 items)	Brazil	Primary students	5 years	137	0.85
Low (48 items)	Thailand	Primary students	7 years	669	0.84
High (40 items)	West Africa	Secondary students	9-10 years	282	0.75
High (48 items)	Thailand	Secondary students	10 years	715	0.82

*With the exception of the last entry, all are KR-20 coefficients. The Thailand High form estimate is a test-retest figure.

The High form has had much wider use, serving as an all-purpose selection device at the higher educational levels. It has been used for general university admissions, for postsecondary technical and commercial training institutions, and, to a limited extent, for postuniversity professional courses. Its range of difficulty appears to be adequate to accomodate this variety of practical applications.

General Description

The format of the Reading Comprehension Test is shown in Figure 5. The examinees are to read each paragraph, and to decide which of the alternatives listed for each of the blank spaces is the word that has been omitted. The Low and the High forms include 40 and 42 items, respectively, and most of the examinees finish in the 25 minutes allotted. Because the task is an especially easy one to explain, the total administration time seldom exceeds 30 minutes, and the one-page paper test can be scored by machine.

The Adaptation Procedure

The major problem in the development of the Low form of this test was that the standard technique for measuring reasoning ability

FIGURE 5

Sample Items of the I-D Reading Comprehension Test

A boomerang is a curved club which has been used for hundreds of years in Australia. Although in the past it served only as a weapon, there are now two kinds of <u>21</u> . A small one, used only for sport, will return to the thrower when it is <u>22</u> by a skilled person . The <u>23</u> war boomerang does not <u>24</u> when thrown.

21.	weapons	boomerangs	types	Australians	curves
22.	hit	over	dropped	time	thrown
23.	larger	faster	powerful	curved	metal
24.	spin	return	kill	miss	break

Rocket and jet motors are very similar in that both <u>36</u> the vehicles in which they are <u>37</u> by expelling particles at a very high velocity. Such particles must have not only <u>38</u> , they also must have weight to provide the necessary reactive force. A torch light does expel particles at the speed of light, but the particles lack <u>39</u> so that the reactive force is almost <u>40</u> . The primary difference between rocket and jet motors is that, whereas jets must burn oxygen from the air, rockets carry their <u>41</u> with them so that they can fly above the <u>42</u> .

36.	carry	propel	transmit	guide	operate
37.	mounted	controlled	moving	loaded	guided
38.	power	fuel	energy	force	speed
39.	heat	velocity	weight	force	volume
40.	constant	negligible	dispelled	exhausted	inflammable
41.	power	bombs	missiles	oxidant	astronauts
42.	enemy	jets	planets	world	atmosphere

within the format of a reading exercise—which is to write items that require the examinee to draw logical inferences from the information presented—is difficult to apply with examinees who have only minimal skills in the language in which they are being tested. It was difficult to find paragraphs that were simple enough for the examinees to read and understand and yet meaty enough to permit reasonable test items to be written. And, given suitable paragraphs, it was difficult also to devise items that required some element of reasoning without exceeding the capabilities of students with only a primary school education.

The first sample item in Figure 6 illustrates the kinds of issues that are encountered. The last two sentences of this paragraph contrast two types of boomerangs, and the test construction objectives were the following:

1. To leave enough of the original content of these sentences intact to enable the examinee to see that the features of the two boomerangs that are different are being compared; and

2. To measure whether the examinee is able to infer that any feature of one of the boomerangs that has been replaced by a blank must be just the opposite of the other boomerang's characteristics.

The features that are contrasted are sport-war, small-large, and return-not return, and the question was which member of each pair to delete from the original paragraph in writing the items.

To answer this question, several tryouts were needed. It was found that in the sport-war pair neither word could be deleted because this contrast was too difficult for the examinees, and that in both of the other pairs it was the second rather than the first feature mentioned that should be deleted. Apparently, the task of answering a question on the basis of information presented <u>later</u> in the paragraph was also too complex for the examinees.

In the development of the Low form, then, a fairly lengthy series of tryouts and item analyses was required. For the High form, this was much less of a problem, since more complex paragraphs and associations could safely be used, as illustrated in the second sample item of Figure 6. In reviewing this item, incidentally, it should be noted that all of the questions can be answered without any advance knowledge of rocketry whatever, even though the paragraph gives a fairly technical explanation.

Administratively, the test presented no problems, as the examinees readily understood what they were to do. Further, the standard I-D visual aid was fully effective in explaining the marking procedure.

Intercountry Modifications

Because the contextual clues on which these items depend would seem to have limited generalizability from one language to another, it had been thought that direct translations of this test would probably not be effective. But the results of the two translations that were attempted turned out to be as good as those obtained from the original version, and suggest that this type of test is much less dependent on language idiosyncracies than had been suspected.

The Low form was translated only into Portuguese, and the High form only into Korean. No changes were made in either country; and, as will be seen presently, the estimates of reliability and validity that were obtained were entirely adequate to warrant the operational use of these verbatim translations.

Typical Results

The estimates of reliability typically obtained for the Reading Comprehension Test are summarized in Table 3. They are at approximately the same level for both forms and across all three locations.

TABLE 3

Typical Reliability Estimates of the I-D Reading Comprehension Test

Form	Country	Group	Education	Number	r*
Low	West Africa	Primary students	6-7 years	1,572	0.73
Low	Brazil	Primary students	5 years	139	0.80
High	West Africa	Postsecondary	11-14 years	295	0.74
High	Korea	Telecommo trainees	Mixed	138	0.77

*All are KR-20 coefficients except the Brazil estimate, which is an odd-even coefficient of correlation.

In West Africa, the validity of the Low form against the criterion of grades in the early years of secondary school was in the range of .45-.50 when the test was applied to students already selected. In Brazil the validity of the Low form for seventh-grade students against end-of-year grades was .55; in general, an estimate of .50 is a reasonable expectation.

The validity of the High form against grades near the end of secondary school or in the first two years of postsecondary education was slightly above .50 for a sample of more than 700 West African students. For a small sample of students in university-level commercial courses in West Africa, this figure dropped to .30; for the telecommunications trainees in Korea, an estimate of .47 was obtained. For planning purposes, results near .50 for general academic courses and near .40 for advanced specialized training can be projected.

INFORMATION TESTS

The chief purpose of the I-D information tests is to measure the examinee's interests in and aptitudes for certain broad categories of occupations. The rationale underlying these tests is that every individual accumulates a fairly large amount of "incidental" information outside of school as a result of his hobbies, readings, and everyday observations, and that each will tend to acquire more detailed information about topics that he finds interesting and rewarding than about topics that he does not. By measuring his knowledge of topics pertinent to a particular occupation, an information test should provide an index of his inclinations toward this type of pursuit.

The I-D Mechanical Information Test, which has already been discussed to some extent in an earlier chapter, is the lowest-level information test in the I-D series. It is intended for examinees with only six to nine years of education, and serves mainly as a selection device for the skilled trades.

The I-D Science Information Test and the I-D World Information Test are companion instruments, intended for use at and above the secondary-school-graduate level. They are designed for selection into the science and the arts curricula, respectively, of universities or other postsecondary institutions.

I-D Test 7: Mechanical Information

The I-D Mechanical Information Test has proved to be the most consistently effective of the I-D tests for vocational selection at the postprimary level. Because of its essential simplicity, however, its range of applicability does not extend to examinees who have had more than two or three years of postprimary education, and it cannot normally be used for selection into advanced technical courses. For such applications, a more difficult form of this test should be constructed, using similar developmental procedures.

General Description

The Mechanical Information Test consists of pictorial items about which the examiner asks questions orally, one at a time, as illustrated in Figure 6. There are 56 items, and approximately 35 minutes are required to administer the test, including the pretest instructions. The test is printed on a single sheet of paper and can be scored by machine.

The Adaptation Procedure

Developing a sufficient number of questions suitable for youngsters

FIGURE 6

Sample Items of the I-D Mechanical Information Test

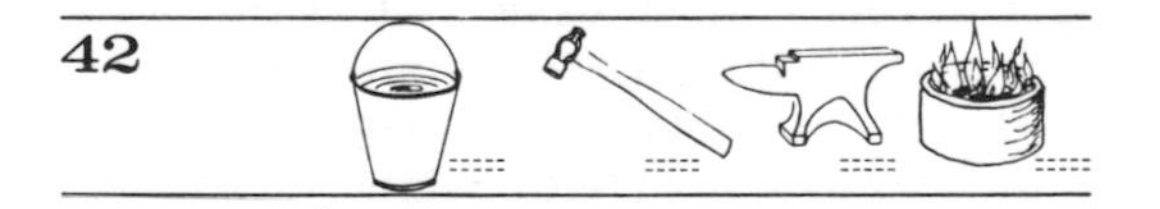

When the examinees reach this item, the examiner says, "When a blacksmith shapes brass, which one of these things does he use first: the water ... the hammer ... the anvil ... or the fire? Mark the one that the blacksmith uses first."

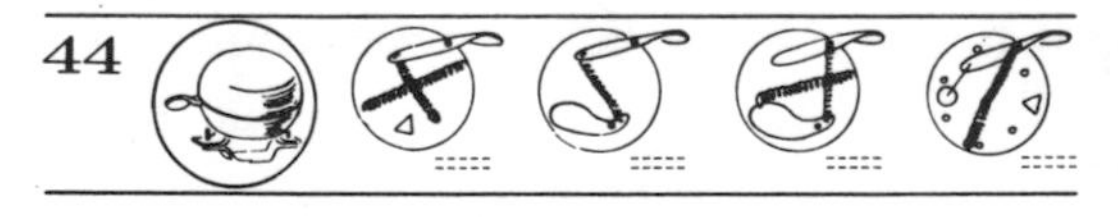

When the examinees reach this item, the examiner says, "If you remove the top of a bicycle bell and look inside, which picture best shows what you would see inside a bicycle bell? Mark one."

from rural locations required nearly a year's time, as earlier noted. The first step was to list as many phenomena as the staff could think of that are sufficiently universal to serve as topics for technical items, irrespective of the degree of local modernization. This list included natural phenomena, such as weather; common household procedures, such as the uses of fire; and basic commodities, such as candles or mirrors, which were known to be found in all parts of the country. The second step was to visit a large sample of villages, and to look for other common amenities that could safely be added to the initial list. This suggested such additional topics as bicycles, blacksmith shops, sewing machines, and even trucks, which (though perhaps not observable everywhere) were prevalent in at least those locations that were likely to generate applicants for vocational courses. And the third step was to prepare the trial test items, and to carry out the numerous item analysis studies that eventually produced the final version.

In accordance with the basic rationale of this test, the approach insofar as possible was to try to devise items of the type illustrated in Figure 6. In the first example, the notion is that all youngsters have an opportunity to watch the local blacksmith at work, but that not all of them will be sufficiently interested in this kind of activity to note and recall what he actually does. In the second, the intent is to identify those youngsters who are sufficiently curious about the gadgets they use to try to find out what is inside. Both answers depend on observations of phenomena quite different from those studied in school.

The procedures used for administering this test were patterned after those used with the Similarities Test, and are highly effective. Having the examiner read each question aloud ensures that the examinees will be able to interpret the drawings correctly and yet does not confound the skills that this test is intended to measure with the reading skills that would be introduced by printed instructions. This approach also paces the test, so that all of the examinees attempt every item.

In all other respects, the characteristics of the test and the methods for administering it follow the standard I-D procedures.

Intercountry Modifications

The Mechanical Information Test was administered in all three countries without substantive modifications. The instructions were translated into the local language, and in two of the countries (Korea and Thailand) certain of the line drawings were changed to equivalents more familiar to the examinees.

Whether these kinds of changes are sufficient to permit the use of this test in a different culture, or whether the content also must be adapted cannot be determined from the limited data so far assembled. The results to date show that the original Mechanical Information Test was a reliable measure of "something" in these three countries, but have not yet confirmed that this "something" is in fact related to performance in vocational courses. Pending further validity studies, little can be said about the generalizability of the specific items developed in West Africa for use in other cultural settings.

There is some evidence, however, that the use of printed instructions, as was tried in Thailand, does change the character of the test and should probably be avoided. When scores on the original version of the test were compared with the grades of ten classes of seventh-grade students in their major academic courses, an average correlation coefficient of approximately .25 was obtained. But when the same comparison was made for ten classes which had been given the test with printed instructions, this coefficient jumped to .43, indicating that more scholastic ability (and perhaps less mechanical aptitude) was being measured. This suggests that the oral administration procedure should be used for vocational application, even when the test can be given in the first language of the examinees.

Typical Results

The reliability estimates typically obtained for the Mechanical Information Test are shown in Table 4. They are reasonably uniform and show that at least the reliability of the instrument was not affected by transplanting the items to a new cultural setting.

The validity of the test in West Africa has been in the range of .45-.55 for trainees in a variety of skilled trades, as determined through both concurrent and follow-up studies of grades in practical courses. In the subsequent study at the Malawi Polytechnic which was discussed at some length in Chapter 2, a coefficient of .59 was obtained. But in Brazil a validity of only .28 was obtained in a study of 127 technical trainees rated for purposes of the research by their instructors. To what extent this more modest result was attributable to the criterion problems that were encountered, and to what extent it indicates needs for item modifications has not been determined. The Brazil study, moreover, was the only application of this test

TABLE 4

Typical Reliability Estimates of the I-D Mechanical Information Test

Country	Group	Education	Number	r*
West Africa	Primary students	6-7 years	2,033	.79
Brazil	Craft trainees	Mixed	203	.70
Korea	Textile workers	Mixed	144	.76
Thailand	Primary students	7 years	30	.73

*The West Africa and Thailand figures are KR-20 coefficients. The other two are odd-even coefficients of correlation.

to the skilled trades that was made in countries outside Africa, and an estimate of its probable validity for other locations therefore cannot yet be projected. Within Africa, figures near .50 can normally be expected.

That the test is not suitable for use for applications below or above the level of the skilled trades was demonstrated in both Thailand and in Korea. The tryouts carried out in these two countries with students in the eleventh and twelfth grades and the additional tryouts carried out in Korea with semiskilled workers gave uniformly poor results, confirming the West Africa findings. The utility of the Mechanical Information Tests appears everywhere to be limited to selection for the skilled trades at the postprimary level.

I-D Tests 17 and 18: Science and World Information

These tests were among the last of the I-D tests to be developed, and have so far had only limited practical applications. They may be used separately for selection into specific curricula—Science Information for such fields as chemistry or physics, World Information for such fields as economics or public administration—or they may be used jointly, to constitute a "general information" test of the type often found useful for admission to the general program of higher-level educational institutions.

General Description

Both tests contain forty multiple-choice factual items of the type shown in Figure 7. When only one is administered, approximately 30 minutes are required; when given serially, approximately 50 minutes suffice for both. Each test is printed on a single sheet of paper and can be scored by machine.

FIGURE 7

Sample Items of the I-D Science and World Information Tests

14. Women usually sing at a higher pitch than men because their vocal cords are

smoother.	softer.	longer.	tighter.	flexible.

15. The chief ingredient in window glass is

nylon.	amber.	cellulose.	quartz.	sand.

76. The main concern of UNICEF is

disease.	children.	argiculture.	disarmanent.	world law.

77. Bamako is the capital of

Angola.	The Gambia.	Mali.	Niger.	Gabon.

The Adaptation Procedure

Since these two tests are used only at the higher educational levels, and since their content is limited to straightforward factual questions, no adaptation of the standard format of information tests was required. The only problem was to find a sufficient number of suitable items—the same problem encountered in the development of such tests in any cultural setting.

In the Science Information Test, the problem was to minimize the effects of the science courses the examinee had taken in school so as to measure how much "incidental" information he had acquired in accordance with the basic test rationale. Eliminating the effects of formal education was of course impossible, since all aspects of science are taught in school and any examinee could have learned the answer to any question that a test might include in one of his prior courses. But because most students take courses in only two or three science subjects, it seemed feasible to reduce these effects by covering a much broader range of topics than any of them was likely to have encountered in school alone, thereby requiring incidental information in addition to formally acquired knowledge for the achievement of a high test score. A miscellany of items concerning anatomy, astronomy, medicine, biology, chemistry, physics, and mathematics was included in the test; and, as will be seen from the sample items in Figure 7, an effort was made to select topics that, though taught, are not normally stressed in formal courses.

The major problem in the development of the World Information Test was to generate reasonable hypotheses about the categories of information that might be predictive. For the kinds of incidental information that would be indicative of inclinations toward "nonscience" pursuits are not nearly so easy to specify as those that relate to the more homogeneous body of things scientific. Eventually, it was decided to focus on events, places, people, and organizations that are discussed regularly in the local newspapers because of their importance in national and international affairs; this approach was found to be reasonably effective. Much of the information in the resulting test was, of course, highly specific to the interests of the African countries, since it was the newspapers of West Africa that were used as the primary source for the development of the questions.

A second problem posed by this test was that the current events type of item, which is one of the best from a measurement point of view, is frequently obsolete by the time the test is given; the early versions of this test had to be updated in advance of virtually every testing session. Accordingly, an effort was made to replace the more frangible items; the present form of the test is based mainly on topics with a reasonable life expectancy, as illustrated in Figure 7.

Both tests required a number of item analysis studies as part of the development process, to identify questions of the right level of difficulty for the examinees. The present level appears to be most appropriate for individuals with twelve to fourteen years of education, at least in the African countries.

Intercountry Modifications

Because of its heavy emphasis on African affairs, the World Information Test was judged unsuitable for use elsewhere, and was not administered at any of the three other locations. It is likely that a totally new form would be required for South America, and one or two still-different forms for the Asian countries.

The Science Information Test would seem to be less dependent on cultural factors, and a translation of this test was prepared for use in Korea. It appeared to be reasonably satisfactory in the one study in which it was applied, but considerably more data must be assembled to determine whether or not the original items should in fact be used without modification.

Typical Results

The estimates of reliability that have been obtained for the Science and World Information Tests are summarized in Table 5. The reason for the very high figure obtained in Korea is almost certainly the heterogeneity of the examinee group, which ranged in education from the elementary to the university level. An overall estimate of .70-.75 for university-level students seems appropriate for both of these tests.

Validity estimates for the tests used individually in West Africa and in Malawi were in the range of .30-.55, against grades in science and in Business Administration courses and against overall grades in the undergraduate level. The estimate in the Korean study of telecommunications trainees was .44 against grades in practical courses, but this result was probably inflated for the reason noted above. For planning purposes, an estimate of approximately .35 seems appropriate for this type of test.

NUMERICAL TESTS

The I-D series contains one test that is entirely numerical and one test that combines quantitative abilities with related perceptual skills. Both are intended for use in scholastic, technical, and commerical selection programs whenever quantitative skills are required.

TABLE 5

Typical Reliability Estimates of the I-D Science and World Information Tests

Test	Country	Group	Education	Number	r*
World	West Africa	Secondary	11-12 years	188	.73
World	West Africa	Postsecondary	12-14 years	105	.74
Science	West Africa	Secondary	11-12 years	188	.54
Science	West Africa	Postsecondary	12-14 years	105	.73
Science	Korea	Telecommo trainees	Mixed	138	.94

*The Korea estimate is based on an odd-even coefficient of correlation. All others are KR-20 coefficients.

The I-D Arithmetic Test can be used from the primary school up to the university level, and has given good results for all three of the above applications throughout this entire range. But because its apparent simplicity is sometimes resented by the more advanced applicant groups, it is preferable to administer a seemingly higher-level test to examinees who have completed nine or more years of formal education.

The I-D Graphs Test is suitable for use with students in the later years of secondary school, and is sufficiently difficult to be used up to and including the university level. At these higher levels, it is an appropriate replacement for the Arithmetic Test, with which it has a moderately high correlation.

I-D Test 14: Arithmetic

Although the Arithmetic Test is based entirely on simple numerical calculations, its purpose is not that of predicting the accuracy with which the examinees will subsequently perform the arithmetic operations that their courses or jobs will require. Rather, the rationale is that one of the characteristics of individuals who have a generally high aptitude for working with things mathematical is that they are able to perform elementary calculations at high rates of speed, and that their scores on a simple test of mental arithmetic can therefore serve as a "symptom" from which this more general aptitude can be inferred. The Arithmetic Test should be regarded as a fairly broad-spectrum test that uses the vehicle of computation problems to approximate the examinees' overall aptitude in the quantitative domain.

General Description

The Arithmetic Test consists of addition, subtraction, multiplication, and division problems, as shown in Figure 8. It is divided into two separately timed parts of 75 problems each; the time limit of five minutes per part is designed to be sufficiently long to yield reliable scores but too short to enable any of the examinees to work all of the problems correctly. The total administration time is 20 minutes and the single-page test paper can be scored by machine.

The Adaptation Procedure

In writing the problems for the Arithmetic Test, a deliberate effort was made to keep them at the simplest possible level—two-digit

FIGURE 8

Sample Items of the I-D Arithmetic Test

90	+	35	=	65	125	55	120	121
56	+	31	=	86	25	97	75	87
48	-	35	=	18	13	3	15	23
97	-	59	=	39	16	38	36	48
64	x	7	=	568	450	448	442	508
69	x	5	=	344	355	345	346	335
408	÷	8	=	50	68	58	51	41
128	÷	2	=	64	57	68	63	79

numbers for the addition and subtraction exercises, one-digit multipliers and divisors for the two more difficult operations. Because of the large differences in the quality of education provided by the many primary schools throughout the country, it seemed important to restrict the content to exercises that all of the examinees would have practiced for years, irrespective of the merits or deficiencies of the particular school each had attended. And more difficult problems were not really necessary to satisfy the requirements of the above rationale.

Explaining these very familiar exercises to the examinees naturally presented no difficulties whatever. But encouraging them to work these exercises rapidly required more careful programming in the case of the Arithmetic Test than in any of the other tests of the I-D series. For the approach to arithmetic that the examinees had been taught in their classes frequently was incompatible with the one that the Arithmetic Test requires, and these highly practiced habits had to be overcome as part of the test explanations. The practice of chanting computations in a fixed rhythmic pattern is one example of the approaches incompatible with the rationale of the Arithmetic Test that was encountered.

Teaching the desired approach required a three-step procedure. The first was to administer the Arithmetic Test as one of the last tests of each session, when the concept of time limits was already well understood. The second was to stress speed throughout the examiner's pretest instructions. And the third (and most effective) was to let the examinees attempt to solve twelve practice exercises in a one minute warm-up session which demonstrated the rate of speed necessary to complete even half of the test. That completing the entire test was impossible was, of course, also explained in advance.

To compensate for the differences in strategy that persisted despite these careful instructions, the standard I-D correction for speeded tests was applied. As noted in a preceding chapter, this was to subtract the number of wrong answers from the number answered correctly, so as to increase the comparability of the scores of the more reckless and the more conservative of the examinees.

Intercountry Modifications

The Arithmetic Test was administered experimentally in all three countries. Because of the universal applicability of computational problems, no changes in the original items were thought necessary or attempted.

Typical Results

The reliability estimates typically obtained for the Arithmetic Test at various levels of education are summarized in Table 6. They are consistently high, as would be expected for this type of test. The lower figure in Thailand may be attributed to the fact that this is a different type of estimate, and perhaps also to the use of printed rather than oral instructions, which might have been less effective in communicating the speed that this test requires.

Validity estimates against course grades at the secondary school level were in the range of .30-.35 in West Africa, for students already selected, in part on the basis of other arithmetic tests. In Thailand, comparable estimates for comprehensive school students were in the range of .40-.50 against grades in the regular academic courses. In studies at the primary school level, the estimate of .15 obtained in Brazil and the estimate of .62 obtained in Thailand are widely divergent, probably a result of differences in the criteria that were applied. Overall, a projected figure of .35 would seem to be a conservative estimate of validity for admission to the general academic program of secondary level institutions.

TABLE 6

Typical Reliability Estimates of the I-D Arithmetic Test

Country	Group	Education	Number	r*
West Africa	Primary students	6-7 years	3,684	.88
Brazil	Primary students	5 years	135	.85
West Africa	Secondary	11-12 years	138	.88
Thailand	Commercial students	11 years	61	.73
Korea	Technical students	12 years	228	.86
Korea	Telecommo trainees	Mixed	138	.85

*All coefficients except the Thailand estimate are based on the correlation between the separately timed halves of the test. The Thailand figure is a test-retest coefficient.

For selection into technical or commercial courses, results comparable to the West African validity estimates of .40-.50 were obtained in eight of the nine similar studies carried out in Thailand and in Korea. In the ninth study the validity estimates were appreciably lower, but it seems that on balance an estimate of .45 for vocational selection is an appropriate projection.

I-D Test 11: Graphs

A test of speed and accuracy in reading graphs was included in the I-D series for two reasons. The first was that this type of test has been a highly useful predictor in the United States for selection into advanced technical courses and for a number of other careers. The second was the hope that this test might substitute in part also for the more general tests of mathematical reasoning that are normally used at the higher educational levels, but that could not be adapted for use in West Africa because "word problems" introduced too high a verbal ability factor with second-language examinees. And, in this more general role as well as in the measurement of higher level technical skill, the Graphs Test has in fact proved to be reasonably effective.

General Description

The Graphs Test consists of thirty problems related to the graph illustrated in Figure 9 and of a second part of thirty additional problems related to another similar graph (not shown). In each item the examinee is to look at the value given in the shaded portion, and then to find the corresponding value of the other variable as quickly as he can by correctly reading the graph. The time limit of four minutes per part is set so that no examinee will finish the test; and the total administration time is approximately 25 minutes, including practice and explanation. The test is printed on a single sheet of paper and can be scored by machine.

FIGURE 9

Sample Items of the I-D Graphs Test

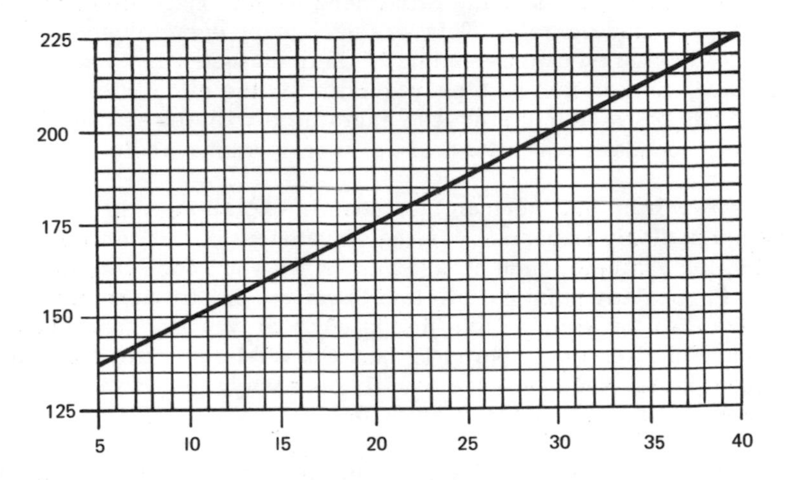

36	223	203	215	220	22.5
175	20	200	15	208	120
165	20	16	18	11	15.5
145	4	13	8	7	20
18	167.5	160	165	174	170

The Adaptation Procedure

As illustrated by the sample items in Figure 9, several complexities were introduced into the graph-reading operations that the items of this test require. It will be seen that the ordinate dimension of the graph is scaled by units of five, while the abscissa is scaled by units of one; that sometimes the examinee is to find the ordinate value corresponding to a given abscissa value, and sometimes vice versa; and that certain problems require interpolation between adjacent lines of the grid. The intent was to require the examinee to attend simultaneously to a number of factors, both numerical and spatial, in solving each of the items, and thereby to obtain a measure of his general facility in coping with quantitative relations.

As a result of these added complexities, the development of suitable instructions was the main difficulty encountered in designing the West African version. Full use had to be made of all of the I-D explanation procedures, and a fairly lengthy demonstration and practice session preceded the test. This was necessary even for students who had already studied graph-reading in their mathematics courses; such prior study may in fact be a prerequisite for the effective use of the test. Attempts to administer it to examinees with fewer than three years of secondary education were generally unsuccessful.

The words that the examiner uses in explaining this test appeared to be particularly important. In the explanation of the concept of graphs, for example, such phrases as "when you reach this line you are at 40" or "any point on this line leads you to 40" were much less effective than the simple "this line is 40" that was eventually adopted. Such careful attention to phrasing (and the trial and error that finding the right phrase requires) are usually necessary for the more complex test operations, as noted in Chapter 5.

The only other difficulty encountered in the use of this test was the practical one of reproducing the test paper at locations at which suitable duplicating equipment could not be provided. Because of the complexity of these items and the pressure of the brief time limit permitted, most examinee groups are understandably distressed when the lines are fuzzy or the points of intersection unclear; poor-quality reproductions are for this reason not fully effective. Access to multilith equipment or electronic stencil-cutting devices is a mundane but necessary prerequisite to the use of this test.

Intercountry Modifications

The Graphs Test was tried experimentally in Thailand and in Korea without substantive change. In both countries the original version was found to be fully effective.

In a recent study in Micronesia, an attempt was made to reduce the complexity of this test so that it can be administered to examinees at a lower educational level. The same scale was used for both dimensions, the size of the grid was enlarged, and no interpolation problems were given. These changes made it possible to administer the test to eighth-grade students, but their effects on the test's predictive properties have not yet been determined.

Typical Results

The estimates of reliability typically obtained for the Graphs Test are summarized in Table 7. As in the case of the Arithmetic Test, the low figure obtained in Thailand is probably attributable to the nature of the coefficient, and to the use of printed rather than oral instructions.

The validity of the Graphs Test against academic course grades at the upper secondary school levels was in the range of .35-.40 in West Africa and in the range of .30-.35 in Thailand. In Korea the validity against grades in telecommunications training was .45; but in the study of technical institute students, the validity of the Graphs Test (as of all other tests) was of negligible proportions. For general academic selection a figure of .35 may be projected.

For selection into advanced technical or commercial courses, the results in Thailand were consistently higher than the West Africa figures. Validity estimates in the ranges of .40-.50 and .30-.40, respectively, were obtained at these two locations; an estimate of .40 is a reasonable projection.

TECHNICAL APTITUDE TESTS

Three of the tests in the I-D series are addressed specifically to the perceptual skills that technical occupations require. One is designed for use at the semiskilled level; two are designed for selection

TABLE 7

Typical Reliability Estimates of the I-D Graphs Test

Country	Group	Education	Number	r*
West Africa	Secondary	10-11 years	147	.83
Thailand	Commercial students	11 years	61	.50
Korea	Technical students	12 years	228	.78

*The Thailand estimate is a test-retest coefficient. The other two are based on the coefficient of correlation between the separately timed halves of the test.

into the skilled trades or other postprimary technical courses. They are normally used in combination with a number of other tests so as to obtain a balanced index of ability with respect to both the perceptual and the nonperceptual components of job performance.

The I-D Checking Test is the lower-level instrument, used jointly with the Similarities Test and the Marking Test to comprise the I-D semiskilled series. The I-D Boxes and the I-D Figures Tests are used at the skilled level, in combination with such tests as Verbal Analogies and Mechanical Information and one of the two dexterity measures.

I-D Test 8: Checking

The I-D Checking Test will be discussed only briefly because its use was extremely limited in all of the countries. As noted earlier in the discussion of the Similarities Test, there were few practical needs for low-level screening tests, and most of the research was devoted to the more advanced ability measures.

General Description

The Checking Test consists of sixty items of the type illustrated in Figure 10. Four of the five drawings in each item are identical, and the examinee is to go through the test as quickly as he is able, marking the one object in each set that differs from all of the rest.

FIGURE 10

Sample Items of the I-D Checking Test

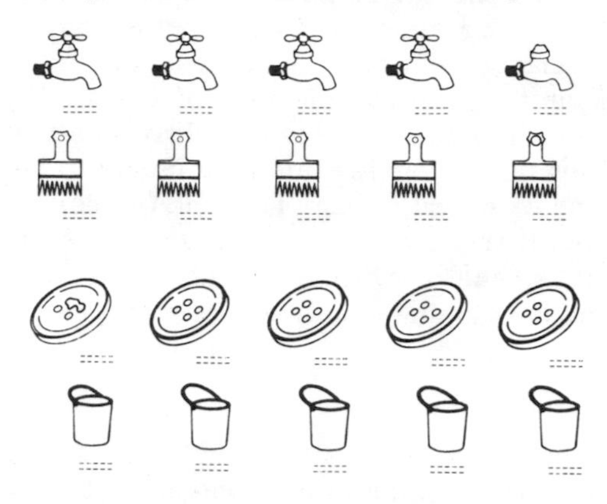

The test is divided into two parts that have time limits of only two minutes each, and the total administration time seldom exceeds ten minutes, including the pretest instructions. The one-page test paper can be scored by machine.

The Adaptation Procedure

The development of this test illustrated the hazards of jumping to conclusions about "obvious" cultural modifications, as was earlier noted. It had been assumed that objects familiar in the West African setting would have to be used as the basis for the drawings in these test items, and a variety of more familiar drawings was developed as the first step in the adaptation procedure. But, as reported in Chapter 4, it was found that the nature of the object in fact made no difference to the utility of the item—perhaps because neither strange nor familiar objects were interpreted correctly by the groups that were tested. The standard test items tried were as suitable as the especially prepared versions, and the selection of content for this test posed none of the problems that had been expected.

Nor was there any problem in explaining the task to the examinees. The concepts of "same" and "different" were readily understood, and only three demonstration exercises and six practice items (to show the rate of speed that was desired) were necessary, even for nonliterate groups.

The one problem that this test does raise, however, is that

virtually flawless printing is an essential. Since most of the drawings are not interpreted as representations of real objects by the examinees, any imperfection in the reproduction of one of the drawings will make it as "different" from the others as will the defect intended; if an examinee's score on an item depends on whether he notices the deliberate or the inadvertent difference first, the test results will be distorted. Thus, in the first sample item of Figure 10, an unintentional break in the bottom line of one of the five drawings may seem to an examinee who does not recognize this as a faucet to be the defect that he was to discover, and he may not look further and see that the missing handle is clearly the answer intended. The high-quality reproduction that is necessary to avoid such problems may be difficult to ensure in some developing countries.

Intercountry Modifications

The only other country the Checking Test was tried in was Korea. No changes were made in the content of the items or in the testing procedure.

Typical Results

The reliability estimates obtained in West Africa and Korea are shown in Table 8. No comparable estimates have been made for groups below the primary school level.

In West Africa, validity estimates of the Checking Test were not attempted. In the Korean study of textile workers, zero validity was obtained against the criterion of proficiency evaluations made by the foremen of the workers who had been tested. The potential applications of this test and its probable accuracy cannot be projected.

TABLE 8

Typical Reliability Estimates of the I-D Checking Test

Country	Group	Education	Number	r*
West Africa	Primary students	6-7 years	2,920	.72
Korea	Textile workers	Elementary	144	.81

*Both coefficients are based on the correlations between the separately timed halves of the test.

I-D Test 9: Boxes

The Boxes Test is a measure of three-dimensional visualization, which is one of the basic abilities necessary for most technical occupations. From a methodological point of view, its development was perhaps the major accomplishment of the initial AID/AIR research in that it demonstrated the feasibility of devising pencil-and-paper measures of skills that had been thought to require apparatus tests in the African setting. But its suitability for widespread operational use has been limited by the demands it makes of the examiner, who must be given special training and practice in the fairly complex demonstration procedure that the effective administration of this test requires.

General Description

The Boxes Test consists of 48 items of the type illustrated in Figure 11. The object at the left of each item is a "pattern" that will form one of the two cubes at the right when it is folded to bring the six faces together; the examinee is to go through the test as rapidly as he can, indicating which of the two cubes will be formed when this folding operation has been completed. The test is divided into two parts of equal difficulty, with time limits of four minutes each; but because of the lengthy demonstration procedure, a total of 40 to 45 minutes overall is required. The one-page test paper can be scored by machine.

The Adaptation Procedure

The major problem in measuring spatial skills with a pencil-and-paper device is that the representation of three dimensions on a two-dimensional surface is a special convention that has to be

FIGURE 11

Sample Items of the I-D Boxes Test

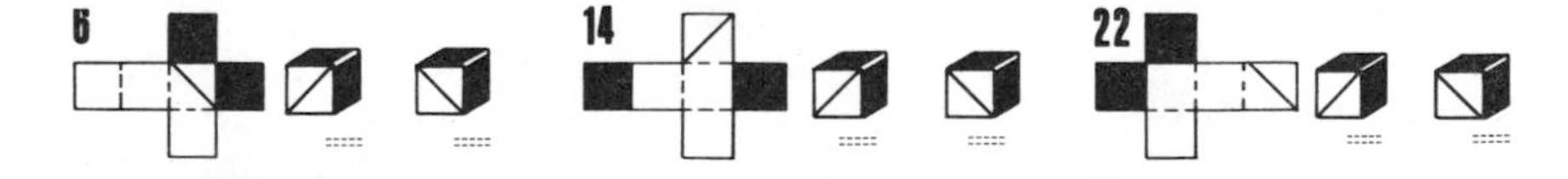

especially learned. An examinee who has grown up surrounded by drawings is thoroughly familiar with this convention, and will interpret the test problems correctly. But an examinee unaccustomed to drawings will see them the way they actually are—i.e., as "flat" two-dimensional representations. And because prior research had shown that uneducated African examinees generally do interpret such drawings as having no depth, apparatus tests involving solid objects rather than drawings were traditionally used to measure spatial visualization.

As a starting point for devising a suitable pencil-and-paper test, it was assumed that the correct interpretation of three-dimensional drawings would have to be taught as an integral part of the testing procedure. And since it was clear that teaching the examinees to interpret a broad range of drawings in a few minutes would be impractical, it was necessary to simplify the standard test items to reduce the amount of teaching that would be required. This led to the use of only two cubes, identical in all ways but one, as illustrated in Figure 11.

The next task was to devise an effective teaching procedure. This was done largely through trial and error, by testing small groups and noting which aspects of the procedure were not understood. Eventually, the complex sequence now used emerged. It includes giving each examinee plastic models of the cubes that he can look at and manipulate while watching the demonstration; drawing a sketch of these cubes on the blackboard, to relate the faces on the solid model to the faces drawn on a plane; relating these sketches to the mock-up of the test paper that is used as a visual aid; relating this mock-up to the exercises on the examinee's own practice sheet; demonstrating the idea of the items by removing the first pattern from the mock-up, and folding it into a cube; relating this newly formed cube to the corresponding cube on the blackboard, mock-up, and paper; and repeating this demonstration for the remainder of the sample items and for each of the practice exercises after the examinees have tried to solve these items alone. This procedure was longer than that used in any of the other I-D tests, but was necessary to ensure comprehension with many of the groups that were tested.

The test items themselves are arranged in increasing order of difficulty with respect to the degree of visualization required. The early problems (such as Item 6 in Figure 11) require no visualization whatever; an examinee who understands the basic idea can pick out the correct answer without "mentally" folding the pattern at all. The intermediate exercises (such as Item 14) can be done with a single fold, in that the dark face at the left can be ignored in solving the problem. The most difficult exercises (such as Item 22) require true three-dimensional visualization. This arrangement was adopted so that the examinees with lesser spatial ability would not become discouraged at the very beginning of the test, but is useful also in determining the degree to which the instructions have been understood. An examinee who cannot solve an exercise such as Item 6 clearly has not understood what it is that he is to do.

For examinees already familiar with drawings in three dimensions, these elaborate instructions are not required. But, inasmuch as there were no visible signs of boredom or restlessness on the part of the more advanced groups, at least in West Africa, the entire sequence was used at all levels to ensure uniform comprehension.

Intercountry Modifications

The Boxes Test was administered in its original form in all three countries, but for experimental purposes only. It was felt that the examinee groups typically being tested in these countries would have no difficulties in interpreting three-dimensional drawings, and the research effort was soon shifted to standard tests of visualization. In Brazil a standard cube-completion test gave good results with groups at higher educational levels; in Thailand, a standard block-counting test was found to be a poor predictor of performance in eleventh-grade shopwork courses. But the data so far compiled are too fragmentary to permit an adequate evaluation of the suitability of standard visualization tests in these countries.

Typical Results

The estimates of reliability typically obtained for the Boxes Test are summarized in Table 9. That higher estimates were obtained for groups of heterogeneous educational backgrounds is normal for most types of tests.

Estimates of the validity of the Boxes Test against performance in practical shop courses were in the range of .30-.45 in West Africa, for a variety of skilled trades; and the estimate of .37 subsequently obtained at the Malawi Polytechnic was consistent with these results. In the other countries the estimates were .40 for the telecommunications trainees in Korea, .35 for automotive trainees in Thailand, and .29 for trainees in four skilled trades in Brazil. In general, a figure near .35 can be projected.

TABLE 9

Typical Reliability Estimates of the I-D Boxes Test

Country	Group	Education	Number	r*
West Africa	Mixed	6-7 years	3,460	.72
West Africa	Mixed	8-9 years	1,050	.76
Brazil	Craft trainees	Mixed	231	.84
Korea	Commo trainees	Mixed	138	.83

*All coefficients are based on the correlation between the separately timed halves of this test.

I-D Test 10: Figures

The Figures Test is intended for the same types of applications as the Boxes Test and is also a perceptual measure. But because it is limited to two-dimensional representations, it does not require nearly so complex an administrative procedure. The correlation between the two tests is generally low, and they are normally used together.

General Description

The Figures Test consists of forty items of the type shown in Figure 12. In each of the drawings, one of the five shapes at the top may be found amid other lines that tend to disguise it; the examinee is to go through the test as quickly as he can, identifying the shape "hidden" in each of the items. The test is divided into two parts, administered with a time limit of five minutes each. The total administration time is 20 minutes and the one-page test paper can be scored by machine.

The Adaptation Procedure

Although this test did not entail the spatial visualization difficulties encountered with Boxes, the use of drawings in any form generally required some adaptation of the standard test items, and Figures was no exception. Three major modifications of the standard approach to tests of this type were required.

FIGURE 12

Sample Items of the I-D Figures Test

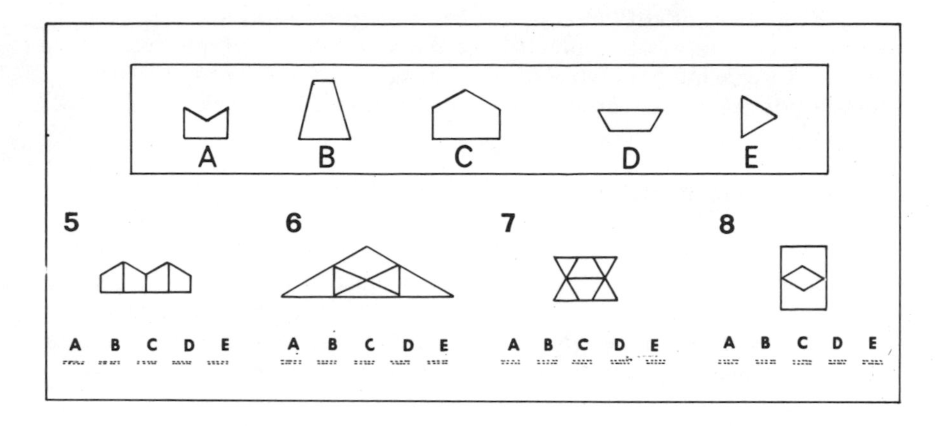

The first modification was to simplify greatly the complexity of the drawings that are frequently used. When the shapes were embedded in a large complex of criss-crossing lines, the examinees had to spend an average of one minute per item to solve the problems, and this was too long for practical test applications. Items that include the bare minimum of lines necessary to disguise the shapes were developed, as illustrated in Figure 12.

The second was to eliminate the complexity of the standard "rule" that permits shapes to be hidden by turning them sideways or upside down within the drawings that comprise the items. All of the shapes in the Figures Test appear within the drawings exactly as they appear in the key at the top of the page, and this is explained explicitly in the pretest instructions.

The third was to teach what is meant by "same size" and "same shape" as part of the demonstration procedure. Without special instructions, most of the examinees in West Africa would select Shape C as the one hidden in Item 5 of Figure 12, for example, or Shape B as the one hidden in Item 7, probably because they are not accustomed to precision in matching sizes and forms exactly. To teach this concept, a visual aid was developed that permits the examiner to remove the shapes from the key and to superimpose them on the sample and practice items, to demonstrate the precise fit that is required.

With these modifications, the test could be administered effectively to examinees at all levels. Even examinees with minimal education could work the problems at an average rate of fifteen to twenty seconds per item, instead of the sixty seconds that the standard versions required.

Intercountry Modifications

The Figures Test was administered experimentally in all three of the countries. The only modification required was to use letters of the local alphabet rather than Roman characters in Korea and Thailand, and in Korea it was thought better also to number the items from left to right rather than vertically, as on the original version.

Typical Results

The estimates of reliability typically obtained for the Figures Test are summarized in Table 10. Again, the high Brazil and Korea estimates are attributable to the heterogeneity of the examinee groups;

TABLE 10

Typical Reliability Estimates of the I-D Figures Test

Country	Group	Education	Number	r*
West Africa	Mixed	6-7 years	3,978	.70
West Africa	Mixed	8-9 years	1,282	.72
Brazil	Craft trainees	Mixed	239	.84
Korea	Telecommo trainees	Mixed	138	.85
Thailand	Primary students	7 years	30	.54

*All coefficients are based on the correlations between the separately timed halves of this test, except the Thailand estimate, which is a KR-20 coefficient.

the low Thailand estimate, to the use of a different type of coefficient and of written rather than oral instructions.

The estimates of the validity of the Figures Test against performance in shopwork courses were in the range of .30-.40 in West Africa; the estimate of .38 subsequently obtained in the study at the Malawi Polytechnic was consistent with this result. In the other countries, the estimates were .24 for the telecommunications trainees in Korea, .32 for automotive trainees in Thailand, and .32 for trainees in four skilled trades in Brazil. Overall a figure of .30 can be projected.

CLERICAL APTITUDE TESTS

Three of the tests in the I-D series are addressed to speed and accuracy in routine operations, as required in many clerical job functions. Although of somewhat different levels of difficulty, all three can be used at the postprimary level, and they are normally used jointly for such applications.

The I-D Coding Test is the most elementary of the three, and is normally dropped for the more advanced groups, who are apt to be bored by the strictly repetitive operations required. The I-D Names Test and the I-D Tables Reading Test can both be used up to and including the university level. In combination with Verbal Analogies and Arithmetic, these three tests comprise the I-D clerical aptitude series.

I-D Test 12: Coding

The Coding Test is primarily a measure of clerical speed, although some elements of accuracy and of memory are also required. Historically, this type of test has sometimes been used as a nonverbal "intelligence" measure, but in these studies it was neither intended nor evaluated for such applications. It was included in the I-D series purely as a job element test that attempts to replicate the clerical task of rapidly copying data from source documents, to prepare a new listing or tabulation.

General Description

The test consists of 150 items of the type illustrated in Figure 13. In the blank spaces under the symbols, the examinee is to write the corresponding symbols as rapidly as he can, using the key at the top of the page. The time limit is two minutes for each half of the test, and the total administration time is 15 minutes, including instructions. This is one of the few I-D tests that cannot be scored by machine.

The Adaptation Procedure

The only difficulty encountered in the development of this test was to find the right words to explain the association between the symbols on the top and the bottom lines of the key. There was considerable confusion in the early tryouts; this was eventually traced to the use of the same word ("symbol" or "mark" or "thing") to refer to entries both above and below the line, blurring the distinction between those that are the stimuli and those that are the responses. Accordingly, the revised instructions begin with the explanation that the pictures above are called "symbols" and the pictures below are called "marks," and that the symbol-mark pairs shown in the key "always belong together." Then, the examinees are shown that on their test papers the marks are missing, and told that they are to fill them in with their pencils so that the right symbols and marks will be together. This simple change was fully effective.

As in the other speeded tests, the use of an adequate number of practice problems also proved to be highly important. Two lines of practice problems are used to show the examinees that they are

FIGURE 13

Sample Items of the I-D Coding Test

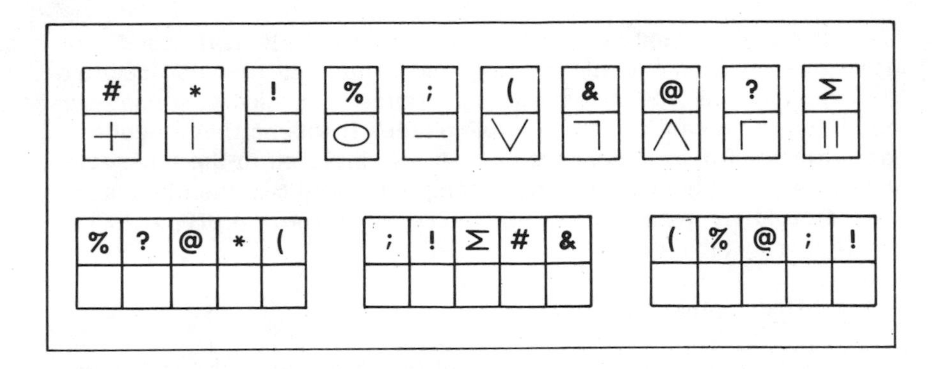

not to stop and wait after the first block of five, nor at the end of each line, and that working at top speed is essential to complete a large number of items. All three of these points represented common misunderstandings that an expanded practice session corrected.

Intercountry Modifications

The Coding Test was administered in a different way in each of the three countries. In Korea the original version was used without modification. In Brazil the original item form was retained, but administered with printed rather than oral instructions. In Thailand, certain of the symbols were changed, and a multiple-choice version was also developed to pave the way for machine-scoring. On the basis of the data so far assembled, the effectiveness of these various approaches seemed to be approximately the same.

Typical Results

The estimates of reliability typically obtained for the Coding Test are summarized in Table 11. All of the estimates are reasonably high, as is usual for tests that depend largely on speed.

The validity estimates against grades in business and commercial courses and against ratings supplied by the supervisors of clerical workers were in the range of .30-.35 in the West African studies. In commercial and secretarial courses in Malawi an estimate of .32 was obtained. In Thailand an average estimate of .28 was obtained for students in commercial courses. In Brazil and Korea, criterion data on clerical performance were not collected. In general, a figure near .30 can usually be expected for trainees or students, and somewhat better results for clerks already employed.

I-D Test 13: Names

The Names Test differs in intent from the Coding Test in that it is entirely perceptual, and in that the primary emphasis is on accuracy rather than on speed. Like Coding, it is a job-element test, addressed to the specific ability required for proofreading, for checking numerical entries, or for other functions in which close attention to detail is important.

General Description

The Names Test consists of 60 items of the type illustrated in Figure 14. The examinee is to scan the list as quickly as he can

TABLE 11

Typical Reliability Estimates of the I-D Coding Test

Country	Group	Education	Number	r*
West Africa	Mixed	6-7 years	3,770	.87
West Africa	Mixed	8-9 years	895	.86
Brazil	Commercial trainees	Mixed	230	.81
Korea	Telecommo trainees	Mixed	138	.86
Thailand	Commercial students	11 years	61	.89

*All of these coefficients were based on the correlation between the separately timed halves of this test, except the Thailand estimate, which is a test-retest coefficient.

and indicate whether or not the two spellings of each name are exactly the same. (The words "correct" and "different" were used so that a separate form would not have to be printed for tryouts in the French-speaking African countries.) The test is divided into two parts with a time limit of two minutes each, and the total administration time is 15 minutes, including instructions. The one-page test paper can be scored by machine.

The Adaptation Procedure

No difficulties were encountered at any point in the development of this test. The names were selected from newspapers, telephone books, and other African sources; errors were introduced by changing a letter, deleting a letter, inserting an extra letter, or transposing two letters of the original version. The initial list developed was found to be satisfactory, and further improvements were not attempted.

The concept of same-different was thoroughly understood by all of the groups that were tested, and only a brief explanation of the task was therefore required. To demonstrate the correct marking procedure and to emphasize the importance of speed, the standard I-D techniques are applied.

Intercountry Modifications

Because of the emphasis on African and European names, the original version of this test was considered unsuitable for use in the

FIGURE 14

Sample Items of the I-D Names Test

Abeni O. Olukoya	Abeni O. Olakoya	CORRECT	DIFFERENT
Albert Fowode	Albert Fowonde	CORRECT	DIFFERENT
Donald Strickler	Donald Strickler	CORRECT	DIFFERENT
H. G. Biyoque	H. G. Biyoque	CORRECT	DIFFERENT
Jean Reynaud	Jean Reynaud	CORRECT	DIFFERENT
A. S. A. Gbajabiamila	A. S. A. Gbajabiamila	CORRECT	DIFFERENT
Ziado Dabbagh	Ziadu Dabbagh	CORRECT	DIFFERENT

other countries. Modified forms, based on local names, were developed in Brazil and Thailand; in Korea, a test of this type was not tried.

The Brazilian version gave results comparable to the West African findings. However, the Thai version was ineffectual and was replaced with a similar test based on comparisons of numerals rather than names. It would be interesting to know whether the failure of this test in Thailand was attributable to certain characteristics inherent in the Thai alphabet, or whether it was the result of certain idiosyncracies of the particular items selected or of the examinee group with which it was tried. There would seem to be no logical reason for this test to have different properties with different alphabets, but the matter was not pursued.

Typical Results

The estimates of reliability typically obtained for the Names Test are summarized in Table 12. For the Thai numerical version of this test, a test-retest coefficient of .83 was obtained.

The estimates of validity against grades in business and commercial courses and against ratings supplied by the supervisors of clerks already employed were in the range of .35-.40 in West Africa; for students in commercial and secretarial courses in Malawi, a figure of .28 was obtained. In Thailand the validity of the version later discarded was effectively zero for eleventh-grade clerical

TABLE 12

Typical Reliability Estimates of the I-D Names Test

Country	Group	Education	Number	r*
West Africa	Mixed	6-7 years	3,675	.73
West Africa	Mixed	8-9 years	976	.76
Brazil	Commercial trainees	Mixed	230	.81

*All of these coefficients are based on the correlation between the separately timed halves of this test.

courses; in Brazil, criterion data on clerical performance could not be assembled. Overall, an estimate in the range of .30-.35 can be projected, at least for countries in which the Roman alphabet is used. For countries that use other alphabets, the potential of this type of test is unknown.

I-D Test 15: Table Reading

The I-D Table Reading Test is the most difficult of the clerical series. It requires not only accuracy and speed, but also an element of the spatial orientation involved in the graph reading test. In the higher-level I-D commercial test series, Table Reading has replaced the Graphs Test, which was used before this test was developed.

General Description

The Table Reading test consists of 80 items of the type illustrated in Figure 15. It is divided into two separate parts with a time limit of two-and-a-half minutes each, and can be administered in a total of 20 minutes overall. The one-page test paper can be scored by machine.

The Adaptation Procedure

After an initial false start, few difficulties were encountered in completing this test. The initial problem was that numerals had been used both as the tabular headings and within the body of the table

FIGURE 15

Sample Items of the I-D Table Reading Test

DAY	NUMBER OF TESTS GIVEN AT EACH SCHOOL SCHOOL														
	A	B	C	D	E	F	G	H	I	J	K	L	M	N	O
MON.	106	347	114	318	682	159	218	477	138	509	153	127	424	382	114
TUE.	84	255	152	358	869	437	164	458	104	637	229	191	358	425	695
WED.	127	208	559	546	796	716	143	286	173	327	306	255	273	573	509
THU.	340	598	191	273	521	682	410	509	152	816	381	318	255	694	417
FRI.	170	127	530	410	476	371	237	764	183	417	573	410	208	796	306
SAT.	255	122	306	851	634	152	293	229	156	521	764	546	153	819	509

DAY	SCHOOL	NUMBER OF TESTS				
FRI.	I	183	764	156	509	152
WED.	N	509	417	694	273	573
TUE.	E	682	437	869	796	318
SAT.	G	229	237	293	152	371
THU.	C	255	208	559	530	191

itself, and this profusion of numbers confused many examinees. The change to the use of days of the week and letters as the tabular headings, so that numerals appeared only within the cells, resolved most of the initial difficulties that had been noted.

When used at the primary school level, the test continued to require highly detailed explanations, however. It was necessary to assume that at least some of the examinees had never seen a table before, and to explain the concept as though this were true of the entire group. The fastest way to do this, it was discovered, was to teach the examinees to place one index finger on "Tuesday" and one on "School E," and then to bring the fingers together to find that "869" is the answer required. After a few problems have been worked using this finger method, the examinees understand the concept of tables, and the test can be given.

Intercountry Modifications

The Table Reading Test was translated into Portuguese, Thai, and Korean with no substantive changes. And, although only limited data were assembled, these direct translations appeared to be sufficiently effective that the test could be considered ready for use without further modification.

Typical Results

The estimates of reliability typically obtained for the Table Reading Test are summarized in Table 13. Because studies of clerical samples were not done in Korea, reliabilities for the Korean version were not computed.

The estimates of validity against grades in business and commercial courses and against ratings supplied by the supervisors of clerks already employed were in the range of .35-.50 in the West African studies. In Thailand most of the estimates were in the range of .30-.40 for grades in clerical and business courses; in Malawi the test was ineffectual as a predictor of performance in clerical and secretarial training. Overall, it appears that figures of .35-.40 can normally be expected.

TABLE 13

Typical Reliability Estimates of the I-D Table Reading Test

Country	Group	Education	Number	r*
West Africa	Mixed	6-7 years	362	.91
West Africa	Mixed	8-9 years	497	.87
Brazil	Commercial trainees	Mixed	230	.73
Thailand	Commercial students	11 years	61	.72

*All coefficients are based on the correlations between the separately timed halves of this test, except the Thailand estimate, which is a test-retest coefficient.

MANUAL ABILITY TESTS

Three of the I-D tests are addressed to manual skills of the type required in some semiskilled jobs and in all of the skilled trades. One is an extremely simple test of virtually pure motor speed and is intended for use in screening illiterate or semiliterate examinees. The two others require skilled eye-hand coordination and are intended for vocational selection at the postprimary level.

The I-D Marking Test is the lower-level screening device, suitable for jobs that require high speed but little skill, such as certain assembly-line operations. The I-D Manual Dexterity Test measures dexterity in using the larger arm muscles, and the I-D Finger Dexterity Test measures similar skills in the use of the finger muscles alone. One of the other of these two tests is included in selection programs for the skilled trades, in accordance with the nature of the manual skills that the trade to be learned requires.

I-D Test 21: Marking

The Marking Test is part of the I-D semiskilled series that also includes the Similarities and Checking Tests. Like these other two instruments, it has so far found little practical application, and will be described only briefly.

General Description

The Marking Test consists of 300 squares arranged in rows of ten, as illustrated in Figure 16. The task is simply to mark an X in each square as rapidly as possible, and the score is the number of squares completed. The test is administered in two parts of 150 squares each, with a time limit of two minutes per part; the total administration time is fifteen minutes, including instructions. The Marking Test cannot be scored by machine.

The Adaptation Procedure

Because of the simplicity of the task, this test is especially easy to explain, and has even been administered with pantomime instructions. The only important requirement is to communicate the rapid pace at which the examinees are to work, and this is

FIGURE 16

Sample Items of the I-D Marking Test

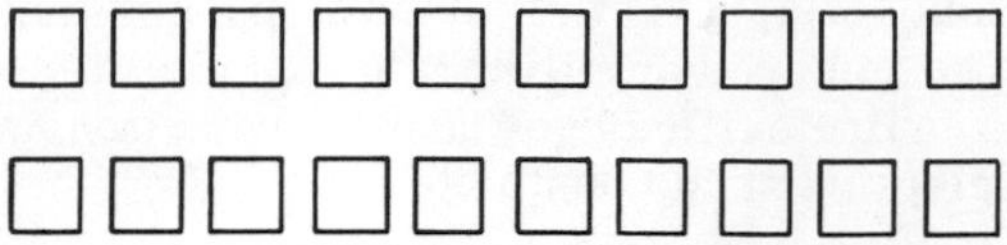

accomplished by a brief demonstration, in which the examiner himself fills in the squares on a large visual aid, working at frantic speed. Also, the entire test is in effect administered twice, the first time for practice, to teach the examinees how quickly a two-minute time limit elapses. No adaptation problems of any kind were encountered.

Intercountry Modifications

In the other countries, the Marking Test was administered in only Korea. No modifications had to be made.

Typical Results

The typical estimates of reliability obtained for the Marking Test are summarized in Table 14. They are high, as is to be expected of a test that depends mainly on speed.

The validity estimate obtained in the Korean study of textile workers was low; in West Africa, validity studies were not undertaken. No projection of validity for the screening of semiskilled workers can be attempted.

I-D Tests 19 and 20: Manual and Finger Dexterity

Both of these tests are attempts to measure dexterity with a pencil-and-paper device rather than with special apparatus of the type more commonly used. In general, the results in these countries were comparable to those obtained from similar pencil-and-paper tests in the United States. The Manual Dexterity Test has proved to be the more effective of the two for selection into general vocational courses, and is used in preference to finger Dexterity for such

TABLE 14

Typical Reliability Estimates of the I-D Marking Test

Country	Group	Education	Number	r*
West Africa	Primary (girls)	6-7 years	44	.87
Korea	Textile workers	Elementary	144	.92

*Both coefficients are based on the correlation between the separately timed halves of this test.

applications. The latter is most effective for trades such as that of electrician, in which precise finger movements are particularly important.

General Description

Sample items of both tests are illustrated in Figure 17. The Manual Dexterity Test consists of two exercises, each approximately 6" x 5" in size; the examinee is to draw a continuous line inside the 1/8" shaded path, beginning at the arrow, and approaching as near to the numeral 100 as he can within the time limit of two minutes per part. His score is the value of the numeral he reaches minus the number of times he strays outside the shaded path. The Finger Dexterity test consists of 90 similar but much smaller exercises, each about 5/8" x 1/2" in size. It is administered in two parts with a time limit of two minutes each, and the examinee's score is the number of exercises completed correctly. The total administration time for each test is fifteen minutes; neither can be scored by machine.

The Adaptation Procedure

The major problem in the development of the instructions for these tests was to teach the examinees the appropriate blend of care and speed that is likely to result in a maximum score. This blend is apt to be different for different examinees, and for this reason could not be demonstrated adequately by the examiner in the sample problems he works on the large visual board. A more effective approach was to let each examinee "discover" this blend for himself by giving the entire test first for practice and letting him evaluate

FIGURE 17

Sample Items of the I-D Dexterity Tests

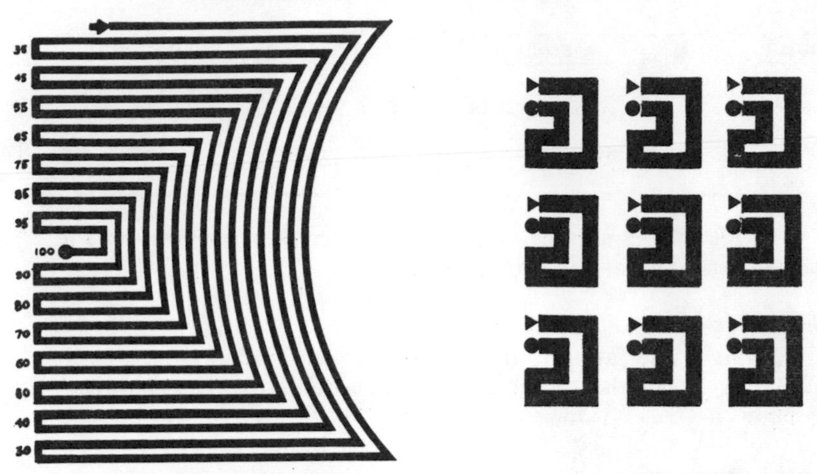

Manual Dexterity Finger Dexterity

the results he achieves in each successive attempt. Thus, at the end of each practice exercise of the Manual Dexterity Test the examiner tells all those who finished before time was up to count the many mistakes that they made, and cautions them to work more slowly; similarly, he tells those who did not reach the numeral 80 that they must work more quickly to obtain a top score. This method of successive approximations proved to be an effective teaching device for these tests—at least for examinees who had the basic manual abilities that are required.

Even more challenging than the development of the testing procedure, however, was the development of an efficient techniques for scoring the papers. Many approaches were tried; none was entirely adequate for large-scale practical applications. One attempt was to treat the papers chemically, so that any marks outside the path would make corresponding marks on the reverse side of the paper, which could then be easily counted. But this was too dependent on the pressure the examinee applied when tracing the path to be sufficiently trustworthy for practical use. Another was to print a replica of the path on a transparent film, so that only the examinee's errors would show through when this was superimposed on his paper. But registering the overlay exactly was too time-consuming. A third was to try to train scorers to approximate the result by comparing the general appearance of the paper with a graded series of models representative of the levels of performance typically attained by examinees at different ability levels. But not all scorers could be trained to make sufficiently close approximations.

The present procedure is to use yellow papers on which the path is printed in blue, and to supply the examinees with red ball-point pens to use for the dexterity tests. The marked change in the color of the line when it moves out of the blue path into the yellow enables a scorer to count the errors much more quickly than when pencils were used, and the scoring task is a reasonable one for fairly small applications. But for mass testing programs, the cumbersomeness of scoring remains the most serious limitation of these dexterity measures.

Intercountry Modifications

Both tests were administered without modification in Thailand and in Korea. Translating the instructions into the local language was the only change that was required.

In Thailand, a new idea was developed for easing the scoring burden. This was to score only a quarter of the grid of the Manual Dexterity Test and to use this sample to estimate the examinee's total test performance. The correlation of .91 that was obtained between these estimates and the actual scores suggests that this may well be the best solution so far developed.

TABLE 15

Typical Reliability Estimates of the I-D Dexterity Tests

Test	Country	Group	Education	Number	r*
Manual	West Africa	Mixed	6-7 years	2,422	.83
Manual	Korea	Textile workers	Elementary	144	.85
Finger	West Africa	Mixed	6-7 years	2,335	.89
Finger	Korea	Textile workers	Elementary	144	.91

*All of these coefficients are based on the correlation between the separately timed halves of these tests.

Typical Results

The estimates of reliability typically obtained for the two dexterity tests are summarized in Table 15. It will be seen that both tests are highly reliable despite the many subjective judgments that have to be made in the process of scoring.

Examinees in the skilled trades were tested only in the African studies. Validity estimates for the Manual Dexterity Test against grades in shop courses and against foreman evaluations were in the range of .35-.40 for a variety of trades (except that of electrician), and in the subsequent study at the Malawi Polytechnic a figure of .55 was obtained. The validity of the Finger Dexterity Test was consistently lower for all groups except electrical workers, where the estimate of .37 far exceeded that of the Manual Dexterity Test. In general, figures near .40 can be projected.

CHAPTER

7

DEVELOPMENT OF OPERATIONAL TESTING PROCEDURES

The design of an operational testing program involves two further developmental procedures. The first is to determine which of the available tests should be used for this particular application to obtain the highest possible accuracy within the practical constraints on time and cost that usually limit the total number of tests the applicants can be given. The second is to formulate an appropriate procedure for combining the separate test scores that will be obtained into a single index of the applicants' respective potential. Both raise issues and problems that require attention as careful as that paid to development of the actual testing procedures.

This chapter begins with a brief overview of these issues and of the approaches that were adopted for resolving them in the AID/AIR research. Then this developmental procedure will be illustrated for scholastic, technical, and clerical selection programs, drawing on the actual applications of the I-D tests for all of the statistical data required.

BASIC DEVELOPMENTAL PROCEDURES

Once the individual tests have been developed, the methods used in designing an operational testing program are entirely independent of cultural variations. The programs that are produced by these methods may vary from country to country, as a result of culture-tied differences in the tests' measurement characteristics. But the methodology itself need not be adapted.

Thus, the techniques described in this chapter are all standard approaches. They are included partly for purposes of continuity, and partly because adequate descriptions of a number of these techniques are not available in many developing countries.

Comparability of the Test Scores

One basic characteristic of composites of scores is that superior performance on one test will compensate for poor performance on another when the scores are all added together. If one applicant earns ten points more than another on Test A but ten points less on Test B, the two will appear to be equally able when the results on Tests A and B are combined into a single index of their potential. That a ten-point difference on Test A is equal to a ten-point difference on Test B is the implicit assumption.

But this assumption is usually false for the raw scores that the applicants earn on two or more separate tests. And the practice of adding the "marks" obtained on a set of different examinations, common in many developing countries, almost always introduces distortion.* Before test scores can be combined, they must be converted to a uniform scale on which seemingly equal differences such as the above in fact are the same.

Many methods for converting scores to a uniform scale have been developed. The method used in the AID/AIR studies was the "stanine" approach, which affords both a solution to the scaling problem and a simplification of the data for purposes of processing and reporting. It consists of dividing the total range of raw scores earned by the examinees into nine approximately equal segments, and converting every score that falls within the same segment to the same stanine score. Each score in the lowest segment is converted to a score of 1; each score in the highest segment to a score of 9; and each score in the intervening segments to the corresponding integer between these extremes. The middle interval straddles the mean, so that there are four and one-half intervals both above and below the midpoint of the overall distribution.

---

*If the tests are equally reliable, the amount of distortion depends on the degree to which the tests differ with respect to the dispersion of the examinees' scores. When the scores are widely dispersed, a ten-point jump represents a much lesser gain in performance than when the scores are bunched fairly closely together.

If the distribution of raw scores is perfectly normal, the resulting scores will have the properties illustrated in Figure 18. Each segment will contain a range of raw scores equal to one half of one standard deviation, and the percentages of examinees earning each of the nine stanine scores will be as shown. A score of Stanine 9 will indicate performance superior to that of 96 percent of the total examinee population; a score of Stanine 7 will indicate superiority to 77 percent of the population; and so on, throughout the entire range.

Since the distribution of the scores of a finite sample of examinees is not apt to be perfectly normal, however, some deviations from these figures must be expected. But these discrepancies are generally small and, at least for the I-D tests, close fits to the theoretical distribution have consistently been obtained, even for samples of only 100 examinees.

FIGURE 18

Stanine Conversion of a Perfectly Normal Distribution

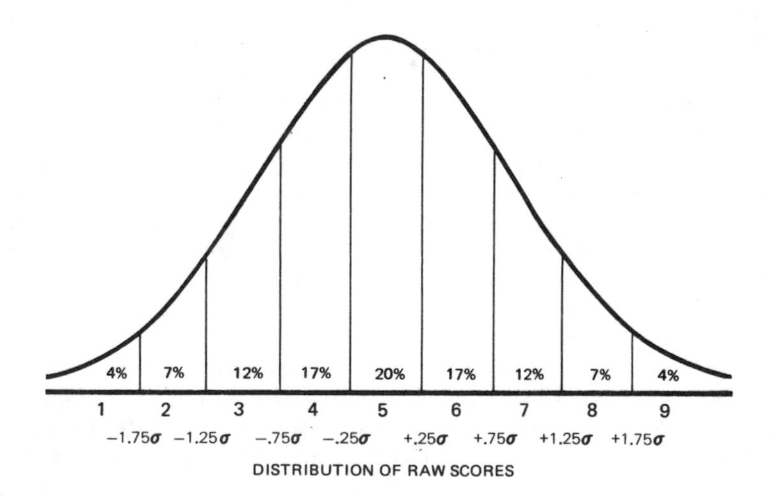

Mechanically, the conversion to stanine scores is best accomplished by using not the standard deviation values of Figure 18 (i.e., giving the examinees who score from .25-.75 σ's above the mean a converted score of Stanine 6), but the percentage values of examinees within each segment, as follows: Array the raw scores in order, from highest to lowest, and identify the Stanine 5 group by counting 40 percent down from the top and 40 percent up from the bottom of this distribution. If exactly 40 percent is not feasible (because too many examinees have the same score at the point of division), use a percentage somewhat higher or lower, such that the numbers of examinees above and below the Stanine 5 interval will be most nearly the same. Then, follow the same procedure to identify the scores of Stanine 7 or higher and of Stanine 3 or lower, by counting 23 percent down and 23 percent up, again adjusting these percentages if necessary to make the two groups most nearly equal in size. Next, split these two groups into three intervals each, balancing insofar as possible the number of Stanine 9 scores with the number of Stanine 1 scores, the Stanine 8's with the Stanine 2's, and the Stanine 7's with the Stanine 3's, at the same time trying to keep the ranges of raw scores included in these intervals most nearly the same. Finally, inspect the results and make any further adjustments in the points of division that will achieve a closer fit to the theoretical model in Figure 18. This can be done as part of the standardization studies, if test norms are developed, or separately for each applicant group after they have been tested.

The stanine scores on two or more tests can be added together to obtain a meaningful composite score. But this sum should not then be divided by the number of tests to obtain an "average" stanine score. Rather, the distribution of the summed scores should itself be subjected to the above procedure, so that they also are converted to single-digit stanine results. This final stanine is then an appropriate index of the applicant's overall performance on the various tests he was given.

The loss of precision that results from grouping applicants who in fact have somewhat different raw scores is seldom a drawback in practical test applications—a nine-point scale is adequate for the decisions that are to be made. The simplifications afforded by one-digit scores are especially attractive in a developing country, where there may be limited access to high-speed computers, and much of the data processing may have to be done by hand.

Overlap in the Abilities Measured

A second important characteristic of programs based on a number of tests is that the resulting scores are not independent. Partly because the abilities that the tests are intended to measure may tend to occur together in human performance, and partly as the result of similarities in the testing procedures (such as the requirement for speed, for example), most pairs of test scores are positively correlated to a certain extent. If this correlation is high, the two tests will provide so much overlapping information that the use of both will give results only slightly more accurate than can be obtained from using the more valid one only.

For this reason, the intercorrelation of the available tests is an important consideration in the selection of those that should be applied. After the one or two most valid tests have been selected, the next most useful test will frequently turn out to be not the one with the next highest validity, but a somewhat less valid test that also has less overlap with the instruments already selected. To design an efficient testing program, knowledge of the test intercorrelations is almost always essential.

Many techniques for reducing the information provided by the correlations among tests into a form more readily interpreted have been developed. Of these, the techniques of factor analysis earlier mentioned have been the most widely used. A more recently developed statistic is a coefficient of the "uniqueness" of each of the tests in a series that will be used together.[1] Such data reduction can be helpful, but in the AID/AIR studies it was found adequate in designing a practical testing program simply to examine the raw correlational data, especially when there was no ready access to a high-speed computer. The kinds of conclusions that can be drawn from these data are described in the illustrative applications that follow this background discussion.

Differential Test Weights

Because of the differences in the validity and overlap of the various test scores, the accuracy of a testing program is generally increased by combining the scores with different weights, so as to obtain an overall index that is maximally predictive.* Mechanically, such weighting is accomplished simply by multiplying each of the

---

*Tests can be differentially weighted in accordance with their respective reliabilities to improve the accuracy of the composite index obtained. But when the tests to be used vary greatly in reliability, it is usually more effective to improve the tests that are less reliable than to adjust for this with a weighting procedure.

stanine scores by the desired weighting factor before they are added together. The problem is to determine the set of weights that should be used for each practical application.

The difficulty arises not in the mathematics of computing the weights that are most consistent with the available validity and intercorrelational data. Through multiple regression analysis the optimum weighting scheme inherent in this information can be determined precisely. Rather, the problem is one of generalizing these weights to future applicant groups, for regression analysis cannot differentiate between the "true" characteristics of the tests and the many chance fluctuations that also affect any set of correlational data; it generates weights that will be optimal also for the next set of applicants only if the effects of these many chance factors again turn out to be exactly the same. In practice, this is never the case.

Accordingly, the effective use of test weights is constrained by two major limitations. The first is that the weights obtained from the initial regression analysis cannot be used to estimate the validity of the testing program for future applicant groups. A validity estimate based on a "multiple" correlation coefficient can easily be twice as large as the result that will in fact be obtained when the tests are administered to another group; this (unfortunately common) misuse of multiple regression must be avoided. The correct estimate of the effectiveness of a set of regression weights is the coefficient of correlation they yield in subsequent applications.

The second limitation is that a fairly large sample of examinees must be tested before the apparently optimum weights are actually used for selection decisions. Because empirically developed weights are so highly dependent on chance fluctuations, the "optimum" values can vary greatly from one administration to the next, and it is only when the proportionate effect of chance has been reduced as a result of large samples that reasonably stable results can be expected. A sample of several hundred examinees should generally be available before regression analysis is attempted.

In the AID/AIR projects, the approach to test weights was as follows:

1. To compute all estimates of validity without the use of any differential weighting scheme whatsoever, and

2. To suggest to the users of tests that they develop weights over time, as a result of experience with the effectiveness of the tests in their individual institutions.

Thus, the validity estimates cited in the illustrative applications will uniformly be minimum estimates, improvable to some extent by appropriate weighting procedures.

Reliability of a Test Combination

The overlap among the separate tests that limits the validity available from the composite has exactly the opposite effect on the reliability of the overall index obtained; each pair of overlapping tests will provide two separate estimates of the ability common to both and thereby increase the overall accuracy of its appraisal. Even tests of only moderate reliability can in combination result in a highly reliable score.

The reliability of a composite can be computed by formula from the individual test reliabilities and the inter-test correlations. The computational procedure is illustrated in the following example, which incorporates the lowest reliability estimate (that of .54 for the Science Information Test for last-year secondary school students) obtained in the West African studies.

The three tests to be used in combination are the High form of the Reading Comprehension Test (RDH), the Science Information Test (SCI), and the test of World Information (WLD). They are to be given to West African students in their last year of secondary school, as an estimate of further academic potential.

To estimate the rel:ability of this three-test series, the first step is to prepare a matrix of test reliabilities and intercorrelations at this educational level, as illustrated in Figure 19. The reliability

FIGURE 19

Illustrative Reliability and Interest Correlation Coefficients

	SCI	WLD	RHD
SCI	(.54)	.34	.36
WLD	.34	(.73)	.49
RHD	.36	.49	(.76)

estimates are shown in the diagonal in parentheses; each intercorrelation is written twice.

The second step is to add these nine values together. A sum of 4.41 is obtained.

The third step is to replace each of the three reliability figures with the value 1.00, and to sum the matrix again.* A result of 5.38 is obtained.

The last step is to divide the first sum by the second larger result. The quotient of .82 is the estimated reliability of the composite.

For composites of four or more tests, the same procedure is followed, using a correspondingly larger matrix of coefficients.

Thus, another important characteristic of tests in combination is that modest reliability should not preclude the inclusion of a test that has proved to be a reasonably effective predictor. When the selection decision will be based on an overall index, it is the reliability of this score and not of the individual tests that should be the primary consideration.

Validity of a Test Combination

The most difficult task in the design of a validity study is to find or develop a criterion measure that will provide an adequate index of performance in the course or job for which the applicants are being selected. This is a more complex problem of test construction than is the development of ability measures because the uniformity of instruction, supervision, and evaluation that can be built into a testing session cannot be achieved in a live classroom or job situation. And rare indeed is the test constructor who is satisfied with the criterion measures at his disposal.

---

*The value 1.00 is appropriate only when the test scores have been converted to stanines or other scores that result in uniform standard deviations. When the standard deviations of the tests vary, or when differential weights are to be applied, these and all of the other values must be adjusted.

Nevertheless, there are a number of practical guidelines for the design and use of criterion measures that proved useful in the United States and that were found to be entirely generalizable to research in a developing country. These general guidelines—applicable to the evaluation of individual instruments as well as composites—will be summarized first; then the issues peculiar to combinations of tests will be considered.

Criterion Measures

From the point of view of research design, there are two broad categories of criterion measures. The first are those that have already been established as standards of performance by the educational or training institution, and that must be used in the study to provide operationally meaningful evaluations. The second are those that are developed specifically for purposes of test validation, and that are administered as an integral part of the research procedure. The degree of control that the test constructor can exercise is quite different in these two situations, and they therefore have different design implications.

Fixed-Criterion Studies

When the students or trainees are required to pass a certain examination or maintain a specified grade-point average as a prerequisite for graduation, any alternative index of their performance is necessarily a less meaningful criterion measure. For, even if it can be shown that another index will provide a better indication of their performance "later in life," selecting students who have the highest ultimate potential but will never realize it because they are unable to pass the course clearly is self-defeating. Until the existing standards are changed (perhaps as a result of a study that demonstrates their poor correlation with later performance), the established criteria should be applied.*

In these situations the most important guideline the test constructor should follow is to base the selection of tests on a detailed examination of the criteria that actually will be applied. The title of

---

*The use of additional indexes, so as to select students who will pass the course and <u>also</u> perform better later is, of course, an improvement. The point of the discussion is that established standards cannot be ignored.

the course and the stated teaching objectives are seldom adequately descriptive. The content of the curriculum, the emphasis of the instructors, and the problems typically included in proficiency tests should be inspected so that the abilities in fact critical to success in this particular course can be identified before the tests are selected.

One illustration of the importance of this step is the following African experience, variations of which occurred in also the other developing countries.

An improved selection program was to be developed for the skilled trades training program of an industrial firm. At first, it seemed that the I-D tests normally used for this purpose would be entirely suitable because the graduates of the course would be assigned to standard types of skilled occupations. But closer study showed that the curriculum was as heavily weighted with "theory" as with "practical" courses, and that passing a course in trigonometry would be required of all of the trainees selected. An unusually high degree of academic potential was necessary for the curriculum that this firm (rightly or wrongly) adopted, and corresponding emphases had to be incorporated into the selection procedure.

A testing program based on the critical requirements normally associated with such course titles as "welding" would have resulted in at best marginal accuracy in this particular application.

Apart from such careful selection of the predictors to be applied, there is little the test constructor can do in the fixed-criterion situation to improve the accuracy (or the apparent accuracy) of the testing program developed. Even the collection and processing of the criterion data will usually be carried out as part of the institution's routine operations, without the special checks and controls that may be desirable for purposes of the research.

Optional-Criterion Studies

When the criterion measure is not prescribed, an appropriate instrument must be developed. This is usually the case when data on the established criterion will not be available until the final year of the course, and an earlier validity estimate is desired; or when the sample consists of employees whose proficiency is not being evaluated so systematically as is that of trainees or students in formal courses.

In these situations, the test constructor has considerably more flexibility in designing the study but is still limited by the typically small budget that can be devoted to criterion development and by the fact that the resulting measure must be accepted unequivocally by the officials of the institution for which the program is being developed. As a result of these practical limitations, the opportunity for innovation that is afforded by these more flexible situations is seldom exploited. Most specially developed criterion measures consist of indexes based on grades or ratings or other subjective evaluations.

The AID/AIR studies did not venture beyond these basic kinds of subjective measures. But it was found that certain of these approaches were more effective than others, and eventually all validity studies were carried out with one of three data collection approaches. They provide successively better results, and are successively more expensive.

The first of these was the use of <u>course grades converted to a comparable scale</u>. Grades were used only when considerations of distance or time made expediency essential, or when a comparison of this type was specifically requested. Depending on the curriculum, grades in four to seven separate courses were obtained for each of the examinees, and then combined into a single index of overall classroom performance.

When the grades were expressed in the form of percentages or similar units, they were converted to stanine scores before they were added, for the reasons earlier noted. When the stanine approach was impractical because the grades were already grouped into an even smaller number of categories (e.g., letter grades from A through E), an equivalent procedure was used.

Assume that the classroom performance of the individual students is normally distributed, and that each grouping of grades therefore represents a segment of an underlying normal distribution. On the basis of this assumption, the position of each segment along the normal curve can then be determined by consulting a table to the normal probability distribution.

In Figure 20, for example, the tabulation at the left shows the distribution of grades that a group of 200 examinees obtained in one of their courses. By consulting a table of the normal curve, it can be determined that the 10 percent who obtained A's represent an interval beginning 1.28 standard deviations above the mean, because this is the interval that contains the top ten percent of a normal distribution. Similarly, it can be determined that the interval that contains the next highest 30 percent begins at 0.25, and so on, for each of the five letter grades. A pictorial representation is shown at the right.

FIGURE 20

Normalizing a Distribution of Course Grades

Grade	No. of Students	Percent of Students	Normal Curve Segment	Height of Curve at Segment Ends
A	20	10	1.28 →	.175 and .000
B	60	30	.25 to 1.28	.386 and .175
C	90	45	−1.04 to .25	.233 and .386
D	20	10	−1.64 to −1.04	.103 and .233
E	10	5	← −1.64	.000 and .103

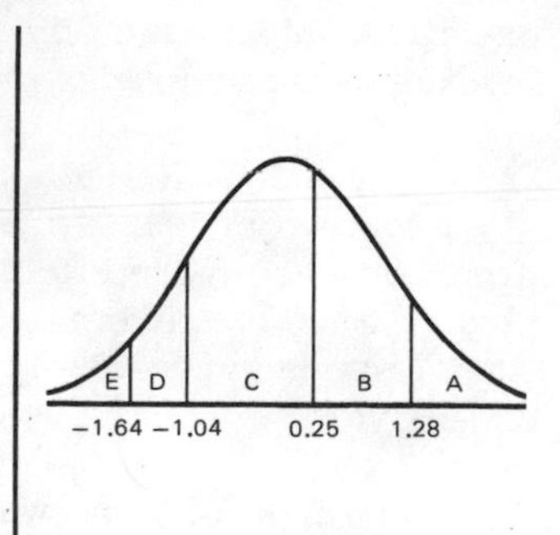

To convert the grades to normalized scores, the ordinate of the curve at each of the division points must also be found, again by consulting the table. As shown in both the chart and picture, the height of the curve is .175 at 1.28, .386 at .25, and so on for the four points of division.

With this information, the average value of each segment can be computed. (Because there is a different number of examinees at each point of the interval, its mean will not be at the exact center.) The procedure is to divide the difference in the height of the curve at each end of the segment by the proportion of students this segment includes. Thus, the average score of the A students is .175-.000 divided by .10, or 1.75 standard deviation above the mean. The average score of the B students is .386-.175 divided by .30, or .70; the average score of the C students is .233-.386 divided by .45, or -.34; etc.

The five quotients obtained are the average normal scores corresponding to the five letter grades, and can legitimately be added to similar scores for other courses. The composite scores obtained for the examinees can then be converted to simpler numbers by using the stanine approach.

This procedure is considerably more cumbersome than the computation of grade-point averages, but avoids the generally false assumption that the difference between an A and a B is equal to the difference between a C and a D, within the same course and across different courses. In the illustrative applications that will be presented, the above approach was used for all validity studies based on these types of criterion measures.

A second and generally more satisfactory procedure was to obtain teacher or supervisor evaluations especially for purposes of the research, using an alternate ranking procedure. Rankings are usually preferable to ratings because the evaluators are forced to make decisions that provide a reasonable distribution of scores, and cannot give the majority of the group an average or somewhat above average score, which is the most common outcome of rating procedures. Whenever practicable, it was ranking data that were collected.

The alternation procedure is a mechanical device for simplifying the complexity of arraying 20 to 30 examinees in descending order. Each of the evaluators is given a roster of the examinees he knows well enough to compare, up to a maximum of 30 or 35 overall. He is also given a ranking form which consists simply of two columns of blank spaces, as illustrated in Figure 21.

FIGURE 21

Form for Alternate Ranking Procedure

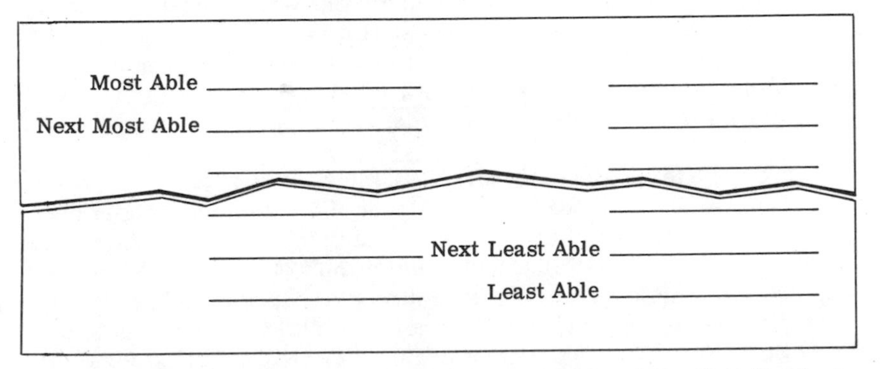
Most Able ____________ ____________
Next Most Able ____________ ____________
____________ ____________
____________ ____________
____________ Next Least Able ____________
____________ Least Able ____________

The first step is to pick out the most able of the N individuals listed, to write his name on the top line of the ranking form, and then to draw a line through his name on the roster. The second step is to pick out the least able of the N-1 individuals whose names remain on the roster, to write his name at the bottom of the ranking form, and then to cross him off the list. Then, the most able of the N-2 individuals still to be ranked is selected, followed by the least able of the remaining N-3, and so on until the entire roster has been completed.

At each point, "most able" or "least able" is the only judgment required, and this is one of the simplifications afforded by this procedure. A second is that the evaluation of the individuals between the extremes, which is usually the most difficult task, is deferred until the list has been reduced to more manageable proportions.

For best results, three or more independent evaluations should be obtained for each examinee, although adequate distributions can sometimes be obtained from just two. The same evaluators need not be used for the entire group, and, in fact, should not be if the sample includes a number of sections taught by different instructors.

To combine the rankings, their numerical equivalents can be added to obtain a composite score, which may then be normalized by means of the same procedure described above for course grades. Usually, the distribution of composite scores will consist of a number of distinct clusters that can be treated like letter grades as indicative of successively higher performance levels.

Whenever practicable, this was the data collection procedure used for optional-criterion validity studies.

The most common situation in which this approach is not applicable is in studies of employees who work in a number of different departments and sections, so that any one supervisor is familiar with the work of only one or a few, and cannot rank a significant percentage of the entire group. In these instances, it was necessary to fall back on ratings, with varied success. Most effective has been the procedure in which the data collector serves as a middleman to try to ensure the comparability of the assessments made by the many separate judges.

Ratings are obtained in individual interviews of up to one hour each. The evaluator is asked first to rank the examinees whom he supervises with respect to each other, and then to compare them with his other employees, with the individuals who held these jobs in the past, and with employees of other sections he happens to know; and in this way to try to approximate their relative standing in the entire force of employees throughout the organization. If he considers an employee exceptionally able or especially incompetent, he is asked for specific examples of his accomplishments or shortcomings; this extreme judgment is then confirmed or softened through discussions with the data collector.

After each employee has been fully discussed in this manner, the rating form is introduced and completed jointly. Because a single data collector conducts each of these sessions, a degree of comparability not available from a general explanation of the procedure above is provided.

Because of the demands of this approach, it was used only occasionally, but uniformly excellent results were obtained.

Design of the Validity Study

In either the fixed or the optional criterion situations, the optimal design of the validity study is as follows:

1. To administer the experimental tests to the group of applicants from which the students or trainees will be selected;

2. To ensure that the test results are not used as a basis for these selection decisions; and

3. To collect the criterion data in a follow-up study, after sufficient time has elapsed to assess the relative proficiency of the individuals who were selected.

From the correlation between the test scores and demonstrated proficiency, the improvements that would have resulted from the use of the tests can then be estimated with reasonable precision. Had the tests been used as part of the actual selection process, only applicants above a certain cutoff score would have been admitted; and the difference between the proficiency of students at these scores and the proficiency of the students in fact selected is the magnitude of the improvement that would probably have been effected. Whenever possible, this is the design that should be applied to validity studies.

In many situations, however, waiting for the results of a follow-up study is unrealistic. This is generally the case in the validity studies of individual tests carried out during the initial development of these procedures, since it is quite impractical to wait one year or longer between successive revisions. This is also the case in any subsequent application in which the results are to be used for an immediate decision, as in a feasibility study to assess the payoff of a proposal already pending. In these situations the estimate must be based on a concurrent validity study, in which the tests are given to a sample of individuals already in the course or the job, so that criterion data on the examinees' demonstrated proficiency can be collected at once.

This approach is also indicated when the test constructor is prepared to wait for follow-up data but the institution that will apply the tests is not. When there are strong pressures for immediate improvements, many organizations will want from the first to use the scores for selection decisions; this spoils the design because no applicants with the lower test scores will be included in the follow-up group. Some estimates can be made, but it is usually safer to rely instead on a concurrent validity study, carried out by testing not only applicants but also a sample of present students or workers.

The estimates obtained from concurrent studies are generally less accurate than follow-up findings for two major reasons. The first is that there is no entirely satisfactory group of students or workers for use in this type of research. If relatively new entrants are tested, they will be maximally similar to the applicants for whom the tests are intended, but will not have been in the course or job long enough to be evaluated adequately on the criterion measure. If more senior groups are used, their proficiency can be gauged more precisely, but their test scores may not be representative of the performance of applicants who have not had nearly the same amount of experience and training. Either way, some loss of accuracy cannot be avoided. In the AID/AIR studies, the option usually selected was to test the more junior samples, compromising the quality of the criterion data for the sake of representative scores.

The second problem is that a group tested after it has been in a course for one or more years will generally not include individuals at the very lowest ability levels, because these would either have been rejected by the current selection procedure or have failed or dropped out as their lack of ability became apparent. The validity estimate obtained from such studies therefore is lower than would be obtained from an unselected applicant group, which would typically include a larger number of less able performers. There are statistical adjustments that can be made to extrapolate the estimate that is obtained to the more heterogeneous applicant group. But in the AID/AIR studies it was decided to avoid such more hypothetical measures because of the complicated explanations that would be required. Instead, the findings reported ignored the effects of dropouts and failures, and showed the result actually obtained as a minimum estimate of the validity available in addition to that provided by the current selection procedures; this was readily understood.

Computational Procedure

After the tests have been administered, the computation of the validity obtained from the composite is identical to the procedure used for a single test, since it is in fact only the single index of overall potential obtained after the scores have been combined that is compared with the criterion measure. But when the probable validity is to be estimated in advance, on the basis of the validities typically obtained from the individual tests, a somewhat more complex approach is required.

The approach that is used is highly similar to that earlier described for estimating the overall reliability of a test combination. It is illustrated below using the same three tests that were used in this earlier example. The first step again is to prepare a matrix, as illustrated in Figure 22. This time it is the validity rather than the reliability coefficients that are inserted in the diagonal cells.

The second step is to add the validity coefficients, exclusive of the intertest correlations. A sum of 1.16 is obtained.

The third step is to total the entire matrix, using the value 1.00 in place of each validity coefficient. The result of 5.38 is the same as that obtained from the corresponding step in the reliability example. But in the validity computation, it is necessary to use the square root of this sum rather than the total itself. A figure of 2.32 is obtained.

The last step is to divide the sum of the validities (1.16) by this square root. The quotient of .50 is the estimated validity of the composite.

In this illustration, the gain in validity attributable to the use of the two information tests in addition to the Reading Comprehension Test is negligible, as a result of the fairly high intertest correlations. The reliability of the overall score will be improved however, as earlier noted.

FIGURE 22

Illustrative Validity of Intertest
Correlation Coefficients

	SCI	WLD	RDH
SCI	.36	.34	.36
WLD	.34	.31	.49
RDH	.36	.49	.49

Converting Validity Coefficients to Operational Measures

There are many ways in which a validity coefficient can be translated into a more meaningful operational measure. One common approach is to express the improvement in terms of the criterion measure that was applied, such as the increase that can be expected in the average course grades the students will earn when the tests are used for selection. A second is to compute the increase in the probability that the average entrant will attain or exceed a fixed minimum proficiency level. There are numerous other related approaches.

The procedure used in the AID/AIR studies was to use the proficiency of the trainee at the midpoint of the present proficiency distribution as the baseline statistic, and to compute the percentage of the entrants selected by the new tests who could be expected to attain or exceed this median level. This had the advantages of simplicity and of applicability to all types of criterion measures. For the proficiency of the median trainee can be determined even from rankings or other measures that are not intrinsically meaningful when expressed in absolute numbers.

On the assumption that both the test scores and the proficiency levels are normally distributed, such percentage equivalents can be determined from tables of the bivariate normal distribution. The results for a range of validity coefficients are summarized in Table 16, in accordance with the stanine score on the newly introduced selection tests that is the cutoff point for admission. Thus, if a composite of tests has a validity of .60, and if only applicants who score at or above Stanine 7 are admitted, one can expect that 83 percent of the selectees will exceed the level of proficiency that is currently being attained by only 50 percent of the group. Further examples are given in the following illustrative applications.

SCHOLASTIC SELECTION PROGRAMS

As earlier noted, admission to secondary school is the crucial decision-point in the educational systems of most of the developing countries. To illustrate the design of school admission programs, therefore, it seems most useful to use selection at this level as the major example, and then to point out the ways in which this basic approach must be changed at the higher levels of education.

TABLE 16

Conversion of Validity Coefficients Into Operational Improvements

Minimum Requirement for Admission	Percentage of Selectees Likely to Become More Proficient Than Present Average Trainee				
	r=.45	r=.50	r=.55	r=.60	r=.65
Present requirements only	50	50	50	50	50
Present requirement and Stanine 6	68	70	72	74	77
Present requirement and Stanine 7	74	77	80	83	85
Present requirement and Stanine 8	80	83	86	89	92
Present requirement and Stanine 9	86	89	92	94	96

Secondary School Admission Procedures

For school admission decisions, scores on scholastic aptitude tests should normally be used in conjunction with two other measures. The first is an index of the applicants' prior academic performance, as shown by tests of achievement in the core primary school courses. The second is an assessment of their personal characteristics, made on the basis of individual interviews by the instructional staff of the institution for which they are being selected. Applicants who have not the necessary academic preparation or who exhibit pronounced personal problems are unlikely to be successful, irrespective of their scholastic potential.

The first step in designing the admission procedure, therefore, is to develop an overall plan for the application of these three separate measures. In practice, this almost always entails the development of a sequential process in which the various measures serve as successive hurdles, so that they can be applied to successively smaller numbers. Because of the typically large ratio of applicants to selectees (as high as 130 to 1 in some of the African studies), evaluating every applicant on all of the measures is, if not totally impossible, at least grossly inefficient.

The considerations pertinent to the design of such a sequential process at the postprimary level are the following:

1. The order of the sequence should be from achievement test to aptitude test to interview, in accordance with the relative costs of these measures and their requirements for specially trained personnel,

2. As many of the applicants as can be accomodated at the aptitude testing stage should be permitted to pass the achievement test hurdle, so as to take account of the limitations of achievement tests at this level, as described in Chapter 1,

3. The use of the interview should be limited to the rejection of applicants who appear to be obviously unfit, because this type of assessment is generally a poor basis for the identification of applicants with outstanding potential.

In addition, these three conditions will generally have to be met, as well as is practicable, within this further constraint:

4. Two separate testing sessions are the most that can be justified, on administrative and logistic grounds, for a secondary school admission procedure.

Asking the applicants to appear for testing on three separate occasions is usually too time-consuming and costly, particularly when considerable travel would be required.

The Three-Stage Selection Procedure

In practice, these conditions mean that a three-stage process is feasible only when the first stage has already been carried out as part of the regular primary school cycle—i.e., when a national achievement examination is administered at the end of the primary course as the basis for certifying successful completion. In this case, the scores of those who decide to apply for the secondary schools can be obtained from the records without extra testing, and can be used as the first screening hurdle. Only two extra sessions, one for the aptitude tests and one for the interviews, need be conducted.

The percentage of the total applicant pool that is invited on the basis of the primary school exit examination to appear for aptitude testing will depend mainly on the capacity of the facilities that can be provided. From a technical point of view, it is appropriate to invite three to five times the number eventually to be admitted, since this will generally guarantee that only applicants with aptitude test scores of Stanine 7 or better need be admitted. The higher the validity of the aptitude test, the more this ratio can be shaved to meet administrative constraints—the result of testing three times the number to be admitted when the validity coefficient is .60 will be approximately the same as that obtained from testing five times this number when the coefficient is .50, for example, in terms of the proficiency expectations of Table 16.

In selecting the applicants to be invited for interviews, two types of strategies can be adopted. One is to interview only as many as will be admitted, and to replace the typically few that will be rejected by inviting an appropriate number of "alternates" for a subsequent interview session. The other is to try to anticipate the number of rejections, perhaps 10 percent at the most, and to invite a correspondingly larger number for the initial session. The relative merits of these approaches depend on the timing of the program, the distances to be travelled, and other local conditions.

The Two-Stage Selection Procedure

When exit examinations are not used at the primary level, the achievement testing component must be carried out as part of the admission procedure. Within the limit of two testing sessions, this means that two of the three measures must be used jointly at either the first or the second stage of the program. If the achievement test is used at the first stage, the aptitude tests and the interview must both be fitted into the second session. If the interview alone is to constitute the second hurdle, the achievement and aptitude tests must be used jointly as the initial screening procedure. Either way, certain compromises have to be made.

If the achievement test alone constitutes the first hurdle, it will generally not be possible to evaluate as many applicants as is desirable on the aptitude tests because all of these applicants will also have to be interviewed, and this is inordinately expensive for large applicant groups. If the interview alone constitutes the second hurdle, this problem is eased, but there may well be comparable difficulties in training a sufficient number of examiners to administer the aptitude tests to all applicants throughout the country. Which is the lesser evil depends on local conditions.

Frequently, the most effective compromise is to split the aptitude tests between the two stages, and to invite only two to three times the number of applicants to be admitted to attend the second testing session. This will result in the administration of the entire series of aptitude tests to somewhat fewer applicants than is desirable, and in the interviewing of somewhat more applicants than is economical, but will tend to prevent either deficiency from reaching unmanageable proportions. It is the approach that was generally followed in the AID/AIR studies when exit examinations were not used at the primary level.

Selecting the Aptitude Tests

Once the overall plan has been developed, the aptitude tests that best fit the technical and practical requirements can be selected. In the case of the I-D series, there are three basic tests related to performance in secondary school academic courses, as will be recalled from the descriptions in Chapter 6. These are the Verbal Analogies (Low), Reading Comprehension (Low), and Arithmetic Tests. Their essential statistical properties are summarized in Table 17, based on the West African data.

If a three-stage selection procedure is to be used, all three of these tests can usually be applied at the second stage. The total administration time is approximately one-and-a-half hours for the entire set, so that each examiner can conveniently test two hundred or more students per day. The reliability of the series is approximately .90, and the expected validity .58, when all three tests are equally weighted.

In administering the tests, the Reading Comprehension Test should be given first, since it is a convenient vehicle for teaching the marking procedure, and involves no other operations unfamiliar to the examinees. The Verbal Analogies Test is second; and the Arithmetic Test, because of its requirement of speed, is the last. Special attention must be given to the teaching of the speed concept in this particular test series, because it includes no tests of intermediate speed to prepare the examinees for the rapidity that the Arithmetic Test requires.

If the testing is to be accomplished in only two stages, the most practicable approach is to administer the Reading Comprehension Test in conjunction with the achievement tests for the initial screening, and then to apply the Verbal Analogies and Arithmetic Tests when the interviews are conducted. Using no more than a single aptitude test at the first stage is usually dictated by the amount of time the achievement tests will require—they generally should include essay tests as well as objective measures, for the reasons earlier noted. And the Reading Comprehension Test is the logical candidate for administration by untrained examiners throughout the country.

TABLE 17

The I-D Postprimary Scholastic Aptitude Tests*

	RDL	RTH	Reliability	Validity
VAL	.44	.34	.87	.50
RDL		.31	.73	.50
RTH			.88	.32

*Details on the numbers of examinees, criterion instruments, etc., may be found in the I-D Technical Manual.

For secondary schools with a technical bias, one of the technical aptitude tests should be added to this basic series. The appropriate choice is the Mechanical Information Test because it is generally the most valid of these procedures and because it requires virtually no examiner training. This will increase the administration time to approximately two hours, but improved validity against overall school performance can be expected.

In general, then, inclusions of three or four aptitude tests in the secondary school selection process can be expected to provide validities of .55-.60 or more, apart from the contributions of the other admission procedures. Translated into operational terms, these gains are shown in Figure 23 for increasingly stringent entry qualifications. One of the advantages of the large ratio of applicants to selectees generally found at the secondary school level, of course, is that admitting only applicants at the Stanine 8 or even Stanine 9 levels is entirely feasible in many locations.

Postsecondary School Admission Procedures

The key simplification in selection programs for sixth forms, universities, and other postsecondary institutions is that the above problems of achievement testing seldom arise. Final examination results are almost always available for use as the first screening hurdle, and can be applied as predictors much more confidently than can similar measures at the postprimary level. And because the absolute number of applicants also is considerably smaller at these higher levels, compromises in the design of the admission procedure are not required. On the basis of the available achievement test scores,

FIGURE 23

Validity of the I-D Secondary School Admission Tests

Minimum Requirements for Admission	Percentage Selected Likely to Perform Above Level of Present Average Student
Present standards only	50%
Present standard and I-D Stanine 6	74%
Present standards and I-D Stanine 7	82%
Present standard and I-D Stanine 8	88%
Present standard and I-D Stanine 9	94%

a "short list" of promising candidates is prepared; and the aptitude tests and interviews are then applied to these candidates in either one or two further stages, whichever is more convenient in light of the numbers involved.

As at the postprimary level, three or four aptitude tests constitute an effective admission series. In the case of the I-D tests, these may be selected from the 5 instruments listed in Table 18, in accordance with the nature of the curriculum to which the applicants will be admitted.

For admission to a general curriculum (e.g., liberal arts), a balance series of verbal and quantitative measure should be applied, since the field of specialization each candidate will eventually enter is unknown. If all five tests are used, a composite reliability coefficient of .87 and a composite validity coefficient of .61 can be expected. But the high degree of overlap between the Graphs and Arithmetic Tests suggests that using both of these instruments is not worthwhile. On technical grounds, the Arithmetic Test is somewhat superior, because of its lower intertest correlations; but the Graphs Test tends to be more advanced examinee groups, as earlier noted. Which one should be applied, therefore, depends mainly on local conditions. Either way, a total administration time of approximately one hour and 45 minutes will be required.

If the curriculum has a science bias, the World Information Test can reasonably be dropped, resulting in a more economical three-test series. Similarly, the Science Information Test is not applicable to curricula that emphasize commerce, administration, or other non-science courses. For these reduced series the Arithmetic Test has been found significantly better than the Graphs Test in the preliminary studies that have been completed, and may be the more appropriate one to apply in all situations.

Overall, the validities for all of these postsecondary applications are approximately the same as those obtained at the postprimary level, and the improvements charted in Figure 23 are again the appropriate projections. At both levels even better results should be obtained when differential test weights consistently effective for the intended application have been developed.

SELECTION FOR POSTPRIMARY TECHNICAL COURSES

Technical selection programs in the developing countries, whether in the context of vocational schools or in-house industrial training courses must take account not only of the related measurement issues, but also of the social status of blue-collar occupations. Typically, these are considered far less desirable than jobs in offices or in government service; and many individuals who apply for technical training do so only because nothing else is available, or because they

TABLE 18

The I-D Postsecondary Scholastic Aptitude Tests*

	GPH	RTH	SCI	WLD	Reliability	Validity
RDH	.34	.14	.36	.49	.76	.52
GPH		.58	.18	.14	.79	.39
RTH			.10	-.03	.88	.37
SCI				.34	.54	.36
WLD					.73	.31

*Details on the numbers of examinees, criterion instruments, etc., may be found in the I-D Technical Manual.

think they may be able to parlay this experience into a more suitable job later. Unless special care is taken to assess the applicants' interest as well as potential, a sizable proportion may wander to other pursuits as soon as the opportunity arises.

One appropriate precaution is afforded by the preselection interview, which can and should be directed mainly toward the applicant's actual aspirations. Interviews for technical training should generally be longer than those used for academic admission programs, and it should be expected that a larger percentage of applicants will be rejected at this stage of the selection procedures.

A second, perhaps less apparent implication is that school achievement tests should _not_ be used as an initial screening hurdle. Even though success in technical training programs will depend in part on the same kinds of characteristics that high academic performance requires, the applicants who were successful in school and yet could not continue their education are apt to be those least satisfied with blue-collar work, and therefore particularly poor risks. To ensure that the trainees selected can cope with the theoretical as well as practical courses, the use of a scholastic aptitude test is a safer procedure.

Thus, selection programs for postprimary technical training include two major components. One is a set of aptitude tests designed to measure scholastic ability as well as technical skills more specifically related to job performance; and the other is a staff interview oriented toward the applicant's long-range aspirations. They may be administered jointly, or separated into a two-stage sequential procedure.

For selection into the skilled trades, the I-D series provides seven relevant tests, as listed in Table 19. Only five of these tests are used for any one application, however. _Either_ Similarities _or_ Verbal Analogies is used as a measure of reasoning skill; and _either_ Manual Dexterity _or_ Finger Dexterity is used as the dexterity measure.

In the choice between Similarities and Verbal Analogies, it is almost always the latter that should be applied. As noted in Chapter 6, the Similarities Test cannot yet be regarded as fully developed; and even an improved form of this test is likely to be less valid for most technical courses than a more orthodox scholastic ability measure. Only when the curriculum contains an exceptionally low proportion of theory courses (as might be the case, for example, in the training of welders) should a less verbal test be considered.

The selection of the appropriate dexterity test for a given application should be based on the kinds of manual skills that this particular job will require. In most of the trades studies to date, the Manual

TABLE 19

The I-D Skilled Trade Selection Tests**

	VAL	MEC	FIG	BOX	MAN	FIN	Reliability	Validity*
SIM	?	.47	.23	.24	.13	.16	.56	.30
VAL		.36	.19	.28	.17	.03	.87	.45
MEC			.36	.28	.20	.23	.79	.45
FIG				.23	.14	.15	.70	.35
BOX					.13	.15	.72	.33
MAN						.47	.83	.38
FIN							.89	.37

*Because the Similarities Test was used in most of the West African studies, the validity of the Verbal Analogies Test is a preliminary estimate, based on data from other locations. The validity of the Finger Dexterity Test is for electrician trainees, that of Manual Dexterity for other trade courses.

**Details on the numbers of examinees, criterion instruments, etc., may be found in the I-D Technical Manual.

Dexterity Test has seemed to be the more relevant, and has in fact turned out to be the more accurate measure. The selection of trainees for electrician courses has been the one exception, and for these courses the Finger Dexterity Test should be applied.

The most commonly used combination of tests, therefore, has been Verbal Analogies, Mechanical Information, Figures, Boxes, and Manual Dexterity, administered in that order. The total time required to give all five is approximately two and a half hours, and specially trained examiners are essential. In accordance with the data in Table 19, a composite reliability of approximately .89 and a composite validity of approximately .63 can be projected. The corresponding gains in trainee proficiency are charted in Figure 24.

If a two-stage selection process is used, the most appropriate tests for initial screening are the Verbal Analogies and Mechanical Information Tests, which do not require highly trained examiner personnel. In this case, the three remaining tests and the interview are applied at the second stage for final selection. Or all five aptitude tests may be used initially, so that the interview alone comprises the final hurdle.

FIGURE 24

Validity of the I-D Skilled Trade Selection Tests

Minimum Requirements for Admission	Percentage Selected Likely to Perform Above Level of Present Average Student
Present standards only	50%
Present standards and I-D Stanine 6	76%
Present standards and I-D Stanine 7	85%
Present standards and I-D Stanine 8	90%
Present standards and I-D Stanine 9	96%

In technical selection programs for occupations other than the skilled trades (e.g., for the various categories of "junior technician" or "technical assistant" courses), the dexterity test is generally inappropriate and need not be applied. A useful substitute is the Arithmetic Test, especially when some of the trainees may later have opportunities for more advanced technical courses. From this revised series, composite validities near .60 can be expected.

Combinations of scores that would permit differential predictions among the various categories of skilled trades have not as yet been discovered. In many applications it is necessary to make not only selection but also placement decisions—to decide who should become a carpenter, who a machinist, who a mechanic, etc.; and a procedure for weighting the tests differently for each trade so as to obtain separate indexes of potential would be most helpful. But consistent patterns of relationships between the individual tests and the various trades have not emerged from the data. And, given the generally poor results of attempts at differential prediction in the industrialized countries, further research of this type is apt to be equally unproductive.

Applications beyond the postprimary level converge to the programs already described for academic admission of curricula with a science bias. None of the seven tests discussed in this section should be used with groups who have had more than nine years of education.

SELECTION FOR CLERICAL COURSES

For clerical selection programs, the scholastic achievement test returns to the ranks of useful screening procedures. Because the language and numerical skills emphasized in the regular school curriculum are directly pertinent to the typical clerical functions, and because the above problems of social stigma do not arise, applicants who were successful in school are generally good prospects for training as office workers. And although it would not be economical to construct special achievement tests for use as selection devices, indexes already available can and should be applied as the initial hurdle.

Final selection is made, as before, on the basis of appropriate aptitude tests and an interview directed at such personal requirements (diction, neatness, appearance, etc.) as may be considered important to the positions that the applicants will be expected to fill. At the more advanced levels, proficiency tests in typing, shorthand, and other skills presumably acquired in earlier courses also may have to be added to the selection procedure. But this poses no serious developmental problems, since proficiency tests do not require "cultural" modifications, and standard techniques can be applied.

If the numbers are large, it is appropriate to administer the aptitude tests and the interviews (plus proficiency measures) in separate stages. But splitting the aptitude tests themselves is not necessary in clerical selection, because these kinds of abilities can be measured reliably in less time than technical skills, and it is simpler to administer the entire series than to set up for two separate sessions.

The I-D tests used for these applications include the Verbal Analogies, Coding, Names, Table Reading, and Arithmetic Tests, administered in that order. Either the Low form or High form of the Verbal Analogies Test may be used, in accordance with the applicants' educational level; and, since the instructions for these two tests are identical, groups of mixed educational backgrounds can be tested at the same time by giving each examinee the appropriate test paper once the explanations have been completed. Approximately one-and-a-half hours is required for the five-test series.

The statistical properties of these tests are summarized in Table 20. From these data, a composite reliability above .92 and a composite validity of approximately .62 can be projected. The equivalent gain in trainee performance is charted in Figure 25.

TABLE 20

The I-D Clerical Selection Series**

	COD	NAM	TAB	RTH	Reliability	Validity*
VAL	.26	.35	.35	.34	.87	.55
VAH	.20	.12	.22	.18	.75	.54
COD		.42	.43	.31	.87	.34
NAM			.45	.39	.73	.39
TAB				.34	.91	.44
RTH					.88	.40

*Average coefficients for samples at varying educational levels.

**Details on the numbers of examinees, criterion instruments, etc., may be found in the I-D Technical Manual.

FIGURE 25

Validity of the I-D Clerical Selection Tests

Minimum Requirements for Admission	Percentage Selected Likely to Perform Above Level of Present Average Student
Present standards only	50%
Present standards and I-D Stanine 6	76%
Present standards and I-D Stanine 7	84%
Present standards and I-D Stanine 8	90%
Present standards and I-D Stanine 9	96%

For vocational schools that offer both technical and business courses, some differential placement is possible on the basis of these tests and corresponding tests of the technical aptitude series. Largely as a result of the high internal consistency of the clerical series, the correlation between a composite of Coding, Names, and Table Reading and a composite of Boxes, Figures, and Manual Dexterity is below .45, which affords sufficient uniqueness for placement decisions. In these applications, the applicants can be screened initially on the Verbal Analogies and Arithmetic Tests, and then given the six-test technical/ clerical series as part of the final selection procedure.

NOTE

1. This coefficient of uniqueness is explained in J. C. Flanagan, _Technical Report, Flanagan Aptitude Classification Tests_ (Chicago: Science Research Associates, 1959).

PART IV

DEVELOPING LOCAL TESTING RESOURCES

CHAPTER

8

THE FEASIBILITY OF A CENTRALIZED INSTITUTION

In many developing countries, testing reform requires not only the test-related investments considered in Chapter 2 but also a substantial expansion of the professional and logistic infrastructure. Additional specialists must be trained, adequate facilities must be provided, and new bureaucracies must be created. The basic mechanisms for effective testing do not exist, and the priority need is for the requisite capabilities and institutions.

In these situations the cost of testing reform is so high that it can normally be undertaken only at the central government level, with a sizable investment of public funds and substantial external assistance. Given these much higher stakes, the cost-effectiveness questions first raised in Chapter 2 must be explored even more thoroughly and extended to a variety of other nontechnical issues.

THE MAXIMUM PAYOFF POTENTIAL

The first step, as before, is to enumerate the benefits that are likely to be realized from the project if it is fully successful. These include the improvements that should result from the specific testing services that will be provided, and such additional benefits as can be expected from the availability of expanded professional resources.

Improvements in Testing

Proposals for testing reform or requests for technical assistance to testing are usually the result of certain specific pressures. Something has gone wrong, and someone reasonably important wants it corrected. The first AID/AIR project, as earlier noted, grew out of the problems of the technical training institutes that the U.S. government was supporting; each subsequent effort has also been triggered by one major need. "We must solve Problem A" has been the normal beginning.

If institution-building is not required, such a proposal can reasonably be evaluated on the basis of the payoff of having better tests to apply to Problem A, and of the cost of developing these better tests, as already outlined in Chapter 2. No other issues need be considered. But if institution-building also must be undertaken, the analysis cannot be this simple; the institution-building component will add an "overhead" figure of perhaps 2,000 or 12,000 percent to the basic cost of the testing program, and the payoff of Problem A will seldom justify so large an investment. A feasibility study based on a single problem will almost always result in negative recommendations.

But countries that have Problem A typically have also a Problem C, a Problem F, etc., and the sum of the payoffs for a combination of these could make institution-building a prudent investment. And it is therefore suggested that the appropriate response to an invitation to help solve Problem A is to offer instead to examine the full range of problems related to testing. A feasibility study of lesser scope will usually turn out to have been itself cost-ineffective.

Thus, the assessment should properly begin with a comprehensive inventory of the testing problems that a professional center might help to resolve in this country. And the procedures of Chapter 2 should then be applied to each of these problems, using the appropriate one of the three methods of payoff projection suggested. As before, improvements in both accuracy and logistics should be considered, and a reasonable degree of quantification should be attempted.

Since the objective at this stage is to obtain a maximum possible payoff projection, virtually all types of testing problems should be included in the assessment. But care should also be taken to ensure that each of the needs that can be evaluated at only the lowest level of payoff projection—i.e., in terms of the magnitude of the problem rather than the probable gain—is in fact a "possible" application. For, in so broad a survey, a number of inappropriate test applications will frequently be suggested.

One class of inappropriate applications consists of expressed needs that, on closer examination, are found not to be problems at all in this particular country. Tests for career guidance are the prime case in point. In nearly every survey that was conducted, the introduction of effective guidance procedures was strongly supported as one of the country's most critical testing needs. And yet, there were only isolated cases in which guidance tests, once developed, actually could be applied. The quantities and varieties of educational opportunity that are the "so what" of guidance did not exist, and the system as a whole did not provide the necessary flexibility for branching to different pursuits. Though guidance could quite properly be considered an essential component of the educational process from a philosophic point of view, it could not be implemented in these countries without a host of accompanying systems changes that were not likely to be made in the foreseeable future. Including improved guidance procedures among the outcomes expected would have distorted the payoff projections.

Similarly, there may be considerable interest in the identification of exceptionally able youngsters in "disadvantaged" rural areas, so that their talents will not be wasted, as seems now to be the case in many locations. In an earlier discussion, it was noted that tests for this purpose can in fact be constructed, and can quite accurately identify talents that are passed over by the traditional examination procedures. But for actual payoff, identifying them is not enough. To transition to a quality school, many of these talented youngsters may need a period of intensive remedial learning—will opportunities for this be provided? To be able to stay in school, they will probably need special financial assistance—is government prepared to grant such support? Unless the results of the new tests can actually be translated into the appropriate action, little payoff can be expected. And the survey must for this reason look beyond the development of tests not now available in the country, and consider also the arrangements that have been made for practical implementation.

A second class of inappropriate applications consists of the unfortunately large number of legitimate test needs which are not yet within the state of the art. That these include some of the more exciting payoffs is regrettable, but should not sway the appraisal, for although it may be within the realm of possibility for the proposed project to achieve the methodological breakthroughs required, this is scarcely the most likely result. The selection of agricultural extension trainees who will be content to work in the rural areas rather than to flock to the big cities, for example, requires the measurement of characteristics that have proved elusive even in countries with long testing traditions, and the survey should not presume that the task will be easier in a developing country. For all payoffs that depend on the measurement of such slippery factors as "personality" or "motivation," past findings suggest a pessimistic appraisal.

Deleting these kinds of unrealistic applications from the inventory initially compiled will reduce the list, but even this reduced inventory will generally result in an impressive profile of payoff potential. At a minimum, it will normally include the improvements attributable to more accurate selection for secondary schools, trade centers, technical institutes, universities, and a wide variety of industrial, civil service, and military training courses; the improvements attributable to more reliable proficiency and certification exams; and the savings attributable to the logistic improvements that would be made in each of these separate operations. The total payoff potential is normally high in any country that has reached the stage at which an investment in modern testing is seriously being considered.

That this estimate is a maximum projection that will probably not be attained is, of course, understood. Establishing a center that can serve both university and military needs may not be administratively feasible, for example; and the above gross projection will have to be further refined in the light of such nontechnical limitations. But it is important to establish the maximum nevertheless, because many of these apparent constraints may in fact be negotiable, as will be pointed out in a later discussion. The most useful feasibility study often is one that does not aim for a flat "yes or no" appraisal, but that instead tries to define the minimum scope the proposed institution must have to make a local investment or external assistance worthwhile.

Impact on Social Change

In addition to the total payoff expected from the various testing services the proposed unit could provide, the very existence of a professional institution in this field can have important by-product effects. And, from a broader perspective than that of the testing specialist, certain of these by-products may well be judged to represent an even higher payoff than that available from the improvement of the country's testing procedures.

The major example of such institutional benefits that is likely to be encountered is in countries that use national or external examinations rather than grades as the basis for awarding graduation diplomas. In these countries, an individual's opportunities for advanced training, his chances for attractive employment, and even the salary that he is paid can depend on the scores that he earns on these certification tests, which remain a part of his personal record for life. And the curriculum of every school and the efforts of every teacher are naturally oriented toward these examinations as the de facto goal of all education.

In theory, this is fully as workable a system as the quality-point grading methods that American educators tend to prefer. If the examination accurately reflects the skills and values that the country's youth should be developing as a result of their schooling, it is in fact the superior procedure, since the school-to-school variations in grading standards inherent in the American system are automatically avoided. But in practice, the actual examinations are typically found to be very much out of date. Their content may emphasize the skills that are appropriate for the tiny minority of the population that will eventually reach the highest educational levels—a carryover from colonialist or elitist days. Their format may encourage the rote learning of assorted factual information—a remnant of former pedagogic approaches. And, where this is the case, the examinations can be legitimately regarded as a serious societal problem that retards perhaps more than any other factor the push for rapid modernization.

Yet, scrapping the examination system, as visiting specialists often suggest, is not a realistic solution. For the examination does help to maintain a uniformity of standards that, given the shortage of qualified teachers, no system of classroom grading could possibly attain. It does serve as a check on the sometimes large proportion of schools that are operated for profit by entrepreneurs. It does provide negotiable credentials for the many students who must obtain higher education abroad. It is the approach that the people themselves understand, accept, and would be reluctant to surrender. And it is in actuality <u>not</u> the examination but the educational objectives on which it is based that are the root of the problem.

A more productive solution, therefore, is to build on the one outstanding advantage of the examination system, which the deficiencies in its implementation sometimes obscure. A rigid examination system is probably the best of all vehicles—better by far than any available in the American system—for making the changes in the educational process that modernization requires. When the national examination is changed, the curriculum and teaching practices throughout the country begin immediately to fall into line; after the initial growing pains have been surmounted, a changed educational product emerges. The hand that writes the examinations truly controls the most effective of all possible levers to sweeping reform.

Thus, the existence of such an examination system provides an opportunity for payoff far beyond the technical improvement of the examination procedures. A professional testing establishment, more than any other education-related agency or organization, can take the lead in bringing about the needed reforms in objectives, curricula, and instructional methods; and thereby have a significant impact on the full spectrum of national development programs. This outcome cannot be taken for granted, of course, since the professionals' control over the content of the examination is by no means absolute. But the probability of educational reform is so much higher where there is an adequate measurement capability than when there is not that a high payoff potential can and should be projected.

This capability for long-range reform, moreover, can also have important short-term effects. In countries that are making substantial investments in educational innovation—by experimenting with comprehensive schools or schools with a technical bias or other new institutions—changes in the curriculum must be accompanied by corresponding changes in the traditional examinations to be effective. The students in these new streams will insist on socially acceptable graduation credentials; and only the inclusion of these courses among the "official" examination papers can serve this legitimatizing function. Twice during the course of the Nigeria project, a major U.S.-supported educational program introduced innovations not yet reflected in the exams, and on both occasions the West African Examinations Council had to take rapid action to solve the very serious problems that were subsequently encountered. The existence of an institution that was capable of taking these actions—and that was sufficiently sympathetic to innovation to actually take them—had the highly significant payoff of safeguarding two large developmental investments.

The magnitude of the gains that might be realized from this impetus for educational reform and innovation depends on the degree to which the present product of education is out of line with the country's needs; such discrepancies cannot be pinpointed precisely. Perhaps the best approach in a preliminary survey is to try to identify the problems that leaders in both the public and private sectors have experienced in using the graduates of the local schools and making them fully productive. The nature and number of the "hurts" reported by senior officials should permit at least a rough estimate of the potential payoff in the country in question.

Other types of social changes that the proposed institution might stimulate also should be considered, such as its impact on the problem of nepotism, for example. In many cultures the granting of favors to kinsmen and neighbors is a long-standing tradition that is not regarded as wrong by the society; the more enlightened leaders therefore cannot easily change it. But a professional testing center may afford a partial solution. A senior official in one country claimed that since the establishment of the national testing center, he has been able to satisfy his many petitioners by telling them that the law requires testing, that there is a long waiting list for testing, but that he would personally arrange an early appointment for the candidate to give him the best possible chance. And the records of the testing center confirmed that he had indeed written many letters of "personal recommendation" for testing, effecting an immediate social change without violating tradition.

Again, these and similar outcomes cannot be taken for granted. But the provision of an alternative in a situation that now offers no other options clearly should be included in the payoff projection.

Other Research Contributions

A third category of payoffs derives from the fact that the skills needed to staff a professional testing center are the same as those needed for a wide variety of other behavioral science endeavors. When there is no other local capability for meeting these more general research needs, the center may be able gradually to expand its charter, and take on these problems as well. This was the expectation of the University of Malawi, which saw the establishment of a testing center as a vehicle for developing skills applicable to many national needs beyond those tests and examinations. And this was what in fact happened in the project in Korea, where the problems now being addressed by the Korean Institute for Research in the Behavioral Sciences (e.g., family planning) offer potential contributions far greater than those envisioned in this organization's initial testing charter.

Such expansions in scope can reasonably be programmed from the beginning, moreover, because testing reform is an unusually good vehicle for launching a multipurpose research institution. Tests, as has already been noted, are an important aspect of life in many developing countries; an institution that begins with a testing mission can count on more general support than can one devoted to issues which, however vital, are less well understood. Also, there is more of an opportunity in the field of testing than in most other "soft" science projects to make fairly rapid and visible contributions, and thereby establish the embryonic institution's credentials. An additional advantage of considerable practical importance is that a testing center can earn fees to help support itself throughout the early stages, when only a modest government subsidy can be expected. Even institutions that begin life with a global charter may find it useful to concentrate much of their initial effort on testing.

The needs and opportunities for the development of a multipurpose research center is another factor, therefore, that should be specifically evaluated in the survey. If there is such a need, and if the project can be given the scope to fulfill it, a broad range of additional payoffs can be projected.

Overall, the three categories of payoff that have been suggested include the following:

1. The combined payoffs of the improvements that could be made in ongoing test operations;

2. The additional benefits available from the existence of a professional testing resource in stimulating educational reform or other societal change; and

3. The further contributions that would be made if the testing center envolves into a multipurpose behavioral research institution.

Depending on the degree of quantification desired (which, in turn, usually depends on the magnitude of the necessary investment), a feasibility study of one week to one month in length should be sufficient to assemble adequate information on these possibilities in a developing country.

THE LIKELIHOOD OF SUCCESS

Which of the many payoffs that have been identified would actually be achieved as the result of the project cannot be predicted with confidence at the time of the survey. Inevitably, certain important factors will have been overlooked, certain situations will change, and certain seemingly foolproof arrangements will manage somehow to go astray. In testing as in all development projects, there are no advance guarantees.

Still, the maximum estimate that has been projected can be refined by considering also the likelihood of each outcome in the light of specific local conditions. And this should be the second step of the survey. The objectives are first, to provide the decision-maker with further evaluative information and second, to identify weaknesses in the proposed method of project implementation that should be renegotiated to increase its potential attainment.

As a starting point for this type of appraisal, the AID/AIR experience suggests a core of seven basic feasibility questions that were found to be particularly important. It can offer also a rule of thumb for evaluating the answers obtained. If the present situation must change in order to achieve the desired payoff, the finding on this aspect is a negative indication that reduces the project's potential. If the payoff will be achieved unless the present situation unexpectedly changes, the finding is a plus that confirms the above projection. And, although there is no mathematical procedure for adding up these pluses and minuses, such additional feasibility data will naturally permit a more realistic decision.

Three of the questions pertain to the feasibility of actually developing and putting into effect the specific testing services that have been projected, and should be applied to each of the potential test applications. The other four are addressed to the even more basic issue of the likelihood of success in developing a viable professional institution in this country at this particular time, and under the specific arrangements proposed.

Feasibility of the Proposed Test Applications

The focus at this stage of the survey is not on the technical feasibility of the proposed applications, since these issues were considered in compiling the list and all unrealistic suggestions were at that point deleted. Rather, it is on the political and pragmatic factors that determine whether or not a technically sound idea is likely to be implemented in the actual operational setting. From this point of view, the following three questions are especially important:

1. Who is it that regards this problem as a serious "hurt" for which a remedy is urgently needed? In compiling the list of testing needs, a wide variety of sources was no doubt consulted. The relative credibility of these sources was presumably checked as part of the survey. Now these sources should be reviewed again, from a more pragmatic perspective. Given the political realities in this country, how much leverage can each of these sources exert in enlisting the needed cooperation to do the research, and in ensuring that the resulting procedures will in fact be adopted? The greater the leverage of the prospective client, the higher the chance of operational implementation.

Lowest on this criterion is any test application that the survey team itself suggested on the basis of its own observations. No matter how serious this need may be in the abstract, it is not until it is perceived as such by the responsible officials that the support necessary to solve it can realistically be expected. The present situation has to be changed by selling the importance of the problem to the people in charge, and success in effecting this change should not be taken for granted. Applications proposed by the team itself should be treated as long-shot payoff projections.

Somewhat more promising are the needs identified by the professional community, such as university staff, since these individuals can be effective partners in gaining support at the decision-making level. But one should not overestimate the influence of the professional in a developing country. Unless he happens to be in an especially favored position, he may actually have greater difficulty in getting a hearing by senior officials than the visitor from abroad. On balance, an application suggested only at the professional level should be regarded as mildly negative on this first feasibility factor.

Applications suggested by the responsible officials themselves should be assigned a fairly high level of expectation, especially when these officials are in a position to provide the support that will be required. Some caution is indicated whenever the enthusiasm for testing reform in a prospective client organization is limited to one top official, since there is considerable mobility at these senior levels in many developing countries. But even in this instance the above rule suggests an optimistic appraisal inasmuch as the prospects will remain favorable until and unless the situation changes.

The most promising applications of all are those that represent problems the organization must solve, irrespective of the personalities of the incumbents involved. The earlier example of a ministry faced with a rise in the candidates who would sit for an examination from 30,000 to 70,000 students is one such situation in which support is virtually assured. It is difficult to visualize any situational change that would eliminate the need for positive action.

The findings on this feasibility question are useful mainly in discounting the magnitude of the payoff that was earlier projected. For the availability of excellent tests will have little value if there is no eager or even willing consumer.

2. Do the administrative linkages between the professional unit that would develop these tests and the operating unit that would apply them already exist or must these be created? Normally, the planning of the project and the conduct of the feasibility study will be carried out under the auspices of a certain government agency, such as the

Ministry of Education. And unless other arrangements are made, the proposed professional unit would naturally be established as part of that organization. A second important feasibility issue is the extent to which it will be possible to cross bureaucratic lines of authority and actually implement those test applications that are not part of this same organizational structure.

The possibilities in this regard appear to vary greatly from country to country. In some countries it is entirely feasible to include even military testing within the planned scope of an education-based testing center. In others, programs sponsored by the Ministry of Education ipso facto rule out the possibility of university participation, and vice versa. Each of the proposed applications should be checked from this purely bureaucratic point of view, and confirmed or discounted in accordance with local conditions.

The best guide to this assessment, of course, is the history of interactions among the organizations concerned. If, as in one country, the ministry and the university share staff, so that many of the senior personnel hold dual positions, services for both organizations can realistically be projected. If, as in many other countries, these organizations have set up separate units to carry out parallel functions, such a projection would be unduly optimistic, for, even though these cooperative relationships may subsequently develop—and, in fact, did in the case of two of the projects—this is not be most probable expectation.

The greatest utility of this appraisal is in renegotiating the proposed project arrangements. Often it can be shown that the project will be a viable one only if it is carried out as a multiagency effort; sometimes this demonstration will proved persuasive. Agreement may be obtained to establish the center under the supervision of a governing board representating of the various organizations; this is a generally effective vehicle for ensuring a broad scope of services, as will be further discussed in the following chapter.

3. To what extent does the logistic infrastructure necessary to implement each of the proposed applications already exist, and to what extent must it be created? Carrying out a large testing program, especially on a nationwide level, requires a wide range of administrative mechanisms and arrangements. Because the employment of full-time personnel to conduct a few testing sessions per year is totally unrealistic, a large corps of field supervisors and proctors available on an as-needed basis must be recruited and trained. Because there will generally be only a limited number of facilities throughout the

country that can accommodate large testing sessions, foolproof provisions for the use of these facilities must be made. Because the security of the tests is always a major concern, tightly controlled transmittal and distribution procedures must be developed. The starting-up costs of a new testing program, and the time that these arrangements require, can be substantial.

Accordingly, each of the proposed applications should also be checked from the point of view of logistic provisions. If the task is simply to introduce new instruments and streamlined procedures into an existing testing program that has been carried out for some years, fairly rapid progress and early payoff can be expected. If the task is to greatly expand or totally reengineer an established program, progress is likely to be much slower. If the task is to introduce testing into a situation in which testing has not been the practice before, a considerable lag to actual payoff should be projected. The separate applications that have been listed can vary widely in this regard.

The main utility of this further appraisal is that it adds a time perspective to the payoff projections. And this should be useful both for the feasibility evaluation and the subsequent scheduling of the activities to be undertaken.

Viability of the Proposed Institution

The other four questions pertain to the likelihood that the institution to be developed—as distinct from the services it will provide—will be successful. The institutions to which AID/AIR assistance has been provided have ranged from dynamic establishments that have increased their scope and professional reputation to perenially struggling establishments that have survived only in the technical sense of not emptying the building and locking the doors. And it is clearly useful to try to assess in advance the status of the situational factors that facilitate or obstruct the development of a viable institution.

Trying to specify all of these factors was, of course, far beyond the scope of the research.[1] But the factors raised in the following questions did seem, at least in retrospect, to explain the differences in institutional development that were observed:

1. Who would serve as the proposed institution's director? The single most important requirement, all of these past studies suggest, is the immediate availability of a competent and preferably charismatic director. Usually, it is during the first two years of an

institution-building effort that its eventual viability is effectively predetermined; the crucial factor in this early stage has consistently seemed to be the quality of the director. He has the most significant direct effect on the program because many of the crucial steps are ones that he personally must accomplish, and a perhaps equally important indirect affect in that outside agencies and officials respond to an organization that has not yet developed its own "institutional character" mainly on the basis of who is in charge.

If one of the country's top professionals will be assigned, and if he is prepared to give the project enough of his time, fairly rapid progress can be expected. If an expatriate specialist with equivalent qualifications must assume these functions while the local specialists are being trained, the results can be equally effective, but a lower expectancy should be projected at the time of the survey. If it is necessary to begin with a director (local or expatriate) of lesser stature, the outcome should be judged problematic. Clearly, this is another aspect of the proposed arrangements on which renegotiation sometimes must be attempted.

2. Is the proposed institution likely to attract and retain top professional talent? That there will be enough trained personnel to staff the project when it begins cannot be expected, and is not necessary for the program's success. So long as adequate time and funds are budgeted—and this is, of course, essential—the present shortage of trained specialists need not in itself be regarded as a major deterrent.

But there are two other aspects of the local personnel picture that should be checked explicitly in the survey, for problems in either of these can reduce the likelihood of success irrespective of the magnitude of the training provisions.

The first is the availability of qualified trainees to enter the special programs that will be established. Is there a sufficient pool of individuals with undergraduate degrees in related fields (e.g., education) who can be released from their present duties to begin a career in testing? Are there at least a few individuals with higher qualifications (e.g., a master's degree in psychology or statistics) who can enter advanced measurement courses? If there are not, the country must be prepared either to invest in an exceptionally long period of institutional development, or to admit that it is not yet ready for a major effort in testing.

In collecting information on these points, it is best to work not with statistics on high-level manpower, but with the names of the actual individuals who are being considered, and to interview a sample of these individuals as part of the survey. Using this approach, it was found in one country that there was but a single individual with an advanced degree at all related to testing, and that even he could not be spared from his present administrative position; in another country the seemingly large pool of available candidates consisted mainly of rejects of other training programs, of professional students who had been accumulating degrees in a wide range of courses, and of individuals who for one reason or another could not leave the country for advanced education. Such more precise information is clearly essential for a realistic assessment.

The second related consideration is the degree to which the proposed institution will be able to compete for the available talent with the many other organizations that would draw on the same resources. From the point of view of the prospective trainee, entering an essentially new field of as yet unknown status in his country entails a much higher risk than pursuing one of the well-established careers; and if the conditions of service are not up to par, he is likely to turn down the opportunity for training, or take it and then look for a better job. What the proposed institution will be able to offer in terms of salaries, fringe benefits, upward mobility, statutory protection, and all of the other conditions that are spelled out precisely for the standard public service positions should be checked as part of the survey, to ensure that a career in testing will be competitive with the candidates' other options. If not, it may prove impossible to meet the projected training quotas with the caliber of people desired.

The fact that both this and the preceding question relate to personnel issues underscores the pivotal role of this factor in the development of a professional institution. A project that cannot assemble the requisite skills will fail, irrespective of the amount of money or equipment or professional assistance that may be provided.

3. Do the testing services that are to be implemented immediately include at least one that is a permanent and highly visible operation? Because institution-building is a lengthy process, another of the basic requirements for success is survival during the developmental phases. Before the institution can become truly viable and self-sufficient, many unanticipated events are likely to threaten the continuity of support on which it is dependent, and there should be adequate safeguards to help it weather these storms. A change in government, the transfer of a minister, a revision of external assistance policy, and the replacement of an AID mission director are examples of the storms the AID/AIR projects encountered.

The most adequate safeguard for institutional survival—recognizing that none can be absolute—is a charter that includes at least one of the testing services that in this particular country is judged essential. Normally, such "essential" services consist of only three applications: the certification examinations of the secondary school level, the entrance examination to the academic curriculum at the secondary school level, and the university admission tests, in that order of importance. All other applications, however much they have contributed to the above payoff projections, are of relatively little significance against the present criteria of survival. And the inclusion of at least one of the essential three in the institution's initial charter should therefore be given considerable weight (and perhaps renegotiated) as a central factor in the likelihood of success.

One drawback to the inclusion of such services as post-secondary certification testing is that these can benefit least from the new methodologies suggested in this handbook, and that the staff time they will consume will necessarily detract from the more innovative types of test applications. But, on balance, it must be concluded that the increased prospects of continuity make this trade-off worthwhile.

4. How appropriate is the institution's proposed organizational affiliation, and how feasible will it be to change this affiliation as the program develops? The two main characteristics of an appropriate "home" for a testing activity have already been noted. The first is that it afford maximum opportunity for crossing bureaucratic lines of authority to provide testing services to other organizations. And the second is that it be able to attract and retain top professional talent. For long-range viability, both are essential.

If the proposed charter is such that the institution will from the first be established within a framework that meets both of these criteria, this final feasibility question need not be further considered. But such charters may well be the exception. None of the AID/AIR projects began with an optimum organizational structure from these points of view, and the same may have to be the case in future efforts in other countries. The decision to begin with a modest scope and then grow as accomplishments mount and capabilities develop is a tempting bureaucratic position; in some instances it may in fact prove impossible to identify the ideal home in advance, at the time of the feasibility study.

Thus, the indicated approach will often be to negotiate for the broadest scope possible along the lines suggested above and in the following chapter, and then to apply this final question to assess the institution's growth potential. Is the proposed organizational structure a reasonable springboard for the development of an influential professional center in this country, or is it more likely to act as a restraining force that will confine the institution to its initial limited charter? What is the most reasonable projection five to ten years into the future?

Specific criteria for answering this question cannot yet be suggested. It would be comforting to believe, in accordance with current doctrine, that ad hoc arrangements which defer the organizational issue are not an appropriate beginning; and that a firm base within a traditional organization should always be sought. But the AID/AIR experience does not confirm this popular view. The West Africa project, which has shown the greatest professional growth, began as a unilateral American effort, was later linked to an established organization, and became an integral part of that organization later still. The Korea project, which has also been highly successful, began as a binational activity with interim organizational links for administrative purposes only, and then grew into a new interministerial organization. The projects that began as an integral part of a traditional bureaucracy have yet to attain much less exceed the initial expectations.

These experiences are not readily generalizable, however. The sample is far too small to overcome the many other local differences in these undertakings. It is also possible that under other organizational arrangements the West Africa and Korea projects might have developed even faster.* But it does seem clear that the opportunities for organizational mobility are important to institution-building, and that they should be evaluated without preconceived constraints in the feasibility study.

COST PROJECTIONS

As in the costing of individual testing programs, there is usually little difficulty in estimating the recurrent costs of operating a testing

---

*An earlier attempt to establish ties with the West African Examinations Council was unsuccessful, perhaps because it was not adequately pursued. But it is also true that the project was a much more attractive one in terms of staff, instruments, reputation, and established clientele at the time this liaison was subsequently effected.

center. Many of the cost elements (salaries, rentals, etc.) are fixed; and the variable costs (travel, supplies, etc.) can be approximated from the scope of activities that has been projected. For this latter component, the guidelines suggested by the experience of other testing establishments may be helpful, and the annual reports of such organizations as the West African Examinations Council or the Korean Institute for Research in the Behavioral Sciences should be consulted.

Estimating the capital costs of developing the institution into a professionally viable organization is more difficult, especially with respect to the external assistance component. There is no easy way to predict how long the process of "professionalization" is apt to require, and the intercountry differences in this respect appear to be large. Only the most general guidelines can be suggested.

Foreign Advisers

The cost of the foreign specialists who may have to be brought in on a resident basis throughout the developmental phases is normally the capital cost that is the most expensive. But, in most of the developing countries, this cost cannot be avoided. For, testing specialists everywhere in the world learn the key job skills on an apprenticeship basis after their formal professional training has been completed; when senior personnel to guide this apprenticeship are not available, they must be specially provided. No one in the United States would assign a new Ph.D. or a Ph.D. without directly related experience to the management of a large testing operation; no one should attempt this in a developing country.

Given the high cost of this component, an estimate of the number of years of outside assistance that will be required must be made as part of the feasibility study. As a general guide, the following procedure may be suggested. Identify the three positions in the proposed institution that will require the highest level of professional skill. Evaluate the backgrounds of the candidates for these three positions, and determine the number of years of formal training that the most junior of these candidates will need to meet the minimum educational requirements for the least demanding of these positions. Then add two years to this figure to obtain an estimate of the number of years of specialist residency that will be required. The result should not be interpreted as a firm figure, but rather as an "order of magnitude" for purposes of the feasibility evaluation.

The number of specialists needed per year should be determined by developing a detailed staffing pattern and training schedule, in accordance with the planned scope and local conditions. In general, two to four outside specialists is an appropriate number during the initial years, depending on the size of the proposed institution.

Professional Training

A second major cost item is the provision of formal training for the professional staff. Normally, this training will have to be carried out in other countries that offer the advanced measurement programs required.

To the maximum extent possible, the amounts and type of training to be provided should be geared to the present qualifications of the candidates and the formal instruction that their new positions will actually require. And, from these points of view, a Ph.D. degree need *not* be considered a minimum prerequisite, as tends to be the case in the highly developed countries. There is much to be gained from a nondegree program that focuses on measurement and related courses, from an assignment to an operational testing center, or from a combined work-study program that includes both applied and academic components. Even "short" measurement courses, such as those offered periodically in Princeton by Educational Testing Services and in Lagos by the West African Examinations Council, can be extremely helpful.

At the same time, however, the importance of an advanced degree as a status symbol also must be considered. In some countries it may be possible to attract able candidates to a program that does not end with the conferral of a diploma. In some, an advanced degree is essential to command the professional respect that both the individual and the institution must have to be effective. The appropriate mix of training must reflect also these nontechnical considerations, and must therefore be developed on an ad hoc basis, specifically for each country.

For purposes of the feasibility study, a reasonable projection is an average of eighteen months for each professional position at a supervisory level. But this general estimate should be refined, whenever possible, in the light of the actual local conditions.

Facilities and Equipment

A testing center, unlike many other types of institutions, does not require a specialized physical plant. The centers associated with the AID/AIR research have been sited in residential dwellings, on a college campus, in an ultramodern skyscraper, and in other structures with entirely adequate working conditions. Special construction costs need not be projected.

The most important type of specialized equipment that is required is adequate duplicating machinery for producing test forms with a minimum of delay. Although the final test forms would normally be printed at a professional printing house, the need for rapid reproduction of trial tests (and perhaps numerous revisions) makes an adequate in-house duplication feasibility essential. Basic multilith equipment or other processes that can accommodate drawings as well as text should be provided from the time the project begins, and the addition of more elaborate units later should be projected.

Next in importance is high-speed data processing equipment, including a document reader for test scoring and a medium-capacity computer. The procurement of such equipment can be deferred until the scope of activities justify the expense but, in light of the long delivery lags, should be planned well in advance. The availability of a computer has many advantages in addition to data processing (e.g., in stimulating research), and methods for obtaining one at the earliest possible time, such as cost-sharing arrangements or the provision of services to other organizations, should be explored. Because it is generally advisable to rent rather than purchase this type of equipment, its cost will eventually have to be subsumed under the center's recurrent expenses, but it can be considered a reasonable capital investment throughout the developmental stages.

Another cost to be projected is that of stocking an adequate professional library, including if possible microfilm readers and records as well as books. Among the recurrent expenses, subscriptions to the major measurement journals also should be included.

Overall, the hardware costs of a testing facility are relatively modest, and procurement can be phased over a fairly long period of time. As earlier noted, it is the professional skills that are the most costly and most crucial component.

Cost Reduction

One of the ways in which the establishment of a centralized testing facility can help to reduce the costs of separately administered testing programs was described in Chapter 2. This is by combining the testing operations of a number of organizations that have similar needs, and thereby lowering both the costs of test development and the recurrent expenses. A second important saving is in reducing the huge sums that many developing countries now must spend to maintain the security of their tests before they are given. Once the institution has developed the necessary logistic infrastructure and is capable of producing alternate forms of the major tests, many of the current costly precautions can be eased, and a sizable saving effected.

Another cost benefit of a multipurpose testing center is that it can provide services to organizations that do not subsidize its operations (e.g., to the private sector), and earn income to help defray other expenses. Such income can be substantial. The earnings of the West African Examinations Council last year from testing fees charged to nongovernment users were in excess of U.S.$30,000—sufficient to pay the rental costs of a computer—and the possibilities of developing an active service component should therefore be assessed as yet another part of the feasibility study.

CHECKLIST OF FEASIBILITY QUESTIONS

There were 11 major questions related to the desirability of an investment in institution-building raised in this chapter.

These may be summarized briefly as follows:

1. What is the maximum payoff that would result from the introduction of the needed improvements in the country's testing programs? After discounting those applications that are technically or administratively unlikely, what is the probably payoff to be projected?

2. What additional payoffs might be realized from the institution's potential impact on educational reform and other societal change?

3. What further payoffs would be realized if this institution expands its charter beyond testing to multipurpose social research? Is such an expansion realistic?

4. In light of the infrastructure and operational mechanisms to be developed, what is a reasonable time frame to attach to the above payoff projections?

5. Will the proposed institution have from the first the services of a capable and charismatic project director?

6. Will the proposed institution be able to attract and retain the professional talent required?

7. Does the institution's initial charter include at least one "essential" program that would help to ensure its survival?

8. Will the institution's initial organizational affiliation be sufficiently flexible to permit change if these linkages prove too restrictive?

9. Using the qualification gap between the planned professional positions and the available candidates for these positions as a guide, how many years of outside specialist services will be required?

10. What mix of formal education, work-study programs, and short courses should be projected? What are the attendant costs and the time required?

11. To what extent will the institution be able to defray its operating costs through earned income for services provided to outside organizations?

A number of these issues will be further explored in the following chapter on organization and operating procedures.

NOTES

1. A research study addressed specifically to the key issues in institution-building was carried out, under AID contract, a few years ago. The final report of this study is Milton J. Esman, The Institution Building Concepts: An Interim Appraisal (University of Pittsburgh Graduate School of Public and International Affairs, March, 1967).

CHAPTER 9
ORGANIZATION AND OPERATING PROCEDURES

Once it has been decided to proceed with an institutional development program, many additional highly specific decisions have to be made. The general structure and scope projected during the feasibility study must be elaborated in full detail; the exact mechanics of implementation must be developed; both short- and long-range activity targets have to be set. And even though many of the decisions are likely to be changed as the institution develops, their influence throughout the initial phase—when the entire concept may be on trial—makes careful planning at this beginning stage especially important.

This chapter describes the different approaches to program implementation that were followed at the various project locations; where possible, it relates these to subsequent accomplishments and limitations. But broad generalizations cannot be attempted, for none of the topics discussed in this handbook is so highly dependent on local conditions as the specific program mechanics, and there may well be as many "ideal" approaches as there are developing countries. The objective in this concluding chapter is simply to present a broad range of alternatives for local consideration.

LEGAL STATUS

The decision that is made about the organizational locus of the testing establishment can have far-reaching consequences, as described in the preceding chapter. Careful consideration should be given first to the selection of the agency or agencies through which the center will be legally incorporated within the government structure, and then to the exact nature of its interconnections with the agency selected. Whether this is to be a permanent or interim arrangement also should be decided.

No two of the testing establishments that were created or expanded as part of the AID/AIR projects are identical in organizational structure. But they can be grouped into four general types of institutions that may be regarded as fundamentally different models for institution-building. The AID/AIR experience with each type will be reviewed from the points of view of (1) ease of establishment, (2) recruitment of staff, (3) research opportunities, (4) practical applications, and (5) overall evaluation.

The Testing Division of a Government Agency or Department

The simplest organizational approach is to establish the testing unit as an integral part of one of the operating departments of the central government structure. This was the model used in both the Liberia and the Thailand projects; in both instances with the National Department (or Ministry) of Education. The Liberia Testing Center was established as part of the Student Personnel Services Unit of the Department of Education, the Thailand Selection Research Project as part of the Teacher Training Department of the Ministry of Education. Technical assistance to the former was provided for a period of nearly four years, to the latter for 21 months.

Ease of Establishment

In both instances, the establishment of the activity posed no special problems. There were some delays attributable to the many steps required to execute a binational assistance agreement, but the intracountry arrangements were far less demanding than in the other implementation approaches. Ease of establishment is one of the advantages inherent in this first model, since a new internal unit typically can be created at the discretion of the agency head without outside approval.

Recruitment of Staff

The professional staff in this model are necessarily part of the regular civil service, subject to all of the standard regulations. This has the advantages of ensuring job security for the staff, and of providing them with the full range of benefits that are the norm in countries in which the government is by far the major employer. But it also has the disadvantage of precluding special incentives for the development of specialized measurement skills, since most governments apply only such advancement criteria as are equally applicable to all positions throughout the service.

Which of these has the greater impact on the opportunities for attracting and retaining staff may depend on the size of the establishment to which the center belongs. In Thailand, the huge reservoir of professional talent that is part of the Teacher Training Department could be (and was) tapped to staff the center—a number of career civil servants with special interests in this field were identified and simply assigned to these positions. Recruitment and retention both were facilitated by the center's status as an integral agency function. But in Liberia, the three-man Student Personnel Services Unit had not comparable in-house resources, and individuals who were not already part of the civil service had to be recruited specifically for these positions. And, here, the inability of the center to offer extra rewards for the extra training required posed recruitment difficulties that never were fully surmounted. Candidates could (and did) opt for positions in other agencies that offered the identical benefits without subjecting them to the rigors of advanced measurement courses.

On balance, civil service positions are superior to positions in less stable organizations, as will be noted in the later discussion of the Nigerian Aptitude Testing Unit. But they may be less attractive than positions in permanent establishments that are devoted exclusively or primarily to testing, and that have the flexibility to reflect this orientation in the conditions of service.

Research Opportunities

Both centers proved to be excellent homes for research, and at both an impressive number of studies has been completed. Part of the reason, perhaps, is that no agency has easier access to large samples of tryout groups than the agency that operates the educational system, and virtually any type of research is readily arranged by a unit integral to this operation. Also, an "official" government center can generally enlist such outside cooperation as may be necessary whenever samples or data not available within its own establishment are required.

The main limitation on the research activities of a unit that is part of an operating branch of government is that some of the staff time that is available for research will periodically be taken up with operational agency functions. In Thailand, for example, the main task of the Teacher Training Department is implicit in its title; it could not release its measurement specialists to the center without requiring that they continue to teach certain measurement courses. And in Liberia also, the staff from time to time had to attend to other departmental duties.

But these were not serious problems—and, at a certain stage in a testing center's development, may not be problems at all. (In West Africa, full-time professional staff are currently being encouraged to take on extracurricular teaching positions, as an apparently useful self-development measure.) A center situated within a government agency should experience no difficulties in carrying out the needed research.

Practical Applications

The main concern about the viability of this model, as noted in the preceding chapter, is the possible limitation that an affiliation with a single agency may impose on the center's scope of operations. It was suggested that the situation in this respect can vary widely from country to country, and the quite different experiences in Liberia and Thailand illustrate this proposition.

In Liberia, the center's location within the Department of Education appeared to have no restrictive effect whatever. The center conducted the national examinations at the junior and senior high school levels, developed admissions tests for use at the university level, administered employment tests for other government departments, and provided testing services to a number of industrial and commercial organizations. Virtually every major test application feasible in a country the size of Liberia has been subsumed within the center's program of operations; and it seems reasonable to conclude that no alternative charter could have provided greater freedom or scope for a Liberian Testing Center.

In Thailand, such a broad range of services was not developed, partly because the introduction of operational applications was not one of the initial project objectives and partly because the external assistance phase was unusually brief. But, even looking ahead, it is difficult to visualize a center integral to the Teacher Training Department conducting the school certification examinations or the university entrance tests or the testing program of the Civil Service Commission. Though there are certain important applications that it reasonably can carry out within its charter, it can probably not grow into an all-purpose national testing center.

This is not meant to imply that an alternative home could have served as a more appropriate center within the bureaucratic structure of Thailand. Any government agency would have comparable difficulty in crossing departmental lines, and the Teacher Training Department does have the important advantage of controlling most of the country's trained measurement personnel. Nor does this imply that a series of separate homes to serve the needs of the various branches of government should be developed. Thailand cannot afford the costly duplication of effort that this would require. It seems as clear now as it did at the beginning of the project that the need is for a centralized testing service that can serve many sectors. But the project did not show how such a center could or should be developed.

Evaluation

The tentative conclusions that can be drawn from this limited experience are that the main strengths of this first model lie in the following:

1. The administrative simplicity of establishing and chartering a new testing center; and

2. The ease of arranging and implementing the extensive developmental research that test construction requires.

Its main weaknesses lie in the following:

1. The potential difficulty of recruiting able staff into the regular civil service structure; and

2. The potential difficulty of extending services to other autonomous organizations.

Resolving both of these weaknesses within the context of this single-agency organizational model may be unrealistic, moreover. The fact that serious recruitment problems but no bureaucratic problems were encountered in Liberia, while in Thailand the situation was just the reverse, may be a function simply of the enormous difference in the sizes of these countries. Small countries that have the professional assets of a Thailand and large countries that afford the bureaucratic congeniality of a Liberia probably are the exception.

Still, some steps can be taken to mitigate these effects. When adequate professionalization within a small country's limited resources remains a continuing problem, the establishment of a multinational base can be considered, such as the links that the Liberia Testing Center has developed with the West African Examinations Council, in which it is now an associate member. When formal interconnections among the independent agencies that use tests are not feasible, an informal advisory panel representative of the major consumers (as was set up at the beginning of the project in Liberia and a number of other countries) may help to bridge the gap sufficiently to provide the center with a de facto interagency charter.

But such inherent weaknesses, rooted in long-standing local characteristics, cannot be overcome completely within the life of the project, and will continue to impose some limitations. And it is therefore important to assess their probable effects at the time of the feasibility study, as stressed in the preceding chapter.

The Testing Division of a Quasi-Governmental Organization

The second model is similar to the first in that the center again becomes part of an organization that has numerous functions other than testing, and that depends on the government for its support. But in this case, the parent organization is not one of the operating branches of the central government structure. And this difference, coupled with the increasing number of such quasi-governmental organizations that are being established in the developing countries, makes it useful to treat this approach as a model distinct from the above.

Two of the AID/AIR projects have had links with these types of organizations. But one of these, in Korea, was an interim arrangement only. It was decided when the Korea project began to attach it administratively to the Central Education Research Institute (which is a private organization that receives half of its annual budget as a sustaining government grant), and to maintain this interim relationship until a permanent home was selected. The relationship lasted for a period of fifteen months and led smoothly to the establishment of the permanent institutional base that had been envisioned.

In Brazil, the project has been permanently institutionalized within the Getúlio Vargas Foundation, which is a large independent organization supported almost entirely by government grants. It operates a number of educational and research institutes in Brazil, and had established an institute devoted to testing fifteen years before the project began. At first, the project was carried out as a research activity of this institute, within the institute's regular organizational structure. Then the foundation decided to establish a new and relatively autonomous testing center within this institute to administer both and AID/AIR project and a separate project supported by the Ford Foundation; and this new center is the institution the project is to help to develop. Technical assistance has been provided for nearly four years, and members of the AIR staff are still serving in Brazil as advisers.

Ease of Establishment

Although a period of approximately six months was required in each of these countries to formalize the arrangements, the agreement in principle had been reached quickly, and the research could be carried forward throughout the administrative negotiations. As in the above model, only a few individuals had to participate in the decisions; and this greatly simplifies the problems of obtaining authorization to proceed.

It should be noted, however, that in both of these instances testing research was already part of the parent organization's ongoing operations, so that a basic policy decision was not required. Had the proposed arrangement required these organizations to expand into a new field (as would have been the case, for example, with such institutions as the Korean Institute of Science and Technology or with the Applied Scientific Research Corporation of Thailand) greater difficulties would probably have been encountered. Both such difficulties need not be a deterrent to the exploration of this type of arrangement in countries that have no institutions chartered for testing, since it might still prove to be the best of the available options.

Recruitment of Staff

Although positions with these types of quasi-governmental organizations are thought to be highly attractive, this proposition was not put to the test in either country. At both locations, most senior professionals typically hold a number of concurrent appointments with separate organizations, and it was easy to obtain staff who would take on these functions in addition to their other appointments. There is some reason to believe that these organizations could also compete effectively for full-time employees, but this has not yet been shown.

One clear-cut advantage that these organizations do enjoy over the regular civil service, however, is that personnel policies can be much more readily changed and adapted. During the course of the Brazil project, for example, it was pointed out that the staff's salaries were not nearly commensurate with their qualifications; the Vargas Foundation promulgated a revised salary schedule for all employees in the "psychologist" job classification. Such changes are at best difficult to bring about in the civil service structure.

A second advantage is that a private organization can more readily obtain staff on a loan basis from other agencies than can an official government unit. In both Brazil and Korea a number of the initial staff needs were met by the "secondment" of personnel from out-side organizations, and this is an especially helpful device for stretching the modest budget with which new testing centers typically begin.

Research Opportunities

Arrangements for developmental research naturally require more effort in this model than in the above because a quasi-governmental organization does not itself control any of the tryout samples required. Each study has to be "sold" individually to the operating agencies concerned; whereas this is seldom a problem when these agencies have already petitioned for assistance with ongoing test operations, it does tend to limit more basic research, such as the methodological studies described in the earlier chapters. A greater number of compromises in the design of the research also may be required.

To a considerable extent, these difficulties can be overcome by drawing on the prestige and personal credits of the senior specialists assigned to the center, and in both Brazil and Korea this was an important avenue to research. But the possibility that the research program developed within this organizational model will have to be more opportunistic than comprehensive cannot be discounted. Although other factors were also involved, neither the Brazil or the Korea project generated as much experimental data as did the "official" Thailand and Liberia centers.

Practical Applications

With respect to the opportunities for practical test applications, the status of the center as a quasi-governmental organization can have both negative and positive effects. The negative aspect, as in the case of the opportunities for research, is that this type of center cannot count on the guaranteed minimum of in-house applications that an official government center has from the beginning, and must develop its entire program itself. The positive feature is that there will generally be no limit on the scope of the program that it can at least theoretically develop, since the interagency tensions that might close doors to an official center should not affect a strictly neutral outside organization. If the center can take full advantage of this theoretically unlimited scope, this second model could easily be the one that ultimately will be the more productive.

The practical question, of course, is whether a large number of operating agencies will in fact turn over their internal testing operations to an outside center over which they exercise no control. For some types of agencies, such as industrial organizations, this poses no special problems. For others, such as the public school system, this may be an extremely difficult thing to do. So far, the operations of the Brazilian unit have not been extended to these more sensitive types of test applications.

Because this center has only recently begun to offer operational services, however, an assessment at this time would be premature. The delicate mechanisms necessary may yet be developed. The potential of this second model therefore is still unknown.

Evaluation

Tentatively, then, this second model appears to be an exceptionally good vehicle for beginning a testing activity on an interim basis when a final decision on the institutional issue must be deferred. As a permanent home for testing it seems to have clear advantages over the official-government model in providing attractive recruitment incentives, but corresponding disadvantages in carrying out a comprehensive program of development research. Its relative merits in affording a broad scope of operational testing services have not yet been determined.

The Largely Autonomous National Center

The third approach differs from the preceding model in two important respects. The first is that the center is not part of a larger organization, but is itself incorporated as a separate institution devoted wholly or mainly to testing. The second is that the major users of testing services participate in the management of the organization, at least at the policy level. Although the main source of funding may still be the government, and although the institution itself may be regarded as quasi-governmental, these two elements of autonomy and consumer control give this third model its distinctive characteristics.

The first center of this type established under the AID/AIR projects was the Nigerian Aptitude Testing Unit, which operated as an independent organization for eighteen months prior to its merger with the West African Examinations Council. The second was the Korean Institute for Research in the Behavioral Sciences, which was the successor to the interim arrangement described above. The Nigerian Unit received technical assistance throughout the entire period of its existence; the Korean Institute throughout the first year of its operations.

Other examples of this model are the four national organizations that comprise the West African Examinations Council, though these were, of course, not developed within the scope of this research. The council was established in 1953, seven years before the first AID/AIR project began.

Ease of Establishment

The establishment of a national testing center has so far proved to be a lengthy and complex operation. The time lag between the drafting of the initial plan for a testing facility in Nigeria and the actual establishment of the Nigerian Aptitude Testing Unit was nearly two years; in Korea, an interim arrangement of fifteen months was required, as noted above. Such slow patterns of evolution may well be inherent in this approach; unlike the preceding two models, this organizational structure requires the agreement of numerous independent agencies, and the development of a well-defined charter acceptable to them all. Time, compromise, and dedication (and, of course, adequate interim funding) may be essential prerequisites to this model in most developing countries.

A complicating factor that was encountered in both countries, moreover, was the ready availability of alternative models that also had strong supporters. In Nigeria, all certification testing was the legal responsibility of the West African Examinations Council; a small program of aptitude testing had been begun by one university, and programs were being planned by two others; and the expansion of the testing capabilities of at least two of the provincial Ministries of Education already was underway. Any of these efforts could have provided a reasonable base for further professionalization. And in Korea, ongoing testing efforts were similarly split among a variety of small units that each controlled a portion of the total professional talent on which a national center would have to draw to be fully effective. In both countries, the development of a framework within which these assets could be pooled and focused was the key challenge to institution-building.

The establishment of the West African Examinations Council itself cannot be compared with these later efforts, since this was done in colonial times, and since its initial charter was simply to act as a local agent for testing centers in the United Kingdom. But its subsequent growing pains in becoming a truly independent and indigenous establishment do provide further illustration of the complexities of developing largely autonomous national centers.

Recruitment of Staff

With respect to professional recruitment, this model is substantially superior to the preceding two. These organizations establish their own salary scales and conditions of service; and, being oriented explicitly toward measurement functions, they can reflect this emphasis in the incentives provided. In both Nigeria and Korea the conditions of service are considerably better than in the other countries, and there have been no problems in recruiting highly qualified staff.

In the Nigerian Aptitude Testing Unit, the peculiar legal basis of this organization did jeopardize staff retention, however. Legally, the unit operated within the statutory charter of the West African Examinations Council rather than being created by statute itself; this meant, as the staff well realized, that it could be dissolved with or without cause, at the council's pleasure. Until the unit was fully integrated within the council, staff retention was problematic. A solid juridical basis may well be one of the main requirements in this approach to institution-building.

Research Opportunities

The opportunities for research in this model are theoretically high because the many agencies that participate in the center's management can (and usually will) provide the operational access required. But the research that is in fact accomplished may be constrained by two other practical reasons.

The first is that institutions of this type cannot generally expect to be subsidized completely, and must devote a substantial portion of their activities to revenue-producing endeavors. In the case of the Korean Institute for Research in the Behavioral Sciences, this may not impose a serious limitation on the time available for research, because it is planned to attract contract research funds as one of the primary sources of outside support. But in more service-oriented organizations, such as the Nigerian Aptitude Testing Unit or the West African Examinations Council, the demands of the operational testing programs to which these units are committed necessarily have to come first. Though numerous research projects may be begun, they can easily become activities that are carried on nominally, year after year, without reaching completion.

A second related reason is that the management of this type of institution is more demanding than the management of the two earlier organizational models, and that the most able researchers are typically assigned to the senior administrative positions. And, as in all organizations, administrative crises regularly take precedence over substantive pursuits.

Thus, it may be that certain special features have to be introduced in the implementation of this model to insure a continuing research emphasis, if this is intended to be a major institutional objective. But the kinds of features that will indeed be effective is not yet clear. The Nigerian Aptitude Testing Unit tried to create a number of staff positions that would be devoted exclusively to research, and to develop a program of subcontracting basic research to the local universities, but neither effort was particularly successful. The present Korean approach of offering research services to outside agencies is too new to be adequately assessed.

Practical Applications

The opportunities that this model affords for meeting the full range of testing needs in a developing country is its outstanding advantage. Both the Nigerian Aptitude Testing Unit and the West African Examinations Council exhibited phenomenal rates of growth; by 1966, virtually all of the major kinds of testing services were available in Nigeria, and actually were being provided to all categories of potential consumers.

An important factor in the rapid growth of the Nigerian Aptitude Testing Unit was the degree to which the major users of testing services participated in the development of the unit, and in the management of its operations. Figure 26 shows the composition of its 23-member governing board, and illustrates the broad range of representation that was achieved. A similar pattern, adapted to local conditions, is suggested as generally desirable for all autonomous national centers.

The Nigeria operations of the West African Examinations Council are governed at the policy-making level by a national committee representative of the education sector that the council was established to serve. But, in addition to this senior committee, the council has also developed a network of subcommittees at both the national and provincial levels, and delegated to these the important task of approving each of the major types of examinations before they are given. This has created a participating role for a large number of key

FIGURE 26

Board of Governors of Nigerian Aptitude Testing Unit

Organization	Representative(s)	
Federal Ministry of Education	Permanent secretary	(1)
Regional Ministries of Education	Permanent secretary of each	(4)
Federal Ministry of Labor	Permanent secretary	(1)
National Manpower Board	Secretary	(1)
West African Examinations Council	Delegates	(4)
Universities	One delegate each	(5)
Employers' Consultative Association	Delegates	(4)
Chamber of Commerce	Delegate	(1)
Any	Chairman of board	(1)
Nigerian Aptitude Testing Unit	Director	(1)

individuals throughout the country, and seems to have been instrumental in developing the present strength and influence of the council. Any center that will have responsibility for certification tests should find this a highly useful model to follow.

Evaluation

The main advantages of a largely autonomous national center appear to lie in the following:

1. The degree to which it can meet local testing needs of all types in all sectors; and

2. The attractive employment opportunities it can offer to career professional staff.

Its major weaknesses are the following:

1. The limitations that its pattern of operations imposes on a continuing program of innovative research; and

2. The lenghty evolutionary process that may be required to bring such a center into existence.

Whenever local conditions permit, it should be regarded as the preferred model for meeting the full range of testing needs in a developing country.

The Largely Autonomous International Center

The final model is that of an independent regional center that serves and is supported by a number of countries. The prime example, of course, is the West African Examinations Council, to which technical assistance on a _regional_ basis has been provided for the past four years, as a continuation of the earlier Nigerian program. More recently, additional AID/AIR projects have been begun with two newly established regional centers in East Africa, which also are patterned to a considerable degree on the West African organization.

Ease of Establishment

As would be expected, the development of a multinational institution is even more complex than that of an autonomous national center. All of the difficulties of organizing at the national level remain, and the further difficulties of accommodating the interests of sovereign states compound the organizational problems that will be encountered. An even longer period of planning and negotiation will almost certainly be required.

Still, this model does afford an opportunity for smaller countries to pool their resources, and gain access to a professional capability that individually they would be hard pressed to develop. This was the decision that Liberia made, as described in a preceding discussion; a similar decision was subsequently made in Malawi. Even for larger countries, such as Nigeria or Kenya or Ghana, the regional approach offers potentially attractive economies that should be explored when geographic, ethnic, and political factors permit.

The establishment of the West African Examinations Council in 1953 sheds little light on the current problems of regional organization, for the reasons earlier noted. But the council's ability to maintain its regional structure through periods of political turbulence since 1953 can probably be attributed largely to its discreet management of this arrangement. The council has not attempted to impose uniform testing practices on the member countries, but has instead adapted its programs in each country in accordance with the decisions of the local committees; in this way it has provided a maximum of benefits with a minimum of control. And such flexibility may generally be essential for the long-term viability of a regional organization.

Recruitment of Staff

Regional organizations are generally in a highly favorable position with respect to the recruitment of staff; they can draw from a large pool of potential candidates and typically offer conditions of service more generous than those in the member countries. This has been the experience also of the West African Examinations Council, which has consistently been able to attract outstanding staff. In this respect, the regional model is probably superior to all of the others.

Research Opportunities

The basic conflict between the needs for research and the demands of ongoing operations that was described above in the context of the national center applies equally to regional organizations. For, even though the larger size of a regional institution does give it greater flexibility in the assignment of staff, the proportionately increased demands of its far-flung testing services may similarly constrain the amount of time that can be devoted to innovative research.

Thus, the establishment within the council of an Office for Test Development and Research that would be freed of all operational responsibilities was probably helpful; but, to date, the activities of this office have in fact had to emphasize the "development" much more than the "research." The routine maintenance of the council's objective achievement tests alone requires the preparation and analysis of 2,500 new test items per year, and this figure will continue to climb as more of the traditional essay tests are converted to objective versions. If research is to receive continuing emphasis—and this, of course, is a policy decision—special provisions may have to be made in the regional just as in the national center.

Practical Applications

That a regional organization can provide a wide variety of testing services to its member countries has been clearly shown in the recent history of the West African Examinations Council. The many services initially available only in Nigeria are now being extended also to the other countries, and the regional model appears to be entirely as effective a vehicle for meeting the full range of testing needs as a separate national center.

Certain aspects of the West Africa experience, moreover, suggest that a regional framework may even accelerate the growth of testing services in the countries it serves. The council's initial plan had been to defer the introduction of aptitude measures until it had accomplished its highest priority task of taking over all of the certification tests that were still being set and marked in the United Kingdom—a demanding and long-term effort that has not been completed even today. But as Nigeria's rapid development increased the demand for aptitude tests, and as this demand led to the creation of the Nigerian Aptitude Testing Unit, and as this unit began to serve an ever larger clientele in the council's largest member country, it had to revise its initial position. Organizationally, it could not ignore the growth of a second testing establishment that in certain fields, notably secondary school admission testing, was being asked to take over services that the council formerly had provided. But legally it could not fully integrate such apparently competitive operations under its regional charter without extending the services available in Nigeria to also the other countries. And in this indirect manner, aptitude testing was introduced in these countries well in advance of the original plan.

The specifics of this experience are probably not generalizable to other organizations in other countries. But the implicit proposition that a regional center must be responsive to the needs of all member countries, and that a need stressed in one will result in the availability of new services in also the others may well be applicable to all multinational service organizations. If so, the regional model could be an especially potent approach to rapid testing reform.

Evaluation

The main advantages of the independent regional organization, therefore, appear to be the following:

1. It can make possible the development of professional testing services in countries that have not the resources to establish separate national centers.

2. Even in larger countries it may offer additional benefits with respect to the expansion of test applications and the recruitment of capable staff.

The main limitations of this approach are the following:

1. The establishment of a regional center is likely to entail a lengthy delay while the necessary arrangements and negotiations are being completed.

2. In many locations the realities of geographic, linguistic, or political factors may make a regional testing service entirely unrealistic.

On balance, the two-stage process of beginning with an interim local arrangement and then transitioning to an independent national or regional center may be the generally most productive model for institution-building.

FINANCIAL SUPPORT

Patterns of financial support will, of course, vary as a function of the basic model of organization that is adopted. But the three basic sources of funds for all models are government grants, center earnings, and external assistance. Each will be discussed briefly from the point of view of the perhaps generalizable ideas that were developed at the various project locations.

Government Grants

The mechanics of government subsidy can take many forms. At the simplest level, when the center is part of a larger parent organization, the latter can simply add the center staff to its rolls as regular employees and authorize the center director to charge other expenditures to its accounts (in accordance with established requisitioning and accounting procedures). This was essentially the approach used in financing the Liberia Testing Center. A somewhat more complex pattern within the same model is to finance a portion of the costs in this manner and to provide the remainder by drawing on the special funds that may be available in a separate government account for the support of externally assisted programs. This was done in both Brazil and Thailand. To subsidize a largely autonomous center the government can provide a fixed sum per annum, as in the case of the Nigerian Aptitude Testing Unit; or it can contribute a variable sum on the basis of a proposed budget the center prepares and submits for review, as is being done in Korea. Or the government can agree to pay the amount of the deficit the center incurs, as the member countries of the West African Examinations Council do to meet the costs of the national programs. To finance the non-national overhead costs of the regional superstructure, these countries also contribute an additional sum, on the basis of a fixed formula of percentage allocations, geared to the relative size of each member country.

Each of these patterns is viable so long as the income and expenditures of the testing center are maintained as a separate account—if not physically, at least on paper. The availability of cost-analysis data is essential to the effective management of a testing center, especially during its developmental phases, when a large number of specific implementation decisions will have to be made or reconsidered. Whenever the expenditures of the testing center were irretrievably merged with other expenses, problems of analysis and planning were subsequently encountered.

A second important requirement is that the testing center be able to accumulate a surplus and carry this forward as surplus to the following year. In the early phases, when the center is likely to be operating at a bare subsistence level, even a modest surplus can serve as a useful contingency fund; in the later phases, continued accrual should permit periodic investments that could not be undertaken within the regular budget.

Center Earnings

The major category of earned income of a testing center, of course, consists of the fees that are assessed for the services being provided. Usually, there are three types of fees to be considered.

First are the fees charged for certification examinations. In most countries, these are paid by the candidates themselves; in some locations, such as West Africa, they are fairly substantial. But when tests must be provided for a large number of courses, including those that only two or three candidates may actually take, and when the papers consist mainly of essay questions, even high fees will typically not pay for the attendant expenses. Policy decisions have to be made about the appropriate partitioning of these costs between the candidate fees and the government grant, and about the desirability of reducing costs by restricting the courses offered or introducing more economical testing procedures. Such decisions are generally made by the government at the highest levels.

A second major category of fees includes those assessed for the entrance examinations to government-operated schools and training centers. These programs can generally be operated at a profit with a low per capita fee, which may be paid by the government (as part of its grant or as an additional assessment), by the candidate directly, or, as in the case of the Nigerian Aptitude Testing Unit, by the individual institutions, which themselves charged a fee to each candidate for admission. In the Nigerian operation, the computation of the fee assessed by the center for such government-related programs took into account the share of the overhead costs that had in effect been prepaid by the sustaining government contribution.

The third major category consists of fees charged for testing services to institutions that do not provide other financial support to the center, such as selection programs for private employers. Here it is reasonable to assess fees that will meet the total costs of the program, and also contribute to the surplus fund of the center. The Nigeria schedule of fees for such applications consisted of a modest per capita fee (approximately U.S.$3.00), an extra "set-up" charge for testing small groups, and any related travel expenses.

Income from services other than testing may also be available as the center expands its capabilities and resources. Contract research, especially if it is directly relevant to the center's program, is the major possibility that should be explored, as the Korean Institute is currently doing. Once the center acquires high-speed data processing equipment and the related programming skills, there should be many other opportunities for services or consultation to improve the center's financial position.

In addition to such cash earnings, a testing center can sometimes obtain also direct personnel and logistic support that will similarly help to meet its operating expenses. The utility of arranging for professional staff on "secondment" from other agencies has already been noted. An expanded opportunity of this type was found to be available in Brazil, where candidates for degrees in psychology have to submit evidence of practical experience as a prerequisite to graduation, and therefore are eager to work without pay to accumulate the required number of hours. In Korea an agency that could not transfer funds to the center to pay for testing agreed instead to do the center's printing in exchange for the services provided; in Nigeria, visual aids were constructed on a similar barter arrangement. Opportunities of these kinds are no doubt available in most developing countries.

A final and perhaps obvious point is that all funds not immediately required for operating expenses should be invested. Short-term deposit plans are offered by many banks, and interest rates in the developing countries tend to be highly attractive.

External Assistance

The requirements for external assistance also can be met in a number of ways from a variety of sources. In West Africa the Agency for International Development is currently providing resident testing specialists and certain commodity support; the Ford Foundation is funding the staff training programs; and the British Council is supplying a subject matter specialist to assist with the development of a new examination. In Brazil the two major projects of the testing center are being supported by AID and the Ford Foundation, as earlier noted. In Korea the Asia Foundation and the Fulbright Commission provided partial funding for a specific research undertaking to supplement the AID contribution of overall institutional support. To the extent that external assistance is needed, all sources available to the country should be explored.

In the early developmental stages, the most appropriate external contributions are technical advisers, training grants, and assistance with capital investments. Later, these inputs can perhaps more appropriately take the form of support for selected projects, granted on the basis of specific proposals prepared by the center. Such arrangements can be mutually attractive if they meet the external organization's own research needs, such as a project to evaluate the effectiveness of Peace Corps teachers, for example.

INTERNAL ORGANIZATION

The basic decision to be made about the internal structure of a testing center is whether to organize along programmatic or functional lines. In the programmatic model, the primary subdivisions of the organization are responsible for the different types of testing services being offered, and each of these divisions manages all aspects of the programs it has been assigned. In the functional model, the primary subdivisions are responsible for the different types of activities that comprise the testing process—development, test administration, and analysis of results—and each division performs these functions for all of the programs that comprise the center's overall testing operations. Hybrid patterns that combine features of both models also can be constructed.

For a small testing center, or a potentially large center just beginning its operations, the programmatic pattern of organization appears to be the better. When there is a limited staff, assigning one professional full responsibility for a program—to supervise the development of the tests, the field tryouts, the printing, the reporting of the results, and all other details—is more efficient than attempts to divide these responsibilities among a number of specialized units. The controls and the coordination mechanisms necessary to implement a functional model cannot yet be provided, and a simple organizational structure is the indicated approach. Figure 27 shows the organization of the Nigerian Aptitude Testing Unit when it first was established; a highly similar structure also was used by the Liberia Testing Center.

Certain of the basic service functions, of course, should be centralized even within this programmatic approach. Thus, the divisions of the Nigerian Aptitude Testing Unit did not have internal test scoring capabilities, but shared a central test scoring section that reported to the director. It was the responsibility of each division head, however, to insure that the scoring of his tests was completed on schedule, even if he had to employ temporary clerical help to supplement the central service section. And this pattern of unitary responsibility seemed to work well.

The programmatic approach is also the one better suited to a multipurpose research organization, such as the Korean Institute for

FIGURE 27

Initial Organization of the Nigerian Aptitude Testing Unit

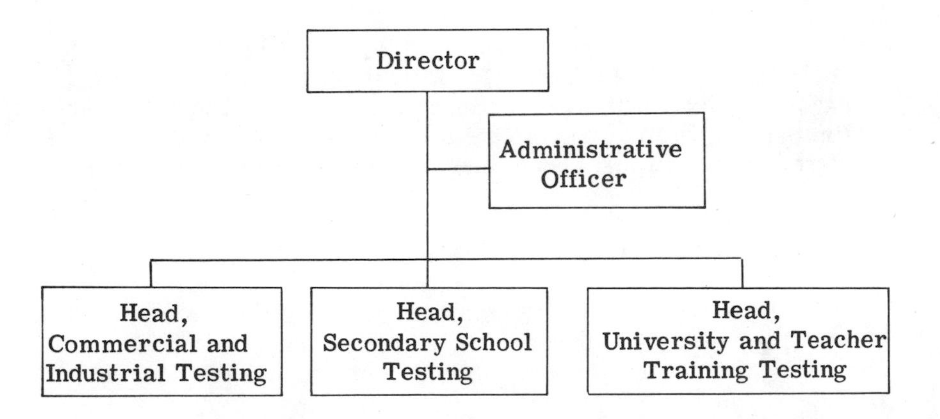

Research in the Behavioral Sciences, that plans to engage in activities other than testing. Here, the Test Development and Research Department is one of four coordinate substantive divisions, defined by program orientation, and then is split itself—again programmatically—into sections devoted to different types of test applications.

For a large testing establishment, such as the West African Examinations Council, either approach can be used. Before its merger with the Nigerian Aptitude Testing Unit, the Council was organized along programmatic lines, with a designated staff member in charge of each program in each member country. Then, as part of the merger arrangement, a functional approach was adopted. The administration of the programs remained the responsibility of the existing structure, the development of tests for these programs became the responsibility of the new Test Development and Research Office, and the statistical analysis functions became a joint responsibility, since these have both administrative and technical components. The partial organization chart in Figure 28 shows the essential features of this arrangement.

The main advantages of this model are that it liberates the technical staff from many of the routine management responsibilities, which should spur a more active program of development and research, and that it provides career opportunities for the talented professional and the talented administrator that are equally attractive. Its main disadvantages are that the administration of the testing programs does not receive the close professional supervision inherent in the programmatic model, and that the technical requirements of standardized testing may therefore not be equally well met. To date, the Test Development and Research Office has in fact retained operational responsibility for the administration of the more demanding aptitude tests, which, it is felt, cannot yet be converted to the functional pattern of implementation.

For a developing testing facility, therefore, the programmatic model is likely to be the generally more effective structure, though it may be less efficient. Applications of the functional approach should be limited, at least initially, to the management of certification tests and other programs that require less direct professional supervision.

OPERATING PROCEDURES

Another important requirement for the effective management of a testing center is to prepare explicit rules and procedures for every aspect of the center's regular operations. These should span

FIGURE 28

Partial Organization Chart of the West African Examinations Council

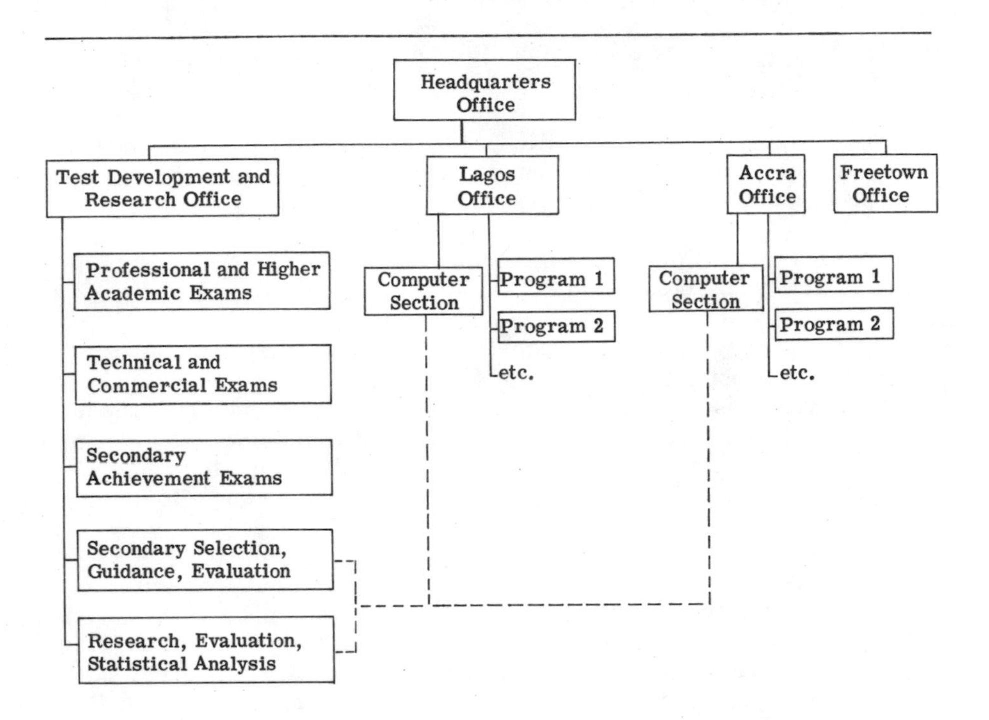

the full range from policy issues to mechanical routines, and should be published in the form of a manual distributed to all staff members. Though the content will be revised and expanded as a function of experience, at least a preliminary draft should be developed as part of the preoperational preparations.

A discussion of the many hundreds of specific issues that might be encompassed in such a manual is beyond the scope of this handbook, but the range of topics to be considered can be suggested. The following is a sample of the topics treated in the manuals prepared at a number of project locations:

1. Personnel. Appointment procedures; position descriptions; salary structure; performance reviews; promotion and transfer; categories of leave; employee benefits; disciplinary actions; separation or termination; travel; payroll procedures; personnel records; etc.

2. Finances. Responsibility; accountability; records, files, and reports; schedule of testing fees; billing procedures; disbursement categories and procedures; amortization procedures; audits; etc.

3. Supplies and equipment. Inventory; ordering procedures; storage; maintenance; library lending procedures; accountability; etc.

4. Security. Building; files, safes, vault; printing procedures; storage procedures; destruction procedures; shipping procedures; inspection of tests by outsiders; etc.

5. Filing. Correspondence; administrative records; tests; forms; length of retention; disposal procedures; access; etc.

6. Testing sessions. Regular, extra, and make-up sessions; requests for testing; staff assignments; advance preparations; checklist of materials needed for each type of test series; material checkout and return procedures; care of forms and equipment; verification of examinee identity; use of examiner's manual; proctoring requirements and procedures; flow-chart of process from request to scoring; etc.

7. Scoring and data processing. Preparation, use, and storage of hand-scoring keys; preparation, use and storage of machine-scoring keys; scoring procedures; check-scoring and quality control; scoring formulas; norms; coding the data; standard statistical routines; sample forms; updating item banks, examinee file, norm tabulations; flowchart of process from receipt of papers to storage; etc.

8. Reporting results. Client relationships; report forms; standard scores; release of scores to others; validity reports; staff publications; regular center reports; etc.

Provisions for regularly updating the manuals should also be made. An extremely useful procedure in this regard is to maintain an error file of breakdowns in center operations, and to use these as a means of identifying needs for revision. A pragmatic trial-and-error approach may be as productive in establishing effective routines as it was in the development of the I-D testing procedures.

ABOUT THE AUTHORS

PAUL A. SCHWARZ is executive vice-president of the American Institutes for Research. During the period 1960-64, he was the director of the research project in Africa that developed the techniques and principles of testing described in this book. During 1965-67, he supervised the extension and application of these techniques to other cultural settings, traveling extensively throughout the developing world. Before assuming his present position in 1970, he spent two years in Thailand developing techniques for measuring social and economic progress in rural locations. His field of specialization is measurement and evaluation. He holds a Ph.D. degree in psychology from the University of Pittsburgh.

ROBERT E. KRUG has had extensive experience in the conduct and management of applied behavioral science research. In 1961, after six years as a member of the faculty at Carnegie Tech (now Carnegie-Mellon University) he became director of the Measurement and Evaluation Program of the American Institutes for Research. He left AIR in 1964 to become director of research for the U.S. Peace Corps and subsequently was director of Plans and Evaluation for Job Corps, Office of Economic Opportunity. In both government positions his major concern was with the development of procedures for assessing program accomplishment.

Since rejoining AIR in 1967, his principal responsibility has been to develop methods for measuring the impact of rural development programs in Thailand. He is currently director of AIR's Asia/Pacific Office in Bangkok.

Mr. Krug was educated at the Ohio State University, where he received his Ph.D. degree in psychology in 1955.